Hitler's Scandinavian Legacy

Hitler's Scandinavian Legacy

The Consequences of the German Invasion
for the Scandinavian Countries,
Then and Now

Edited by
John Gilmour and Jill Stephenson

BLOOMSBURY
LONDON • NEW DELHI • NEW YORK • SYDNEY

Bloomsbury Academic
An imprint of Bloomsbury Publishing Plc

50 Bedford Square	1385 Broadway
London	New York
WC1B 3DP	NY 10018
UK	USA

www.bloomsbury.com

Bloomsbury is a registered trade mark of Bloomsbury Publishing Plc

First published 2013
Paperback edition first published 2014

© John Gilmour and Jill Stephenson, 2013;
Individual chapters © the contributors

All rights reserved. No part of this publication may be reproduced or transmitted in any form or by any means, electronic or mechanical, including photocopying, recording, or any information storage or retrieval system, without prior permission in writing from the publishers.

John Gilmour and Jill Stephenson have asserted their rights under the Copyright, Designs and Patents Act, 1988, to be identified as the Editors of this work.

No responsibility for loss caused to any individual or organization acting on or refraining from action as a result of the material in this publication can be accepted by Bloomsbury Academic or the author.

British Library Cataloguing-in-Publication Data
A catalogue record for this book is available from the British Library.

ISBN: HB: 978-1-4411-9036-9
PB: 978-1-4725-7841-9
ePDF: 978-1-4411-8411-5
ePub: 978-1-4725-0497-5

Typeset by Deanta Global Publishing Services, Chennai, India

Contents

List of Illustrations	vi
List of Contributors	viii
Editors' Acknowledgements	xii

1	Editors' Introduction *John Gilmour and Jill Stephenson*	3
2	Scandinavia in the Second World War *Richard Overy*	13
3	The Nordic Countries and the Second World War: A British Perspective *Patrick Salmon*	39
4	The Obsession with Sovereignty: Cohabitation and Resistance in Denmark 1940–45 *Niels Wium Olesen*	45
5	Closing a Long Chapter: German-Norwegian Relations 1939–45: Norway and the Third Reich *Tom Kristiansen*	73
6	The Case of Sweden *Kent Zetterberg*	101
7	Janus of the North? Finland 1940–44: Finland's road into alliance with Hitler *Oula Silvennoinen*	129
8	'The Five Evil Years': National Self-image, Commemoration and Historiography in Denmark 1945–2010: Trends in Historiography and Commemoration *Claus Bundgård Christensen*	147
9	Hitler's Norwegian Legacy *Ole Kristian Grimnes*	159
10	Realism and Idealism: Swedish Narratives of the Second World War: Historiography and Interpretation in the Post-War Era *Johan Östling*	179
11	Two Shadows over Finland: Hitler, Stalin and the Finns Facing the Second World War as History 1944–2010 *Juhana Aunesluoma*	199
12	Conclusion *Allan Little*	221

Index	233

List of Illustrations

Maps

Map 1	The Nordic region, 1939–45	1
Map 2	Finland, 1939–44	128

Photographs

Figure 1 The Danish crime series 'The Killing II' reaches back to Second World War events familiar to many of its Danish viewers in order to contextualize current issues of violence, freedom and legality. [With kind permission of *DR*, Photo: Rasmus Arrildt, DR.] 2

Figure 2 Gustav Stresemann giving his Nobel Peace Prize lecture in the great hall at the University of Oslo in 1927. [Copyright: Scanpix] 79

Figure 3 *Ministerpräsident* Vidkun Quisling (right) inspecting the First Police Company of the Norwegian *Waffen-SS* embarking on its first tour to the Leningrad front in September 1942. [Copyright: Norwegian Resistance Museum] 95

Figure 4 In Denmark, over 50 years after the war, a 1999 article in the leading newspaper, *Berlingske Tidende*, revealed A. P. Møller's business links with Nazi Germany that shook Denmark and led to a bitter dispute between the publisher and one of its major shareholders. [With kind permission of *Berlingske Tidende*.] *Avisreproduktion v. Statens Avissamling – Statsbiblioteket*, Aarhus, Denmark. 146

Figure 5 Norway's *Dagbladet* headline from 2012: 'Hitler's secret trains through Sweden.' The article re-examines the controversial transits that remain actively recalled and discussed in both countries. [With kind permission of *Dagbladet*.] 158

List of Illustrations   vii

Figure 6 Sweden's *Aftonbladet* in 2000 gives front page coverage of an important milestone in Sweden's post-war response to the country's actions between 1939–45: The Stockholm International Forum on the Holocaust. [With kind permission of *Aftonbladet*.]   178

Figure 7 Finland's *Iltalehti* newspaper in this 2011 special supplement commemorates the wartime service by soldiers and civilians alike in the controversial 'Continuation War' ('*Jatkosota*') when Finnish forces fought alongside the German *Wehrmacht* against the Soviet Union. [With kind permission of Iltalehti/Alma Media.]   197

List of Contributors

Juhana Aunesluoma is an Adjunct Professor of Political History and has worked as the director of The Network for European Studies at the University of Helsinki since January 2010. He defended his doctorate at Oxford University in 1998 and started working as a senior lecturer at the University of Helsinki in 2001. His areas of specialization include Cold War history, international trade and integration policy and Finnish, Nordic and European twentieth century history. His major publications are *Britain, Sweden and the Cold War, 1945–54* (2003), *Understanding Neutrality, The Cold War and the Politics of History* (2008) and *Finlandisation in Reverse. The CSCE and the Rise and Fall of Economic Détente, 1968–75* (2008).

Claus Bundgård Christensen is Associate Professor in the Department of Culture and Identity at the University of Roskilde. His research interests include the Second World War, the First World War, military history, the Holocaust, the *Waffen-SS*, anti-parliamentarianism, Nazism, fascism, history of the Danish police, anti-Communism, crime history, the occupation, the first post-war years and the Cold War. His published work includes *Dansk arbejdetyske befæstningsanlæg* (1997), *Under hagekors og Dannebrog* (1998), *Dagbog fra østfronten* (2005) and he jointly authored *Danmark besat – Krig og hverdag 1940–45.* (2009) His book, *Danskere på vestfronten 1914–18*, won the Danish History book of the Year Award 2009.

John Gilmour is Honorary Fellow in Scandinavian Studies at the University of Edinburgh. His research interests include Scandinavia and the Second World War, the prose literature of Harry Martinson and Björn Larsson, and cultural influences and self-image in present-day Scandinavia. His book on Sweden's experience during the Second World War, *Sweden, the Swastika and Stalin*, was published by the Edinburgh University Press in January 2010.

Ole Kristian Grimnes is currently Professor Emeritus in Modern History at the University of Oslo. In particular, he has worked on the period 1940–45 in Norwegian history. His many publications include *The Rise of a Refugee Community. Norwegians in Sweden 1940–45 (Et flyktningesamfunn vokser fram. Nordmenn i*

Sverige 1940–45) (1969), *The Norwegian Resistance Leadership* (*Hjemmefrontens Ledelse*) (1979), *Norway during the Occupation* (*Norge under okkupasjonen*) (1983), *The German Invasion of Norway* (*Overfall*). Volume 1 of Magne Skodvin (ed.): *Norway at War.* (1984) and *The Road to War. The Nygaardsvold Government's War Decisions in 1940* (*Veien inn i krigen. Regjeringen Nygaardsvolds krigsvedtak i 1940*) (1987). He is a member of the Norwegian Academy of Science and Letters.

Tom Kristiansen is Professor of History at the Norwegian Institute for Defence Studies. He has written extensively on Scandinavian diplomatic, naval and military history in the late nineteenth and first half of the twentieth centuries with a particular focus on the relations between Scandinavia and the great powers, and Anglo-Norwegian relations. His latest books include *Tysk trussel mot Norge? Forsvarsledelse, trusselvurderinger og militære tiltak før 1940* (2008) and *The history of the Norwegian navy 1905-60, Selvstendig og alliert i krig og fred* (2010). Kristiansen is currently working on the history of Norwegian Ministry of Defence 1814–1940.

Allan Little is both a Graduate and an Honorary Graduate of the University of Edinburgh. He is a Special Correspondent at the BBC and the winner of many awards for his reports from abroad, especially from war zones. His postings have included Moscow, Paris, Baghdad, Kuwait and Johannesburg. He spent four years in Yugoslavia in the 1990s, reporting on the Bosnian War, and is co-author of *The Death of Yugoslavia* (1996). More recently, he has reported from Afghanistan. In 2012, he received the British Journalism Review's Charles Wheeler Award for Outstanding Contribution to Broadcast Journalism.

Niels Wium Olesen is Associate Professor in Danish and European twentieth Century History in the Department of Culture and Society, University of Aarhus. He has written widely about the interwar years, the era of the Second World War and the early Cold War. He has participated in several European research projects, the latest being a project about social movements in Europe and the transition from war to peace in 1944–47. He jointly authored *Danmark besat Krig og hverdag 1940–45* (2009) and is currently working on a book on Danish politics in the interwar years. Dr Olesen has made many media contributions in Denmark on both historical issues and current affairs.

Richard Overy is Professor of History at the University of Exeter. He is the author of more than twenty-five books, on the Second World War, the European dictatorships and the history of air power. These include *Why the Allies Won*, *The*

Air War 1939–45, and *The Dictators: Stalin's Russia and Hitler's Germany* (winner of the 2004 Wolfson Prize for History). His most recent publication was *1939: Countdown to War*. His study of the European bombing war will be published in 2013, and he is currently writing a general history of the Second World War. He was elected to the British Academy in 2000 and to the European Academy of Sciences and Arts in 2012.

Johan Östling is a Pro-Futura Scientia Fellow at the Department of History, Lund University, and the Swedish Collegium for Advanced Study (SCAS), Uppsala. He has written extensively on modern Swedish and German history, National Socialism and narratives of the Second World War, historiography and history culture. His dissertation, *Nazismens sensmoral: Svenska erfarenheter i andra världskrigets efterdyning* (2008), was awarded several prizes, including the Clio Prize and the Nils Klim Prize. Östling is joint editor of *Nordic Narratives of the Second World War: National Historiographies Revisited* (2011). He is currently working on a project on the transformation of the Humboldtian tradition and the idea of the university in twentieth-century Germany.

Patrick Salmon is Chief Historian at the Foreign and Commonwealth Office, and Visiting Professor at the University of Newcastle. He is the author of a number of books, including *Scandinavia and the Great Powers 1890–1940* and (with the late John Hiden) *The Baltic Nations and Europe*. He is the editor of *Britain and Norway in the Second World War*. Most recently, he is co-editor of volumes of documents on *Britain and German Unification, 1989–90*, and on *The Nordic Countries: From War to Cold War, 1944–51*.

Oula Silvennoinen is a Postdoctoral Research Fellow at the Department of World Cultures, University of Helsinki. Silvennoinen completed his PhD in 2008 on the subject: Secret Comrades in Arms: The Finnish and German Security Police Cooperation 1933–44. The work documents the establishment of a previously unknown SS-Einsatzkommando within the operational area of northern Norway and Finland. He argues that the Finnish Security Police collaborated with the Germans in interrogating Red Army POWs and identifying communists and Jews, whom they turned over to the Einsatzkommando for execution.

Jill Stephenson is Professor Emeritus and Honorary Fellow of the School of History, Classics and Archaeology at the University of Edinburgh. Her research interests include society and politics in modern Germany to 1945. Her publications include *Hitler's Home Front: Württemberg under the Nazis* (2006), *The Third Reich in Colour* (2002), *Women in Nazi Germany* (2001), *The Nazi Organisation of Women* (1981) and *Women in Nazi Society* (1975). She is a Fellow of the Royal Historical Society.

Kent Zetterberg is Professor Emeritus in the Military History Division of the Swedish National Defence College. He has published widely on Sweden during the Second World War and in the post-war period, including *Liberalism in Crisis: People's Party 1939–45*. He has a particular interest in security policy.

Editors' Acknowledgements

A book of this nature is essentially a collaborative effort and we are indeed indebted to our contributors for their dedication to the task of creating original and insightful history and also for their patience in responding to our many and varied editorial comments.

Behind this stands a further group of people without whom this volume would not have been completed. We have benefited from generous funding from The University of Edinburgh's Centre for the Study of the Two World Wars, Samarbejdsnævnet for Nordenundervisning i Udlandet/ Pohjoismaiden kulttuurin ulkomaanopetuksen toimikunta/Samstarfsnefnd kennslu í Norðurlandafræðum erlendis, the Embassy of Denmark in London, the Royal Norwegian Consulate General in Edinburgh, and the Embassy of Sweden in London. In this connection, we would particularly like to thank the late Jim McMillan, Úlfar Bragason, Lone Britt Molloy, Mona Rohne and Ann Nilsson.

In assembling pictorial material and securing permission to reproduce it, we are indebted to Fredrik Palmqvist of *Aftonbladet*, Lisbeth Knudsen of *Berlingske Tidende*, Henrik Storgaard Sørensen of Statsbiblioteket Aarhus, Mette Quistgaard of *DR* (*the Danish Broadcasting Corporation*), Geir Ramnefjell of *Dagbladet* and Jyrki Vesikansa of *Iltalehti*. Additionally, we would mention Jim Lewis who produced the maps and uncomplainingly endured our frequent revisions.

We have been fortunate in having a patient and understanding editorial team at Continuum and Bloomsbury Academic during the commissioning and preparation of the book: Ben Hayes, Michael Greenwood, Rhodri Mogford, Emily Drewe and especially Frances Arnold to whom we are particularly grateful for her support and understanding.

Finally, we owe an immense debt to our colleagues at the University of Edinburgh for a variety of unstinting contributions and assistance. Paul Addison, Ann Brockington, Susan Halcro, Gunilla Blom-Thomsen, Tom Devine, Arne Kruse, Pauline Maclean, Lesley McLean and Bjarne Thomsen provided much-needed support and advice at various stages of this project and if we have inadvertently omitted anyone from this list, we beg their forgiveness.

Jill Stephenson
John Gilmour
Edinburgh, 2013

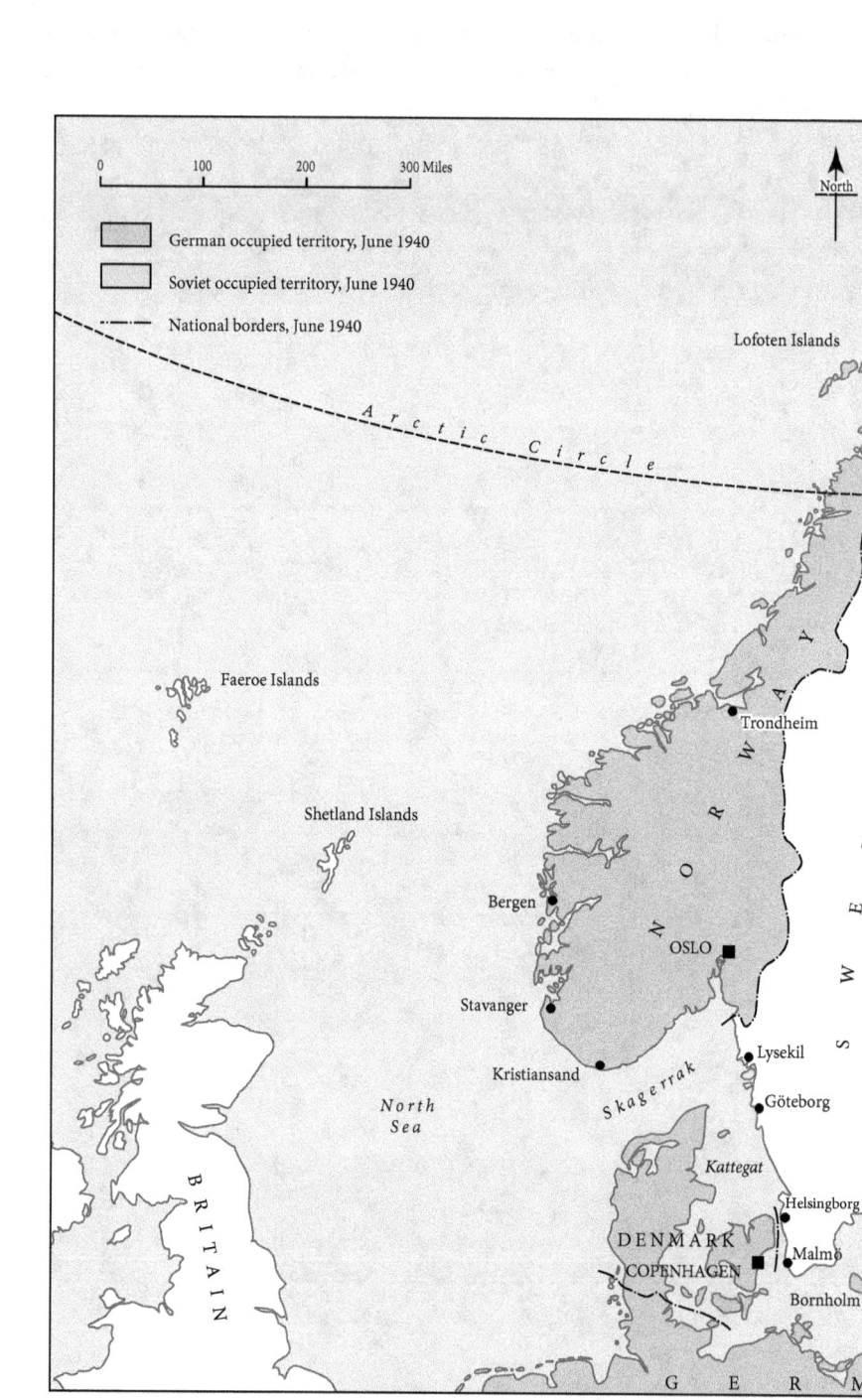

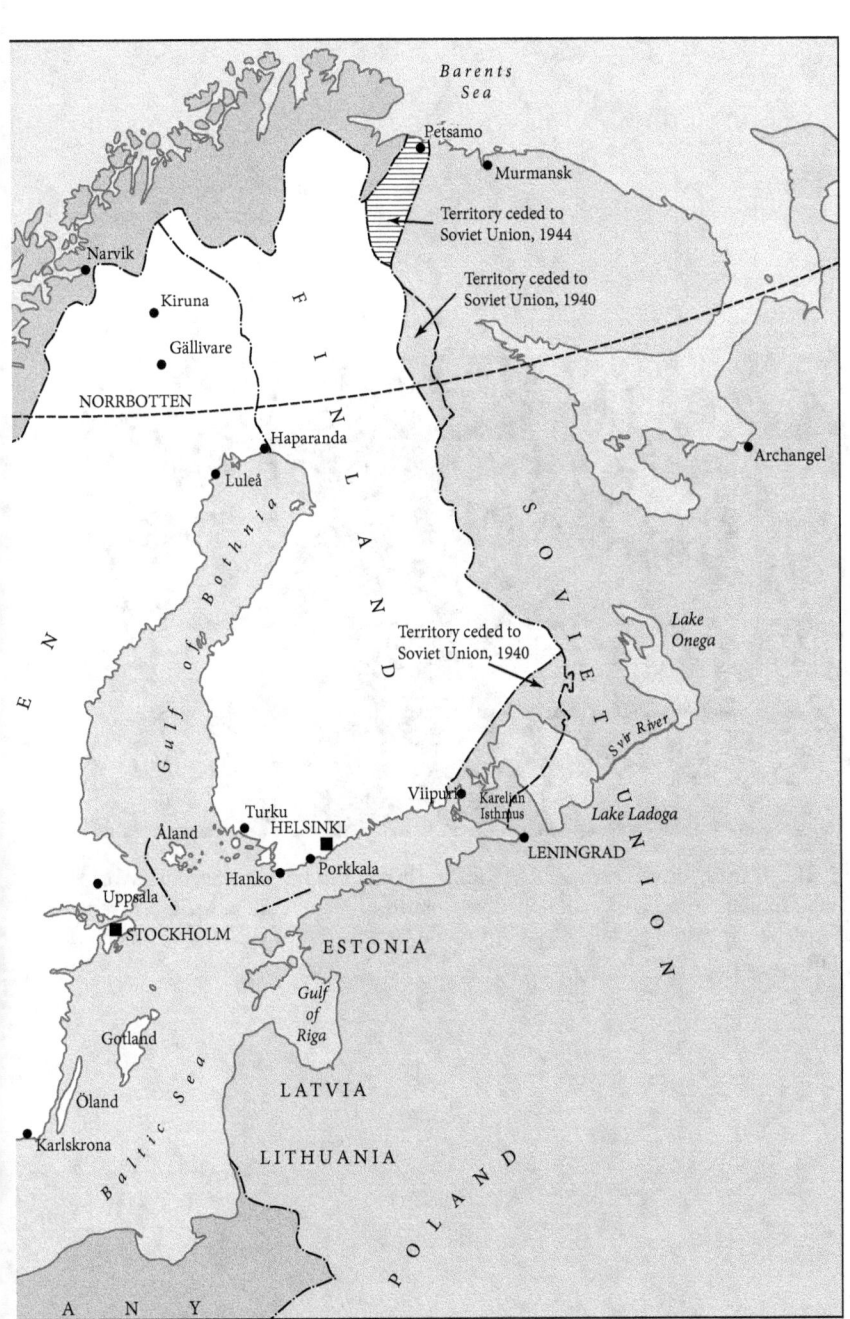

Map 1 The Nordic region, 1939–45.

Figure 1 The Danish crime series 'The Killing II' reaches back to Second World War events familiar to many of its Danish viewers in order to contextualize current issues of violence, freedom and legality. [With kind permission of *DR*, Photo: Rasmus Arrildt, DR.]

1

Editors' Introduction

John Gilmour and Jill Stephenson

Readers may wonder why a stark image from one of television's most successful recent crime drama series, 'The Killing II' appears opposite this page in a book about the legacy of the Second World War in Scandinavia. This picture is no ordinary 'film noir' crime scene setting. It is located in Copenhagen's Ryvang Memorial Park, established in 1945. Here, during the occupation, the Germans tied members of the Danish resistance movement to wooden stakes and executed them by firing squad. They also buried the dead temporarily in this place. Søren Sveistrup, author of 'The Killing II', uses the setting to inject strong imagery linking contemporary violence in Danish society with World War II. In the opening scene, the camera pans over the now-permanent graves of the fallen heroes and flits across Axel Poulsen's monument 'For Denmark: Mother with Her Fallen Son'. The first murder victim is discovered bound to one of the three replica execution stakes.

Sveistrup continues to load this episode with further significant references to the occupation and Denmark's conduct then. In a later scene, the fictional newly appointed leftist Justice Minister, Thomas Buch, is given a 'welcome present' by the right-wing, anti-Islamist People's Party. It is a framed photo, showing German tanks in the streets of Copenhagen, taken during the invasion of 9 April, 1940 which led to the Danish Government reaching an accommodation with Nazi Germany. Their attached message is 'Never again 9th April', meaning that there should be no compromise with the Islamists. The People's Party's fictional leader, Erling Krabbe, is pressing for stronger anti-terrorist legislation to ban lawful Islamist associations. He is accused by Buch of scaremongering. Krabbe responds by emphasizing his democratic credentials using a further reference to World War II: 'My grandfather was in the resistance. He fought for freedom. He ended up in Neuengamme [a concentration camp in Hamburg].'

Buch retaliates in a similar vein in a later scene by insisting that he will not compromise on 'democratic values' and also draws on Second World War events in Denmark as a metaphor. He goes on to tell Krabbe, '. . . as far as I know, a Danish Government has only once before prohibited a legal association'. To emphasize the connection, he then hands Krabbe several photos of the German occupation forces on the streets of Denmark and continues, 'In 1941. The Communist Party. At the time, they (the Government) were being pressurized by the *Wehrmacht*.' When Krabbe retorts that this is not a valid comparison, Buch asks him, 'Do you want . . . to stand alone with an opinion that hasn't been expressed since the Nazis?'

The broader significance of these fictional events and interchanges is that today's Denmark still employs real events and conduct from World War II as reference points for contemporary issues. As we shall see, that characteristic also extends to Norway, Sweden and Finland.

The countries of Scandinavia (in this book conceived as Norway, Denmark, Sweden and Finland) have been regarded generally as backwaters of World War II while gigantic struggles and terrible cruelties took place elsewhere. After 1940, no large-scale military actions occurred there, other than in Finland, but in a European context the Finnish battles of 1944 were slight and not significant. The occupations of Denmark and Norway lasted from April and June 1940, respectively, until the surrender of the German forces on 4 and 7 May 1945, and were characterized by both resistance and collaboration in both countries. Their common neighbour, Sweden, retained its neutral status which the other three countries had unwillingly been forced to abandon by Germany and Russia, but it was subjected to pressures by the belligerents that caused it to flex its neutrality in favour of one side and then the other.

During the German invasion of April 1940, the Danish forces were ordered to surrender before they could offer much resistance, while the Norwegians held out until their inept allies withdrew in June. Increasing resistance in each country was matched by repression against civilians by the occupier. Finnish hostilities were in three phases: a defensive war against the Soviet Union, an offensive war against that country and finally, a reluctant expulsion of the former German brothers-in-arms. Sweden maintained a large conscript army in readiness to repel attack from whichever quarter; Germany, Russia and the western Allies were seen as potential threats to neutrality throughout. On the home fronts in each country, in addition to military considerations, economic and social conditions were characterized by shortages of all kinds of food and materials, and, while hardship was on a lower scale than in the occupied and war-torn territories to the south and east, it nevertheless shaped policies in the Scandinavian countries for occupier and native governments alike.

From these observations, a picture begins to emerge which shows that, for most of the populations of the Scandinavian countries, their position in World War II seemed anything but a backwater. As the 11 authors in this volume demonstrate, the events of the war years were so influential in the development of the respective national psyches that their meaning and importance remain as warmly debated issues today, pervading national politics and media discourse to an extent that might surprise a non-Scandinavian observer drawing his or her knowledge from English-language historiography. That aspect is discussed by *Patrick Salmon* in the context of his survey of current historiography, with additional comments by *Richard Overy* in his review of the war in Scandinavia.

An unfortunate but effective combination of language barriers and Scandinavian reticence have conspired to conceal the importance of the war years for our overall understanding of today's Scandinavia which, at the time of writing, is most famous for *film noir* crime fiction and terrorist outrages. Regarding the latter, Anders Breivik, in his perverted 'Manifesto', even sought to draw in some aspects of Sweden's wartime national narrative.[1] That feature links the concerns of the historian to those of the politician and makes the contents of this book even more relevant to today's discourse about societal consensus, culture and cohesion. The questions remain, however, as to what happened in Scandinavia during the war and what resulted from it – and it is this that the contributors attempt to address. Their essays reveal that a post-war reorientation of political and social self-image evolved which continues today. This was primarily due to the nature and intensity of the wartime experience and the conduct of the politicians, the military, civil authorities, businessmen and civilians, not to mention collaborators and resisters. All were faced with difficult choices due to the unwelcome attentions of the great powers. Pre-war circumstances, as *Richard Overy* explains, were hardly conducive to the maintenance of an optimistic neutrality, and his survey reveals how the events of late 1939 and early 1940 brought the region fleetingly from the periphery to the centre of the stuttering war in Europe. *Oula Silvennoinen* traces the long shadow that the 1918 Finnish civil war cast over the mindset of the leadership during 1940–44. *Niels Wium Olesen* ascribes wartime political continuity in Denmark partly to national stability and homogeneity in the interwar years. In Norway on the other hand, *Tom Kristiansen* reveals the surprising level of pre-war German influence on Norwegian economic, intellectual and cultural life. *Kent Zetterberg* emphasizes the pre-war thinking of a Swedish leadership determined to remain neutral but, if that were not possible, equally determined to come into the war 'on the right side'.

The Molotov-Ribbentrop Pact foreshadowed the beginning of the war for Scandinavia, suspending the traditional balance of power that had offered the region a modicum of security from the predations of its powerful, totalitarian neighbours. *Richard Overy* argues that their actions in Scandinavia were primarily driven by security considerations but that the eventual results of this search for security were poor recompense. The issue was more immediate for Finland. *Oula Silvennoinen* shows how the disillusionment over receiving warm words from the western powers but little concrete assistance during the Winter War against Russia drove the Finnish leadership into the arms of Germany. This unhappy relationship initially delivered Finnish security and recovery of its lost territory from Russia but ultimately led to national participation in a brutal, genocidal conflict that associated Finland with Nazism, despite somewhat naïve protestations to the contrary. In addition, there was an underlying expansionist tendency in Finnish policy which translated into a 'Greater Finland' war aim with associated preparation for 'ethnic cleansing'. *Oula Silvennoinen* delves into previously untouched areas of Finnish wartime history and by thorough research draws attention to previous ambiguities and inconsistencies.

If Finland experienced extensive hostilities and associated casualties, Denmark's armed struggle against Germany's 'protective occupation' could be measured in hours rather than in months, while the 5 years of German presence were characterized by an accommodation with the occupying power that was eventually displaced by increasing resistance to the occupation. *Niels Wium Olesen* details the political and judicial mechanisms and manoeuvres of the accommodation – a constitutional construct that protected all Danes (including Jews) up to the imposition of direct German rule in August 1943 by maintaining Danish domestic sovereignty – but whose anti-constitutional ambiguities contained the essence of its eventual failure and tainted all those associated with it.

Norway fared considerably worse than Denmark due to hostilities on its territory in 1940 and 1944. This was a more brutal occupation, with direct German rule from the outset and a markedly higher level of active resistance both in Norway itself and also by the overseas armed forces. This arose initially from the attempted imposition of Nazism on the country's institutions with the connivance of the right-wing extremist Norwegian collaborationist party, the *Nasjonal Samling*. *Tom Kristiansen's* wide-ranging essay sets out how the 10,000

Norwegians who lost their lives at home and abroad were a part of the support for the overall Allied war effort from an early stage of an invasion whose success for Germany and *débacle* for the Allies led to the formation of the Norwegian government-in-exile and a rejection of any accommodation with the occupiers. While resistance had its successes, the movement's passivity was criticized in London and, unlike Denmark, Norway lost a high percentage of its Jews to extermination without much difficulty for the Germans. The war ended with a country divided by collaboration but vindicated by heroic resistance while abandoning its Germanic associations and neutral posture in favour of the west and NATO.

Neutral Sweden, despite misgivings, remained neutral until the end of the war, but *Kent Zetterberg* demonstrates that its policy of adaptive neutrality was backed up by stronger defences than those of Denmark and Norway, the use of trading advantages to sustain itself and nimble if occasionally unheroic diplomacy to avoid confrontation with the watchful and suspicious belligerents. Sweden faced repeated political and diplomatic crises caused by its adherence to a neutral stance when under pressure to favour now one, then the other belligerent. Yet, the *Realpolitik* which contributed to Sweden's survival as an independent state implied an indifference to the outcome of the war that belied the widespread sentiment among its leadership and electorate in favour of an Allied victory against Nazism while fearing the Soviet Union.

With 1945 and the defeat of the Axis, all the Scandinavian countries discovered, as *Richard Overy* puts it, 'a need to find culprits'. The immediate post-war adjustments and settlements set the tone for the following period well into the 1990s. For Finland, *Juhana Aunesluoma* reviews the trials of Finland's wartime military and political leadership at the instigation of the Soviet Union as self-defeating – if they were intended to demonize – the result being to provide a platform for defence of their policies as legitimate and a basis for their lionization as national heroes. *Claus Bundgård Christensen* recounts that in Denmark, alongside the trials of volunteers for German service, paramilitary groups and collaborators leading to executions and imprisonment, the cohabiting politicians and their parties put out a series of publications intended to exculpate them from any wrongdoing and to justify their wartime policies. These publications led to the so-called 'consensual myth' stressing that politicians and resistance each played their patriotic parts. Norway experienced a tense post-war period of solidarity and strong feelings among those who could castigate the traitors, 'quislings' and collaborators, according to *Ole Kristian Grimnes*. Trials, executions, fines and imprisonment were also meted out legally, as in Denmark, and both countries avoided the lawlessness that had characterized liberation settlements elsewhere in Europe, notably in France. While these prosecutions included passive as well as active *Nasjonal Samling* members, this settlement process ('*landssvikoppgjør*') placed the mainstream population in the 'home front' (thus paradoxically recognizing passive resistance) to form the basis for the collective memory. *Johan Östling* indicates that only a small number of trials and enquiries took place in post-war Sweden in pursuit of closet and real Nazis in the media and the civil service. This assisted in a rapid return to normality, with the government rather than any resistance movement setting the tone for the interpretation of wartime events.

With the onset of the Cold War and Churchill locating the northern end of his symbolic 'iron curtain' just over 100 miles from Sweden ('From Stettin in the Baltic...'), Scandinavian portrayal of wartime events adopted a more purposeful approach to reinforce an impression of post-war national unity in the face of a new threat, this time from the Soviet Union. *Juhana Aunesluoma* outlines how official Finland built on the post-war trials to establish a defensible explanation of Finnish conduct that relied on equating both wartime dictators, distancing Finland from the wider conflict and asserting that the nation lacked 'agency' but instead was 'driftwood' in a torrent of totalitarianism. This narrative has also been the most persistent and deep-rooted in Finnish popular culture. Denmark also quickly adopted a core narrative based on the 'consensual myth' that proved to be remarkably enduring, according to *Claus Bundgård Christensen*. The wartime politicians provided the 'shields' for the resistance to wield the 'swords', but in the late 1950s it emerged that not every resistance group had been given access to a share of the swords; the communists had been undersupplied deliberately. In Norway also, *Ole Kristian Grimnes* identifies the communists as a complicating factor in post-war representations of national unity in wartime. Their reluctance to engage in resistance during the Nazi-Soviet Pact years until June 1941 contrasted with their keenness for sabotage thereafter, an enthusiasm that was not shared by a population fearful of reprisals. The post-war 'master narrative' that quickly took root was based on the concept of national mass resistance in a Manichean struggle that included sabotage and armed interventions.

Sweden's post-war interpretation of its concessionary adaptive neutrality, while it lacked a resistance element, was no less hegemonic than the other countries' narratives. The interpretation, described by *Johan Östling* as 'small-state realistic narrative', was seen as bestowing benefits on Sweden, her neighbours and European peace while avoiding the horrors of war and occupation. Here, too, the Swedish communists had been a complication due to their potential for treachery against Swedish neutrality – ranking alongside the Nazis – but mainstream 'liberal' wartime opponents of the government policy of concessions and engagement were also criticized for rocking the boat at a time when the government was struggling to avoid confrontations with Germany in particular. National unity was paramount.

For most of the period of the Cold War, each country's version of its patriotic narrative was maintained with increasing challenge from new research and assessments. In Finland, *Juhana Aunesluoma* describes how President Kekkonen seized on the rejection of the 'driftwood' theory in the 1970s to emphasize the benefits of his own policy of active neutrality with the Soviet Union, an approach that he believed had been rejected by his predecessors, leading to an unnecessary and disastrous Winter War for Finland. Similarly, Denmark's DNH research project in the 1970s produced two outputs that challenged the unity and effectiveness implied by the 'sword and shield' interpretation, but *Claus Bundgård Christensen* notes that the absence of any resulting alteration to Danish wartime commemoration was 'evidence of the distance between historians and large parts of the population' – something that is not, of course, peculiar to Denmark.

For Norway, *Ole Kristian Grimnes* identifies challenges to the dominance of the master narrative of 'a nation-in-resistance' as coming from the previously stigmatized collaborationists who have more recently been clamouring for an increased share of attention which has struck a responsive chord with those who were uneasy about the 'all-too pervasive character' of that narrative. Shades of grey began to be admitted to the discourse. Sweden also launched a national research project in the 1970s (SUAV) whose outputs *Johan Östling* characterizes as narrow, technical and dominated by 'small-state realism' with the result 'that broad questions concerning Sweden's policy were not addressed in depth'. This missed opportunity created a historiographical lacuna that was to be filled later.

Only in the post-Soviet Union era have the master narratives been tested to destruction, but not always by historians. Journalists and commentators have seized the initiative across Scandinavia and challenged the historians' self-imposed role as custodians of the narrative. Their earlier disregard for the moral implications of the Holocaust has been their undoing in an age where the images of Auschwitz easily displace balanced arguments in the popular mind. *Juhana Aunesluoma* appropriately refers to Auschwitz now being 'the keyhole from which everything else is seen', which challenges the wisdom of Finland's choice in 1941, the somewhat triumphalist view that the ends justified the means and the proclaimed heroism of the national sacrifice. The response to this challenge has been further to attempt to distance Finland's war(s) from World War II. This isolation and distancing has contributed to the maintenance of a strong popular commemoration of the shared heroic past, regardless of the more recent intellectual preoccupation with attributing responsibility for and implication in the Holocaust ever more widely.

The more recently contested interpretation of the wartime years has taken on contemporary political significance in Denmark. *Claus Bundgård Christensen* identifies this as relevant to debates on immigration and foreign military intervention by Denmark, with the policy of cohabitation being closely compared with the acceptance of non-Danish cultures and a failure to intervene against abusive regimes. In 2003, Prime Minister Anders Fogh Rasmussen reversed a 50-year political consensus by rejecting his wartime predecessors' actions as 'a moral betrayal'.

Morality has also intruded into the Norwegian public debate, which *Ole Kristian Grimnes* finds surprising but explicable due to the moral emphasis in the national narrative. He further selects fresh challenges for reinterpretation in the topics of Norwegian collaboration, police, Jews and communists, while he finds that claims of victimization of the collaborationists now challenge the durable heroic image of national adaptation and inclusion. In Sweden, a moral interpretation emerged, according to *Johan Östling*, in the 1990s as part of a larger European change moving from patriotism to universalism with the Holocaust as the catalyst for the shift. This resonated with a political class that wanted no wartime associations to complicate the Swedish position in the EU and so launched a 'warts and all' research project to root out anything previously concealed or overlooked. 'Small state realism' had been eclipsed by researchers taking the Holocaust as their starting point for an account of the war years when Sweden was neutral and unoccupied and did not surrender or lose any Jews to the Nazi extermination programme. On the contrary, Sweden did more than probably any other country to rescue Jews from the Germans' clutches.

Allan Little takes a concluding and uncompromising 'long view' of the entire experience of World War II and its aftermath for the four countries. In his essay, he construes that experience as being in part a moral test. For each country, he explores culpability, mitigation and redemption to reveal a troubling pattern of moral abdication emerging within these countries that had been neutral before the war. The mirror that we as historians and others hold up to national character is problematic in its reflection, redolent of the biblical phrase 'For now we see through a glass, darkly.'

Regrettably, the loss of the historians' role as custodians of narrative for the wartime period has been paralleled by a drift away from balance towards sensationalism, poorly researched articles and programmes where sources are replaced by innuendo and assertion, and where regurgitated half-truths are peddled as a matter of record. Increasingly, this *mélange* forms a 'virtual history' which, while unchallenged, shapes popular perceptions and substitutes itself like a cuckoo in the nest of the source-based national narrative. In sharp contrast to the prevailing trend, this book contributes a valuable riposte to such distortions in which authoritative and leading-edge scholarship by the contributors shines a searching beam into the wartime events and their commemoration, using deep understanding to guide the reader confidently through an apparent maze of fact and ambiguity to present a commanding assessment of this enduring feature, 'Hitler's Scandinavian Legacy'.

Note

1 For example, 'The Swedish Social Democrats were pro-Fascist and pro-Nazi during the 1930s and 40s...' https://publicintelligence.net/anders-behring-breiviks-complete-manifesto-2083-a-european-declaration-of-independence/ accessed 5 October 2012.

2

Scandinavia in the Second World War

Richard Overy

Scandinavia was fortunate not to take part in World War I which so scarred the rest of Europe (though Finland, still part of Tsarist Russia, had to supply troops for the Tsar's army). It was less fortunate in the war that followed. Between 1939 and 1945, the Scandinavian nations were willy-nilly part of the wider European war between fascism, communism and democracy. The impact of that war has remained a contested historical narrative to this day.[1]

The interwar history of the Scandinavian world gave few clues to its later involuntary participation in war. Scandinavia was on the geographical fringes of Europe. Three of the four states – Denmark (still united under the Danish crown with Iceland), Norway and Sweden – were constitutional monarchies. Finland, which won its full independence from Russia in 1918, was a parliamentary republic. There were small parties of the extreme right, some of which drew their inspiration from German National Socialism – including the Swedish and Danish National Socialist Workers' Parties – and some of which like the Finnish Lapua (People's Patriotic) Movement were authoritarian, anti-Communist organizations, but not necessarily fascist. Of the clearly fascist parties, only the Danish National Socialists, with 1.8 per cent of the vote, won seats in parliament.[2] The Norwegian *Nasjonal Samling* [National Unity] party, led by the former cabinet minister Vidkun Quisling, with 1.8 per cent of the vote in 1936, won no seats. Communism had little appeal in any of the Scandinavian states, except Finland (where it was banned); a leading Finnish communist, Otto Kuusinen became Comintern Secretary in Moscow despite the almost complete destruction of exile Finnish Communism in the Stalinist purges of 1937/8.[3] In the other states, the powerful social-democrat movements lived in uneasy and often hostile relation with communism, as they did in Britain and France.

The parliamentary systems survived the economic depression of the early 1930s, unlike other European states, and during the growing international crisis from the mid-1930s onwards the Scandinavian countries remained non-aligned. On 27 May 1938, the four Scandinavian governments signed a declaration of neutrality to make clear their desire not to become embroiled in wider European conflicts. They had small military forces and were not heavily armed, though Finland, bordering its powerful Soviet neighbour, was more prepared for combat than the rest. This powerlessness led the Danish government to sign an inauspicious non-aggression pact with Germany on 31 May 1939, but the other three states refused to enter into any specific agreements.[4] Every effort was made to ensure that neutrality meant what it said, although by the 1930s, as Neville Wylie has argued, the nature of modern war made neutrality a fragile status.[5] Although there were social divisions, each state had a strong sense of national identity and social cohesion, particularly over questions of foreign policy. Scandinavian countries were not like the new states of Eastern Europe, most of which abandoned democracy. These states had serious issues of ethnic conflict and economic crisis and were unable to avoid some level of involvement, voluntary or involuntary, in the expanding ambitions of Germany and the Soviet Union.

Scandinavia was nevertheless caught geographically between the two major dictatorships, Soviet and National Socialist, which bordered northern Europe. As Stalin laconically remarked in 1939: 'It is not the fault of either of us that geographical circumstances are as they are.'[6] Both dictatorships saw security issues as paramount as large-scale rearmament and growing international tension made a second major European war seem possible, if not probable. Soviet leaders looked for enhanced security in the Baltic against possible German incursions and disliked Scandinavian declarations of neutrality, which they interpreted as veiled sympathy for the fascist enemy; Stalin would have preferred a common anti-fascist alliance, but the only treaty the Soviet Union extracted was a non-aggression pact signed with Finland in 1932, which in the end proved as helpful to the Finns as the one signed by Denmark with Hitler's Germany.[7] For the German part, the German Navy worried about the northern flank if it ever found itself at war again with Britain, while German commercial interests in the Scandinavian region found themselves under growing pressure from the expansion there after 1930 of British trade, which challenged the dominant position traditionally enjoyed by German sellers. Although trade rivalry could be exploited to the advantage of the region, it also dragged the Scandinavian states willy-nilly into the growing political confrontation between Britain and Germany and exposed how dependent they might be on secure trade connections in the event of war.[8]

For all these reasons, Scandinavia's eventual involvement in the European war that broke out on 3 September 1939 was the product of geopolitical chance rather than international commitment or political preference.

I

The 'War in the North', a product of German and Soviet aggression, is often marginalized in the general accounts of World War II. Yet it involved substantial military operations and the permanent presence of large numbers of German troops, aircraft and shipping in Denmark, Norway and Finland; it also forced Sweden from a state of relative disarmament to establish forces in order to safeguard independence first from the German threat, then from the powerful Soviet presence in the last years of the conflict. The occupied areas of Scandinavia were also subject to regular air attack by the RAF against targets important to the Germans, while Finland suffered air attack from the Soviet Union three times, in 1939, 1941 and again in 1944.

The onset of warfare in Scandinavia came, nevertheless, from an unexpected source. The strategic significance of the region was made rudely evident to the wider world with the Soviet attack on Finland on 30 November 1939 which heralded the so-called 'Winter War'. Since this was the largest and deadliest of the conflicts in Scandinavia between 1939 and 1945, it is worth looking at the background in some detail. The Soviet Union had been concerned since the early 1930s that Finland might be used as an imperialist outpost in any future conflict; anxiety over the defensibility of the Baltic Sea area resulted in informal contacts between Soviet and Finnish politicians between April 1938 and the spring of 1939, when Soviet negotiators asked for a naval and air base for use in case of war.[9] The discussions lapsed during the Polish crisis over the summer, but under the terms of the German-Soviet Pact of 23 August, Finland was assigned to the Soviet sphere of influence. Only a few weeks before, in July 1939, the Soviet Military Council had drawn up firm contingency plans for an invasion of Finland if it sided with German aggression.[10] The outbreak of the German-Polish war and the Soviet occupation of eastern Poland and the Baltic States utterly transformed the situation confronting the Scandinavian nations, but particularly Finland with its common frontier with the Soviet Union and long memories of Russian domination. In October and November 1939, the Soviet side raised their demands: cession of all Finnish islands in the Gulf of

Finland, a lease on the port on the Hangö peninsula and an area of 2,700 square kilometres on the Karelian Isthmus north of Leningrad, to try to make the Soviet Union's second city more secure. In exchange, the Soviet regime offered a strip of Soviet Karelian territory, roughly double the size of the territory they were demanding from the Finns. Stalin thought this a remarkable concession: 'Does any great power do that? No!,' he told the Finnish delegates.[11] The Finns remained unimpressed. Apart from a number of small concessions, they were not prepared to lose control of sovereign territory.

The Soviet decision to move from negotiation to war had a number of causes. Stalin evidently expected Finland to accede to Soviet requests as the three Baltic States had been compelled to do for their own 'protection' in September and seems to have been influenced by intelligence sources that suggested Field Marshal Mannerheim, soon to be Finnish commander-in-chief and eponymous architect of Finland's border defences, had advised the government to make concessions.[12] This misconception was further fuelled by the belief that Finnish society was deeply divided and that the possibility existed of a pro-Communist movement among the Finnish poor. This suited Kuusinen, who played a key part in drafting the Comintern response to the 'imperialist' war between Germany and the Western powers in September 1939, and who hoped to profit from the sharp change in the balance of power in north-eastern Europe.[13] At some point in November during discussions with the Finns, Stalin began to explore the possibility of setting up a new government in Finland dominated by communists and entirely sympathetic to the Soviet Union. On their side, the Finns also displayed illusion. Some military leaders were unimpressed by the Red Army; political circles in Helsinki found it difficult to believe that the Soviet Union would actually risk a war at such a sensitive moment in Soviet relations with the other major powers. The refusal to accede to Soviet demands, stated a final time at the last Soviet-Finnish meeting on 9 November in Moscow, was not made in order to provoke a war that Finland had no desire to wage but in the hope that Stalin might back down. Patrick Salmon has called this attitude 'unrealistic', but the Finns could see what had happened to small states pressured from Germany or the Soviet Union. Room for real manoeuvre was limited, and defiance was perhaps as sound an option as any.[14]

Stalin left a way out for the Finns right to the end, although military preparations had begun even before the end of negotiations. On the afternoon of 26 November, according to Soviet claims published in *Pravda* the following day, Finnish artillery had shelled a Soviet border village, Mainila, killing four soldiers. Historians still debate the truth of this claim, but it seems evident that it was staged by the Soviet side, though not perhaps as an excuse for war (unlike the Gleiwitz incident on the evening of 31 August on the German-Polish frontier), but as a final opportunity to get the Finns to see sense. Molotov asked the Finnish government to move its forces back 20–25 kilometres as a gesture. Since this would in effect have given the Soviet side unopposed access to the stretch of the Isthmus it had asked for, the Finns argued that they would only do so if the Red Army also pulled back a similar distance.[15] This final rejection of the unilateral Soviet demands, however, accelerated the decision for war. On 28 November, the Soviet side abrogated the non-aggression treaty; the Leningrad Military District completed mobilization and the Russian fleet prepared to act in the Gulf of Finland. At just before seven o'clock on the morning of 30 November, the Red Army began an artillery barrage and a series of air attacks on the Finnish capital without a formal declaration of war. The Soviet side expected a quick victory within 3 weeks or even less; a pro-Soviet puppet government of the 'Finnish People's Republic' was set up at the captured Finnish town of Terijoki headed by Otto Kuusinen. Treaties of 'mutual aid' were signed between the new government and the Soviet Union to prepare the way for Soviet domination of a defeated Finland.[16]

The 'Winter War' was famously a disaster for Soviet forces. The Red Army in the end deployed 1.2 million men, 1,500 tanks and 3,000 aircraft, a force not very different in size from the German assault on Poland in September. The initial attack was launched by 23 divisions, spread along the whole Soviet-Finnish border, with 200,000 troops concentrated in the narrow neck of the Karelian Isthmus. To face this vast array, the Finnish army could mobilize a maximum of 300,000 men in 15 divisions, with a small airforce and almost no tanks.[17] The Finns had the advantage of knowing the terrain, had a prepared defensive line (the Mannerheim Line) across the Isthmus, and highly trained ski troops who could deploy the deadly Finnish 'Suomi' sub-machinegun while on the move. They faced an enemy whose war effort was so clumsy and disorganized, with inadequately clothed and armed troops forced to march in line abreast against fixed Finnish defences, that the failings encouraged confidence in German army circles that a future war with the Soviet Union was winnable. Finnish successes also reduced popular pressure on the Swedish government to intervene on Finland's side; no military help came from Finland's Nordic neighbours, though 10,000–12,000 Swedes gave voluntary assistance and military equipment was sold to the Finnish army.[18] In the end, the sheer weight of Red Army resources flung at the battlefront overcame Finnish resistance on the Line and on 12 March 1940 a peace was signed between the two states in Moscow, conceding most of what the Soviet Union had asked for in the first place, but preserving Finnish independence. The extraordinary resistance of the Finns came at a heavy price for both sides. The Red Army losses have never been confirmed but are estimated at something between 230,000 and 270,000; Finnish losses amounted to some 24,923.[19] Resistance also provided time for the three combatant powers in the West – Britain, France and Germany – to decide on how to respond to the strategic implications of Soviet aggression. The Winter War was in this sense a double problem for the Soviet Union: not only was Finland difficult to defeat, but Soviet aggression alerted the rest of Europe to the potential danger of allowing Scandinavia to remain a merely dormant area.

Germany refused to supply assistance for the Finns, under the terms of the Non-Aggression Pact with Moscow, but it was a reluctant act of self-denial, not only because many Germans sympathized with resistance to Bolshevism, but also because a Soviet victory suddenly threatened German raw material interests in Sweden and Norway. In February 1940, Soviet diplomats assured Germany that the Red Army would confine itself only to the Finnish campaign.[20] What was more worrying for Germany was the sudden interest shown by Britain and France in the Finnish campaign; any direct military intervention by the enemy might threaten German economic and strategic interests profoundly. Moreover, the other Scandinavian states were generally hostile to making any concessions to Germany even to enhance their security. The Western states had indeed been considering some form of intervention as an act of economic warfare, not only against the Swedish iron ore fields, but also against Soviet oil in the Caucasus.[21] The Winter War forced the Western Allies to think about aiding the Finns as a gesture against the two dictatorships, German and Soviet, who were regarded as virtual allies as a result of the Non-Aggression Pact. Britain sold and France gave limited material aid to the Finns (30 British fighter aircraft, 145 French 'planes, 500 heavy guns, 5,000 machine guns). This made little difference to the outcome but it demonstrated to all interested parties the Allied desire to prevent Scandinavia from being divided like eastern Europe between the two dictatorships.[22] From arms supplies, the West began to move towards the idea of active armed involvement to strike a blow at both Soviet and German interests. The British developed two plans, AVONMOUTH and STRATFORD, both approved at the Allied Supreme War Council on 5 February 1940. The first involved sending a small Anglo-French force to Narvik in Norway which would move to northern Sweden and secure the iron ore mines, while a smaller force went on to Finland to give military aid there. The second plan was to send an additional force (eventually of 3 divisions) to establish a defensive line in southern Sweden against any threat from Germany.[23] In the end, neither was carried out. The French were always more enthusiastic than the British, and the London cabinet rejected the plans in mid-March, but their existence almost certainly pressured the Soviet side into accepting an armistice with the Finns rather than occupying the whole country.[24] Stalin had done much to try to avoid entanglement in the larger war, a view he shared with the Scandinavian states. All of them had an interest in ensuring that Allied forces should not try to occupy any part of the region.[25]

From being on the periphery of war, Scandinavia now found itself briefly at its centre. Even before the onset of the Winter War, German leaders had begun to think in terms of military occupation of part of Scandinavia. The German Navy leadership from at least 1937 onwards looked for opportunities to extend into bases on the Norwegian coastline to allow for extended naval operations. In October 1939, Grand Admiral Raeder raised the possibility with Hitler of establishing a submarine base at Trondheim in Norway.[26] Relations with the region had been soured by the help given to Polish exiles after the German-Polish war, and recognition of the Polish government-in-exile.[27] However, only in December, with growing rumours of possible British intervention and following a visit to Berlin by Quisling, did Hitler decide to prepare a possible military operation against Norway, codenamed 'Weserübung', designed to secure bases for the sea war against Britain and to protect the flow of iron ore from Sweden.[28] Raeder and Alfred Rosenberg, the self-styled philosopher of National Socialism, both discussed with Quisling the prospect of launching an internal coup to turn Norway into a pro-German satellite without a conflict. Hitler also met Quisling and was sufficiently impressed to endorse the idea of a possible bloodless takeover of Norway with the help of its national socialists.[29] Like Stalin's misjudgment of Kuusinen, confidence in Quisling was entirely misplaced. Quisling's ideas for a Greater Nordic Peace Union or a Greater Germanic Union were as fanciful as Comintern's hope for a Finnish revolution.[30]

In the absence of any evidence that Norway would voluntarily accept German domination, Hitler issued the directive for Weserübung on 1 March 1940.[31] Occupation of Denmark was also regarded as unavoidable. As in Poland, German occupation of Norway would bring a common frontier with the Soviet Union, whose possible ambitions in the far north were still uncertain and a further reason for invasion. It was a risky operation and was kept so secret that the commander allocated to the operation, General von Falkenhorst, had to buy a Baedeker of Norway to find out where he was supposed to go.[32] In late March, there were unmistakable signs of imminent British action and on 2 April Hitler authorized invasion to begin a week later. By chance both Germany and the Allies were preparing almost simultaneous operations. On 5 April, the Allied governments warned Norway and Sweden that they could not tolerate continued supply of iron ore to Germany and proposed to mine Norwegian territorial waters. Three days later, they began the mining programme just as German ships began to sail for their invasion destinations. At 5 a.m. on 9 April, German forces began the occupation of Denmark, where brief resistance resulted in 16 deaths; the same day paratroops landed to seize Norwegian airfields and troops were disembarked along the southern coast. Quisling began his coup, but it ended in disaster. Norwegian resistance was sustained and on 15 April was joined by a British-French-Polish force which landed in northern Norway in an attempt to seize the port of Narvik. Despite difficulties of supply and severe losses of naval shipping, German forces succeeded in consolidating their position in Norway and after the outbreak of the campaign in the West on 10 May, the Allies gradually withdrew from Scandinavia, one of many British retreats over the next 2 years.[33]

The Norwegian campaign, though entirely successful by early June 1940, when the last Allied troops together with the Norwegian King and ministers sailed for Britain, was a disaster for the small German Navy. Norwegian defences and British sea power accounted for three cruisers sunk, two severely damaged and nine destroyers lost, as well as numerous smaller merchant or transport vessels.[34] The German occupation turned the seas around Norway and northern Sweden into a combat zone for the next 4 years in which much of what remained of the German navy was destroyed by air attack from Bomber Command and Coastal Command or by Royal Naval warships. The German Air Force stationed Air Fleet Five in bases in Denmark and Norway to attack Britain's north-eastern coastline, though it never became the 'German aircraft carrier' that Hermann Göring, air force commander-in-chief, had hoped for.[35] The only major bombing attack came on 15 August 1940 and the losses suffered were so severe that the bombing was never repeated. Bases in Scandinavia proved useful for attacking British North Sea shipping and for reconnaissance, though most of the anti-shipping war was conducted from the French coast.[36] The sea war became important chiefly because the Arctic route to the northern Russian ports of Murmansk and Archangel became one of the main supply arteries for

Lend-Lease aid to the Soviet Union after the German 'Barbarossa' invasion on 22 June 1941. A total of 4.43 million tons was transported by sea to northern Russia (some 22 per cent of all Lend-Lease supplies), of which 7 per cent was lost to German air and naval attack and the atrocious weather.[37] Some of the supply vessels were provided by the large Norwegian merchant fleet, 85 per cent of which had joined the Allies in 1940. By 1945, there were 28,000 Norwegians with 52 ships and 80 aircraft fighting alongside Allied forces.[38]

The third major conflict in the region reversed the first. On 26 June 1941, Finnish forces joined the Axis invasion of the Soviet Union as co-belligerents (but not as allies) in what became known as the 'Continuation War'. This was a difficult decision, given the losses sustained by Finnish society only a year previously and the ambivalence in popular attitudes to National Socialism. Despite Soviet distrust, the Finnish government drew closer to Hitler's Germany during the course of the year after the end of the Winter War.[39] Support for 'Barbarossa' carried the unmistakable risk that relations with Britain and the United States would be compromised or ruptured (and indeed under Soviet pressure Britain declared war on Finland on 7 December 1941).[40] Yet Finland's leaders clearly resented the Soviet defeat in 1940 (and the unmerited intervention of the Soviet government in Finland's internal affairs which had resulted) more than they feared association with German aggression. German forces posted to Finland relied on Finnish assistance in the difficult terrain of forest and swamp and freezing temperatures, but the Finnish army refused to be drawn like the Axis states of Hungary, Slovakia and Romania into large-scale combat with the Red Army. The Finns saw themselves fighting what they called a 'separate war', a view of the conflict that became embedded in popular post-war efforts to justify siding with Germany.[41] Finnish ambitions extended to taking back those territories occupied by the Soviet Union in spring 1940. By 8 September, the Finnish army had recaptured the territory in the neck of the Karelian Isthmus and stayed there instead of helping the German army to complete the capture of Leningrad or to tighten the subsequent siege.[42] Some territory in Soviet Karelia was occupied to extend Finnish control over an area they regarded as properly part of Finland (though its Finnish inhabitants had been deported in 1940 from the frontier regions to the Russian interior), but when the German army asked the Finns to participate in operation SALMON CATCH in summer 1942 to cut the Murmansk-Vologda railway, the Finns refused, uncertain about German success in the wider war.[43] The Finnish army then demobilized 180,000 troops, leaving the 200,000 Germans to use Finland as a route to their northern front.

The Continuation War was renewed in 1944 when Soviet forces at last liberated Leningrad and began to push Axis forces back towards the original Soviet frontier. Finland had been assured in November 1943 through Swedish intermediaries that the Soviet Union would not try to incorporate Finland as long as the government accepted Soviet demands.[44] The Finns hesitated, caught between Soviet and German pressure. To encourage Finnish compliance, the Soviet air force launched three major bombing raids on Helsinki in February 1944, though only three per cent of the bombs actually landed on the capital.[45] Although Finland put out peace feelers, they did not meet Soviet terms. Finnish forces renewed their resistance and the Soviet regime again toyed with the idea of occupation. On 10 June 1944, the Red Army once again attacked the Karelian Isthmus with two large armies. Caught by surprise by an enemy transformed from the clumsy colossus of the Winter War, Finnish resistance crumbled and by 21 June the Soviet army had reached Viipuri with Finland open before them. Although Finnish resistance became firmer, the Finnish government saw that Soviet gains on the southern Baltic coast made further support for the German war effort senseless. On 24 August 1944, the decision was made to abandon the war and an armistice was finally signed on 19 September.[46] Finland had to confirm the concessions made in March 1940 and give up the port of Petsamo on the Barents Sea. Stalin also wanted the Finns to expel German forces from their territory, perhaps as a way of earning their independence from the Soviet bloc rapidly being established in the rest of Eastern Europe. The Red Army drove the northern German forces from Soviet territory as far as the Norwegian port of Kirkenes, which was captured in October 1944, but the Finnish army had to force three German corps to withdraw into a small territory in northern Norway, where they surrendered in May 1945. Finnish forces lost a further 1,000 dead fighting their former co-belligerent.[47] This was Finland's third war, all three against the two major states, Germany and the Soviet Union, and all three survived without the loss of Finnish independence, a remarkable achievement in the context in which small European states had been forced to operate in the 1930s and 1940s.

II

What did the two dictatorships, German and Soviet hope to achieve by intervention in Scandinavia? In both cases, the central issue appeared to be security: for the Soviet Union, action in Finland was designed to strengthen the Soviet strategic position in the Baltic Sea, just as Soviet ambitions against Romania and Bulgaria in the south were to enhance security in the Black Sea region; for Germany, intervention in 1940 was designed to keep the Western Allies away from the northern flank with its essential raw material supplies and to provide a base for the blockade of Britain. German security also meant watching carefully what the Soviet Union was doing while the war in the West was still not won. The placing of German forces alongside Finnish in the campaign against the Soviet Union in June 1941 confirmed that Germany was as keen to protect the iron ore and nickel of the far north from any Soviet threat as it had been from the West.

Yet for both major states the search for security yielded results that were at best ambiguous. The poor performance of the Red Army in the Winter War confirmed intelligence perceptions abroad that Soviet military modernization was a façade, not improved by the purge of competent officers in 1937/8. In a situation where Soviet interests were threatened by Japan, Germany and a possible combination of 'imperialist' states, there was little to be gained by engaging in a conflict that displayed to the wider world just how vulnerable Soviet power seemed and which cost extravagant losses. The Soviet Union was also expelled from the League of Nations as a result of invading Finland, leaving it more politically isolated and encouraging its dangerous embrace of Hitler's Germany. Nor in the end were the concessions wrung from the Finns in March 1940 any real guarantee of security. Leningrad was made no safer for the Karelian Isthmus was easily regained and the city itself surrounded and besieged in a matter of weeks. In the Baltic Sea, German aircraft and submarines could not be prevented from exacting a heavy toll of Soviet shipping, including the complete destruction of a large convoy bound from Tallin in Estonia in August 1941 laden with military personnel.[48]

For Hitler, intervention in Scandinavia came to be regarded as one of two 'decisive' moments in the war alongside the crisis at Moscow in the winter of 1941/2. At dinner in April 1942, he listed the advantages: an effective submarine campaign, intervention in Arctic waters and the bombing of the British Midlands and northern Britain.[49] In fact, most of this list was made possible by seizing the French and Channel coast; the Midlands and north of England could not be attacked effectively from Norway and Denmark, while intervention in the Arctic seas accelerated the final destruction of the German Navy and yielded real success only against the ill-fated Convoy PQ17. Moreover, Germany was compelled to keep 350–400,000 troops and substantial equipment in the north to protect the region and, from summer 1941, to man the northern front line against the Soviet Union. They failed throughout the early years of the war to break the supply lines bringing Lend-Lease goods from the northern Russian ports to the Russian interior further south. Even the economic imperatives that had made intervention seem so important were unevenly rewarded. Swedish iron ore supplied some 21 per cent of iron ore needs between 1939 and 1943, but it is unlikely that without the invasion of Norway the supply would have dried up or been diverted elsewhere. Controlling Norway also produced an economic cost in coping with Norway's food deficiency and transferring substantial capital for projects, such as the ambitious plans for aluminium production, which then failed to materialize. Sabotage did little damage except for the loss of the heavy water plant to British-Norwegian saboteurs in 1943, which might have been avoided if a neutral Norway had been allowed to process and sell the material commercially. The balance of strategic costs and benefits for both dictatorships made the search for security a mixed blessing.

Concern for security in fact masked more substantial ideological and geopolitical ambitions for both the Soviet Union and Germany. Although there were no specific contingency plans in Moscow for constructing a Communist Scandinavia, the regime showed itself willing enough in other parts of Europe to respond opportunistically to changed circumstances. Finnish defiance in 1939 provoked Stalin into escalating the Soviet ambitions from the search for security to creating a Finnish People's Republic, perhaps as a prelude to its incorporation in 1940, like the Baltic States, into the federal Soviet state. A Soviet Finland opened up for the West (and for Germany) the alarming prospect of a possible Soviet presence facing the Atlantic.[50] Occupation of Finland, and indeed northern Norway, was a possibility again in 1944, but Stalin held the Red Army back when occupation, as in Romania or Bulgaria, would have been a simple option. Nikita Khrushchev later claimed that this was a display of sensible politics on Stalin's part; it is certainly the case that the Soviet side had benefited from a neutral Sweden during the war, first as a means to bring pressure on the Finns in 1940 to accept terms, later in 1943 to pressure Finland once again. In this case, as in Greece, Stalin may well have realized the potential costs and risks of creating Scandinavian satellites, 'blinkered not blinded' by ideology, as Geoffrey Roberts has put it.[51] Scandinavia remained during the early Cold War era an uneasy frontier between the two power blocs but one from which the Soviet Union also drew benefits in trade, intelligence and covert contacts.

In the German case, the wartime effort to begin construction of the German 'New Order' in Europe might well have involved Scandinavia in some putative Nordic bloc, or have turned the Scandinavian states into dependencies, entirely reliant on German goodwill to sustain healthy economies and tributary to the imperial centre in Berlin.[52] Hitler's own views on northern Europe were unsophisticated and trivial. 'It seems that the further North one goes,' he told his dinner-time companions in August 1942, 'the more drink people can carry'; and speculating on why the Finns were apparently so prone to mental disease, he explained that it was the summer light, the isolation and too much reading of the Jewish Old Testament.[53] There were nevertheless plans encouraged by Hitler to turn Denmark and Norway into dependent provinces. Norway was to host the largest naval base in Europe at Trondheim, while the development of Norwegian hydro-electric power was designed to make Norway, in Hitler's words, 'the electrical centre of Northern Europe'.[54] As part of a Germanic bloc, Norway would also supply essential materials, including aluminium, to the industrial heartland in Germany. German industrial and construction projects in wartime Norway suggested that the intention was to stay on as the imperial power after a German victory.[55] In reality, the short-term economic exploitation of the region for the German war economy took priority; Scandinavian trade with Germany expanded as western markets disappeared and labour, wood products, metals and metal ores helped sustain German military production until almost the end of the war. Around 100,000 Soviet POWs were sent to Norway to work, housed in 249 camps spread out across the country.[56]

On Finland, Hitler seems to have been content with the idea that the Finns would remain independent defenders of the northern flank of the 'New Order'. The more difficult problem was Sweden. A German occupation was always a possibility, at least up to the point where Sweden was heavily armed enough to resist such an attempt. The small Swedish armed forces at the start of the war, with 79 anti-aircraft guns, no tanks and 300 aircraft, had been transformed by 1945 into an army of 600,000 trained men, boasting 2,750 anti-aircraft guns, 766 tanks and 1,018 aircraft, many of them up-to-date models. This was defence against the Soviet threat as well as the German, but it would have made Sweden a much more difficult prospect for a weakened German army in the north. At times, Hitler was inclined to overcome Swedish objections to German demands for economic or military concessions by occupation, but there were advantages in Sweden's continued neutrality as there were for the Soviet Union. Sweden was an intelligence *entrepôt* during the war, in which German secret servicemen got access to material of use to the German intelligence services (some of it from collaboration with the Swedish intelligence and police forces). It was also a possible conduit for secret negotiations, as it was briefly in the winter of 1939/40 as the German side hoped for a British request for a negotiated peace and again later in the war, when Germany faced the need to find political solutions to a deteriorating war situation. Swedish banks and companies facilitated German international operations, while the flow of iron ore continued uninterrupted into 1944. Although it has often been argued that Sweden avoided occupation only by giving in to everything the German armed forces asked for, there were clear disadvantages in occupying Sweden as there would have been in occupying Switzerland.[57]

For the Allied side, there were also advantages in not having succeeded in 1940 in pre-empting the German invasion with an occupation of their own. The loss of trade proved not to be debilitating, while the political costs of trying to occupy militarily states that wished to remain neutral, as was shown in the brief British occupation of Iceland in 1940–41, were considerable.[58] Moreover, an independent Sweden also gave the British, and later the Americans, an important avenue to intelligence-gathering and covert operations, and a window onto the nearby German enemy. Swedish diplomats and businessmen furnished the RAF with eyewitness accounts (most of them in fact exaggerated, though not deliberately so) about the damage done by Bomber Command to German cities. The British Special Operations Executive operated in Sweden, though only on the understanding that it did not plan sabotage activities in Sweden. This did not prevent SOE from collaborating with the Norwegian resistance from Swedish soil.[59] The German occupation of Norway and Denmark also compelled the German side to keep large forces stationed permanently in Scandinavia (a factor to be exploited in the deception campaign, FORTITUDE NORTH, operated before the Normandy landings), while it gave British special forces a potential ally in the Norwegian and Danish resistance for acts of sabotage and the disruption of German interests.[60] The most strategically significant of these interventions was the partial destruction of the Norwegian heavy water plant at the Norsk Hydro works at Rjukan in February 1943, which undermined the German nuclear research programme at a critical moment. In addition, British bombing of targets in Denmark and Norway, which continued intermittently for most of the war, compelled German forces to keep anti-aircraft guns and aircraft permanently stationed there.[61] British, and later American interest in Scandinavia, compelled a German presence far out of proportion to the effort required of the Allies.

III

The effects of the war on the Scandinavian countries themselves were diverse but substantial. On many of the key issues involved for Scandinavian societies, there is still no historical consensus. A recent study of 'Nordic narratives' has contrasted the patriotic and the universalist, the first, a defence of key decisions and positions taken under the pressure of circumstances, the second, an acknowledgement that self-interest undermined the universal values threatened by the German political and racial remodelling of Europe.[62] The diversity is evident in the fact that the four Scandinavian countries between them represented four different ways of coping under the impact of a German-dominated Europe: one was neutral, one a co-belligerent against the Soviet Union, one a so-called 'model' occupied state, taken over without resistance, and one an occupied state that fought against its occupation. Any narrative of Scandinavia under the impact of war must disaggregate the effect of these differences. Though there were evidently shared experiences, it is striking how little mutual assistance or collaboration the four states gave to one another.[63]

The most immediate effect was physical loss. An estimated 100,000 Scandinavians died during the war, but 89,000 of them were Finns fighting against the Soviet Union, the rest a mix of resistance fighters, political prisoners, bombing victims and a small handful of Finnish and Norwegian Jews who were killed in the Holocaust. The pattern of losses reflects the very different political and military circumstances faced by the individual states. The most unusual was the fate of Iceland, nominally independent but linked by an Act of Union with the Danish crown. The German invasion of Denmark prompted Icelandic leaders to declare a unilateral assumption of the powers still enjoyed by the distant king, Christian X. In May 1940, the undefended island was occupied by British forces to forestall the Germans. An uneasy relationship existed between the two sides, though most Icelanders seem to have been relieved that it was a British occupation. In July 1941, the United States assumed responsibility for the island, partly to minimize the risk of German intervention against the forces of an enemy state. Iceland's leaders used the opportunity to argue for full independence, but the Allies were reluctant to agree. In fact, under the Act of Union, Iceland had the right to declare an end to the link in 1944 and on 17 June that year the Icelandic parliament declared Iceland an independent republic under its first president, Sveirn Bjornsson – a status that was successfully retained at the war's end. In Iceland, political differences were papered over by rising prosperity and the prospect of national independence.[64]

In the four major Scandinavian countries, the political differences were sharper. In Norway, the temporary success of Vidkun Quisling, who became minister president of Norway on 1 February 1942 after a long period in which his political ambitions were frustrated by the occupiers, provoked sharp opposition from much of Norwegian society. Following the failed coup in April 1940 Quisling had had to give way to the German commissar, the *Gauleiter* of Essen, Josef Terboven. In September 1940, the commissar instituted a 'new order' in Norway, abolishing the monarchy, the exile government and all political parties except Quisling's. A commissarial state council was set up and was headed by Quisling and dominated by *Nasjonal Samling* members, but the real authority still lay with the German commissar.[65] Under Quisling's direction, however, a raft of authoritarian legislation was introduced on censorship, the control of the press, race and control of labour. The *Nasjonal Samling* had no more than 50,000 members at its peak, many of them opportunistic fellow travellers. The Norwegian contingents for the SS never numbered more than 1,200.[66] Support for the new regime and its ideology of 'nordicization' was always limited and declined sharply as Germany's fortunes also declined. There was widespread passive resistance and non-compliance in the first year, but a German crackdown pushed the resistance underground following popular protests in May 1941. A military resistance was established, based on Oslo, known as *Milorg*, and although it preferred at first to focus principally on building up an organization to prepare for action at the appropriate moment, rather than armed resistance, it symbolized the permanent rift between Norway's fascist puppets and a more authentic form of Norwegian nationalism.[67] Hitler's relations with Quisling were mixed. Norway's constitutional position was awkward since the King, Haakon VII, and the exile Norwegian government were still Norway's rulers in the eyes of the rest of the world. They had abandoned neutrality in December 1940 by declaring for the Allied cause.[68] Hitler refused Quisling's request for a peace settlement and insisted on supporting Terboven's authority for what Hitler thought was 'the most difficult commissarship of the Reich'. Though Quisling styled himself Norway's *Führer*, he was forced to follow rather than to lead.[69]

In Denmark, the King and government remained in place when German forces entered in 1940 after a short show of resistance by the army in North Schleswig. Up until 29 August 1943, under the loose supervision of the German Foreign Office and the German Army, Denmark kept its constitutional status under a National Government, despite the unsuccessful efforts of the Danish National Socialist Party to benefit from German occupation. The government accepted that the price of the semi-independent status was to agree to the demands made by the German authorities rather than to contest them. In November 1941, Denmark had to sign the Anti-Comintern Pact; 100,000 Danish workers were employed inside the Reich; even before the war Denmark had been heavily reliant on German imports.[70] The arrival of the SS leader Werner Best as German representative in November 1942 created a growing antagonism between the two sides. An election in March 1943 – the only election in the New Order – gave 94 per cent support to the coalition government, a result that the German officials interpreted as anti-German. Efforts to get Denmark to deliver its small population of Jews were frustrated by a concerted programme of assistance that resulted in almost all of the 7,000 Danish Jews escaping by boat to Sweden. Only 52 of those who failed to escape were killed.[71] Some effort was made to harness support for Danish National Socialism and to integrate Denmark with future plans of Germanization, but with limited success.[72]

Following Danish popular protests, on 29 August 1943 Best declared an end to Denmark's special status; Danish military installations were forcibly occupied and political opponents were arrested. Denmark was run by a committee of ministerial heads, collaborating with the German occupation authority. The result here, as in Norway, was to provoke growing resistance. A rival Freedom Council was established and supported by the Danish resistance, working hand in hand with the British SOE, whose chief aim was to destabilize Danish politics through a sabotage campaign and to encourage a German takeover. The Council declared war on Germany, setting Denmark firmly on the Allied side.[73] Active anti-German actions stepped up in 1944 as German defeat appeared imminent. The resistance organization numbered 40,000 by 1945, with perhaps 800 active saboteurs. In Norway, the *Milorg* resistance network also numbered around 40,000 by the end of the war. The growing anti-German sentiment was fuelled by the evidence of Axis defeats, but it was bought at a high cost. Some 40,000 Norwegians were imprisoned or deported, 10,000 of them to concentration camps in Germany, 20,000 to camps in Norway; an estimated 2,500 died in captivity.[74]

In Finland and Sweden, the situation was very different. In neither case was the country united on the decision to collaborate with the German war effort, but in neither case did the government endorse actions that would seriously destabilize relations with their powerful neighbour. For Sweden, the period from the Winter War to the end of the war was one of permanent emergency. A National Government was installed in December 1939 under Per Albin Hansson to cope with the exceptional situation. Public opinion was divided over hostility to the Soviet Union and fear of, or dislike for, National Socialism. For the government, the delicate issue remained how far to go in rejecting or compromising German requirements without undermining Swedish independence. The economic relationship with Germany, like that of Norway and Denmark, was forced by economic reality to fit in with German demands. For Sweden, the more sensitive question was the German armed forces' requirement for transit rights for forces going to Norway or Finland, the right for air force overflights and the supply of military equipment (e.g. the 2,000 army tents sold to the German army in Finland).[75] Each request was treated as an issue for negotiation, rather than something to be taken for granted, though both at the time and since it has been argued that the Swedish government conceded more than was politically necessary or morally justified. The key figure was the Swedish foreign minister, Christian Günther, who from December 1939 had the challenging role of defining the limits of what Sweden would accept without alienating German goodwill. This meant in effect that Swedish 'neutrality' was increasingly nominal, but it also meant, according to Günther, that 'Swedish soil remains Swedish', a moral issue that for many leading Swedes overrode any qualms about helping an aggressive and criminal Germany.[76] The transit rights were only abrogated in August 1943 under pressure from the Western Allies, but German forces continued to move through Sweden in 1944 regardless. Only in 1944 when it was evident that occupation of Sweden was operationally impossible and German forces were in full retreat did it prove possible for the Swedish government and Swedish business to side more openly with Allied needs, but even on the trade question (which did not technically violate neutrality) Swedish producers found hidden ways of maintaining supplies to Germany in the final months of war. The Swedish press and public had always had a more cautious, even hostile view of the German links, but even though by 1944 much Swedish opinion was pro-Allied, there was still an unwillingness to abandon Swedish independence of action.[77] The Enskilda Bank, whose activities in support of German financial and trade policies have now been fully exposed, moved prudentially to cut its ties with the German multinationals IG Farben and Robert Bosch in the winter of 1943–44.[78] Swedish authorities proved willing to allow the Allies access to the secrets of the German V2 rockets that landed accidentally on Swedish soil but on more active assistance remained as neutral as circumstances would permit.[79]

For Finland, the divisions were even more complicated and the decisions related to the war more fateful. Over the Winter War there had been little choice in the face of Soviet aggression, although Finland could have backed down. Yet war with Russia did not automatically turn Finnish opinion or the Finnish government towards Germany, though defeat inclined Finland to a more authoritarian politics. Under president Risto Ryti, elected in December 1940, the role of parliament declined, the press was censored, strikes were outlawed in May 1941 and severe levels of rationing were imposed, which reduced calorie intake to 1,000 a day. Co-belligerency was a difficult decision, and the Continuation War did not provoke the same level of social solidarity shown in December 1939. From 1941, Finnish trade was dominated by German Europe, with 80 per cent of exports and 85 per cent of imports. Finland had to supply billets for German forces on the northern front and to supply other winter requirements. In addition, there was a major refugee crisis when 430,000 people were expelled from the areas occupied by Soviet forces in 1940; despite efforts at resettlement, population flows in 1942 and again in 1944 in response to the war left Finland with almost 450,000 displaced persons in 1945 out of a population of just 3.6 million.[80]

The Swedish and Finnish cases have raised in an acute form the dichotomy of resistance and collaboration. Much of the critical reassessment of the historical legacy of the war in both countries has focused on the failure to find ways of reducing support for the German military and economic machine. As in most European countries touched by the Axis war, the dichotomy is never straightforward. There exists a large grey area between the two positions in which ordinary people as well as officials, businessmen and policemen can limit what they do to assist their common enemy in mundane ways, or withdraw as far as possible from the public sphere in order to preserve their private world and avoid risk. These positions are seldom heroic and can involve difficult moral choices with which those in safety abroad at the time or those born after the event have little sympathy. In Sweden and Finland, independence remained a critical objective. As Hans-Jürgen Lutzhöft has put it, 'much had to be sacrificed in order not to lose everything'.[81] This resulted in a prudential and expedient approach to issues that no Scandinavian country in the 1930s expected to have to make. The novelty of the threat during the war forced improvised and reactive responses where the priority was survival and the minimizing of risk. The moral case can be made both ways in a war not of their own making.

For the Scandinavian populations, however, there was a need to find culprits in 1945. For all the discussion in present-day Scandinavia about the failure to uphold universal human values, there was a strong sense of retribution at the time against those deemed to have failed those values. In Denmark, 34,000 people were punished for collaboration; in Norway, 20,000 were imprisoned and 30,000 lost their civil rights. Quisling was condemned to death, a symbol of betrayal. In Finland, the return of Finnish communists to political life in the autumn of 1944 brought demands for a cleansing of the administration and a Finnish War Trial. Ryti and other Finnish leaders were put on trial and the prevailing public narrative of the war stressed the pro-German treachery of Ryti and his seven colleagues, all of whom were convicted.[82] Only in Sweden did the narrative of what Johan Östling calls 'small-state realism' prevent any political break in 1945 or any wave of political vendetta. Sweden continued to assert its neutrality while Norway and Denmark both looked to a wider European or Atlantic security.[83] Finland was closer to Soviet interests and signed a pact of mutual co-operation in 1948, but retained its independence and close links with the West.[84] None of this is to set aside the acts of betrayal, the search for easy profits or the episodes of exaggerated conciliation which were punished at the time or have been exposed since, but it is necessary to see them in a particular historical context in which choices in everyday life were suddenly, by the rupture of war, invested with a moral significance they do not usually possess. After 5 years, the mundane context of liberal life was restored, deeply scarred by the experience of war, but not irreversibly so. For Scandinavia, the transfer from war to peace was fraught with unresolved conflicts and contested versions of the recent past, but in all four cases the path to a restored parliamentary rule and reintegration into the international economic and political order proved that the war was an aberration, not a consequence of Scandinavia's pre-war international configuration or domestic political pressures, where in the case of Germany, Britain, Italy and France the war was rooted in the experience of the Great War and its unfinished business.

Notes

1. See the important collection of essays in Stenius, Henrik, Österberg, Mirja, Östling, Johan (eds) (2011), *Nordic Narratives of the Second World War: National Historiographies Revisited*. Lund: Nordic Academic Press, especially Chapter 1.
2. For details on the extreme right, see Payne, Stanley (1995), *A History of Fascism 1914–1945*. Madison: Wisconsin UP, pp. 306–11; Lindström, Ulf (1985), *Fascism in Scandinavia 1920–1940*. Stockholm: Almquist & Wiksell. The Lapua movement,

named after a township where violent anti-Communist riots occurred in 1929, changed its name to the Patriotic People's Movement following a failed coup in 1932.
3. Rentola, Kimmo (1998), 'The Finnish Communists and the Winter War', *Journal of Contemporary History* 33: 591-2.
4. Koszel, Bogdan (1991), 'The attitude of the Scandinavian countries to Nazi Germany's war preparations and its aggression on Poland', in Hiden, John, Lane, Thomas (eds), *The Baltic and the Outbreak of the Second World War*. Cambridge: CUP, pp. 124-7.
5. Wylie, Neville (ed.) (2002), *European Neutrals and Non-Belligerents during the Second World War*. Cambridge: CUP, pp. 4-5.
6. Berner, Örjan (1986), *Soviet Policies toward the Nordic Countries*. New York: University Press of America, p. 23.
7. Salmon, Patrick (1991), 'Great Britain, the Soviet Union and Finland', in Hiden, John, Lane, Thomas (eds), *The Baltic and the Outbreak of the Second World War*. Cambridge: CUP, pp. 97-9.
8. Salmon, Patrick (1986), 'Anglo-German Trade Rivalry in the Depression Era: The Political and Economic Impact on Scandinavia 1931-1939', in Recker, Marie-Luise (ed.), *Von der Konkurrenz zur Rivalität: Das britische-deutsche Verhältnis in den Ländern der europäischen Peripherie 1919-1939*. Wiesbaden: Franz Steiner Verlag, pp. 102-6; idem (1991), 'British Policy towards the Nordic Countries between the Wars', in Bohn, Robert, Elvert, Jürgen, Rebas, Hain, Salewski, Michael (eds), *Neutralität und totalitäre Aggression: Nordeuropa und die Grossmächte im Zweiten Weltkrieg*. Stuttgart: Franz Steiner Verlag, pp. 16-17, 19-20.
9. On Soviet attitudes, see Röpstorff, Thomas (1991), 'Finnland zwischen Berlin und Moskau', in Bohn et al. (eds), pp. 93-5.
10. Spring, D. W. (1986), 'The Soviet Decision for War against Finland, 30 November 1939', *Soviet Studies* 38: 213-14.
11. Berner (1986), pp. 23-4; Salmon (1991), pp. 99-101; van Dyke, Carl (1997), *The Soviet Invasion of Finland 1939-40*. London: Frank Cass, pp. 16-18.
12. Kulkov, E. N., Rzheshevsky, Oleg (eds) (2002), *Stalin and the Soviet-Finnish War 1939-1940*. London: Frank Cass, pp. xx-xxi.
13. Dallin, Alexander, Firsov, F. I. (eds) (2000), *Dimitrov and Stalin 1934-1943: Letters from the Soviet Archives*. New Haven: Yale UP, pp. 164-5; on fantasies of imminent social crisis, see also Rentola (1998), pp. 596-7.
14. Salmon (1991), pp. 101-2; van Dyke (1997), pp. 18-21.
15. Spring (1986), pp. 220-1, who argues that the Soviet side displayed considerable equivocation about the risks involved in actually going to war.
16. Dallin, Firsov (2000), p. 164; van Dyke (1997), pp. 56-7.
17. Trotter, William (2002), *The Winter War: The Russo-Finnish War of 1939-1940*. London: Aurum Press, pp. 19-21; van Dyke (1997), pp. 39-40.

18 Magnusson, Thomas (1991), 'Schweden, Finnland und die baltischen Staaten', in Bohn et al. (eds), pp. 209–11. Sweden did mobilize a part of its army, but against the Soviet threat rather than as a prelude to intervention. See also Levine, Paul A. (2002), 'Swedish neutrality during the Second World War: tactical success or moral compromise?', in Wylie (ed.), pp. 314–15.
19 Trotter (2002), p. 263. The official Soviet figure for war dead was 48,745, but it has been revised upwards over the past two decades to reflect more closely what is known of the army's losses.
20 Lutzhöft, Hans-Jürgen (1981), *Deutsche Militärpolitik und schwedische Neutralität 1939–1942*. Neumünster: Karl Wachholtz Verlag, p. 32; Röpstorff (1991), pp. 96–7.
21 Richardson, Charles O. (1973), 'French plans for Allied attacks on the Caucasus Oilfields, Jan-Apr. 1940', *French Historical Studies* 8(1): 130–56.
22 Kulkov, Rzheshevsky (2002), pp. xxii; Salmon (1991), pp. 116–17; Munch-Petersen, Thomas (1991), 'Britain and the Outbreak of the Winter War', in Bohn et al. (eds), pp. 87–9.
23 Kennedy, John (1957), *The Business of War*. London: Hutchinson, pp. 47–8; Salmon (1991), pp. 121–2.
24 Skodvin, Magne (1991), 'Skandinavien in der westallierten militärischen Planung', in Bohl et al. (eds), pp. 75–7.
25 See the discussion of Norwegian hostility to British pressure on neutrality in Salmon, Patrick (2002), 'Norway', in Wylie (ed.), pp. 53–60.
26 'Report of C-in-C Navy to the Fuehrer, 10 October 1939', in *Fuehrer Conferences on Naval Affairs 1939–1945* (1990), London: Greenhill Books, p. 47; Ottmer, Hans-Martin (1991), 'Skandinavien in den marinestrategischen Planungen der Reichs-bzw. Kriegsmarine', in Bohl et al. (eds), pp. 49–50, 64. Raeder hoped that combined German-Soviet pressure might persuade Norway to yield the use of bases without the need for further aggression.
27 Koszel (1992), pp. 132–4.
28 See Salewski, Michael (1991), 'Das Wesentliche von "Weserübung"', in Bohn et al. (eds), pp. 123–4. Salewski argues that Hitler was less worried about British intervention and more concerned about a possible anti-German Scandinavian coalition.
29 'Report of the C-in-C Navy to the Fuehrer, 12 December 1939', in *Fuehrer Conferences (1990)*, pp. 64–5, 67; Salewski (1991), p. 124; Dahl, Hans F. (1991),'The Question of Quisling. Aspects of the German Occupation Regime in Norway', in Bohn et al. (eds), pp. 195–200.
30 Dahl, Hans F. (1999), *Quisling: A Study in Treachery*. Cambridge: CUP, pp. 217–20.
31 Trevor-Roper, Hugh (ed.) (1964), *Hitler's War Directives 1939–1945*. London: Sidgwick & Jackson, pp. 61–4; *Fuehrer Conferences (1990)*, pp. 83–4.

32 This according to Nicolaus von Below, Hitler's air adjutant. See von Below, Nicolaus (2001), *At Hitler's Side: The Memoirs of Hitler's Luftwaffe Adjutant 1937–1945*. London: Greenhill Books, p. 51.
33 For a comprehensive account, see Stegemann, Bernd (1991), 'Operation Weserübung', in Maier, Klaus et al. (eds), *Germany and the Second World War: Volume II: Germany's Initial Conquests in Europe*. Oxford: OUP, pp. 206–19.
34 Details in *Fuehrer Conferences (1990)*, p. 91.
35 Eberle, Henrik, Uhl, Matthias (eds) (2005), *The Hitler Book: The Secret Dossier Prepared for Stalin*. London: John Murray, p. 54.
36 Neitzel, Sönke (1995), *Der Einsatz der deutschen Luftwaffe über dem Atlantik und der Nordsee 1939–1945*. Bonn: Bernard & Graefe Verlag, esp. pp. 58–66, 228–32.
37 Schofield, Brian B. (1964), *The Russian Convoys*. London: Batsford, p. 206, and Kemp, P. (1993), *Convoy. Drama in Arctic Waters*. London: Cassel, p. 235, Appendix 3.
38 Andenæs, Johannes Bratt, Skodvin, Magne, Riste, Olav (1966), *Norway and the Second World War*. Oslo: Grundt Tanum, p. 118.
39 See the details in Röpstorff (1991), pp. 92, 99–101.
40 Koszel (1992), pp. 134–5.
41 Meinander, Henrik (2011), 'A Separate Story? Interpretations of Finland in the Second World War', in Stenius, Österberg, Östling (eds), pp. 55–61.
42 Mawdsley, Evan (2005), *Thunder in the East: The Nazi-Soviet War 1941–1945*. London: Hodder Arnold, p. 129; Trotter (2002), pp. 265–7; Glantz, David (2001), *The Siege of Leningrad, 1941–1944: 900 Days of Terror*. London: Cassell, pp. 34–5.
43 Ibid., pp. 179–80.
44 Berner (1986), p. 35.
45 Medved, Alexsandr N., Hazanov, Dmitrii B. (2000), 'ADD: hyökkäykset Helsinkiin helmikuussa 1944', in *Sotahistoriallinen Seura & Sotamuseo*. Jyväskylä, pp. 134–75. Some 30 Soviet aircraft were lost in the attacks from anti-aircraft fire and accidents. See Trotter (2002), p. 268, who argues that the Red Army still performed poorly once Finnish resistance began to stiffen.
46 Mawdsley (2005), pp. 292–5; Röpstorff (1991), pp. 108–14.
47 Ibid., p. 115; Trotter (2002), pp. 268–9.
48 Mawdsley (2005), p. 83.
49 Trevor-Roper, Hugh (ed.) (1973), *Hitler's Table Talk, 1941–44*. London: Weidenfeld & Nicolson, pp. 438–9, entry for 24 April 1942.
50 Berner (1986), pp. 17–19.
51 Roberts, Geoffrey (2006), *Stalin's Wars: From World War to Cold War, 1939–1953*. New Haven: Yale UP, pp. 47–8.

52 Mazower, Mark (2008), *Hitler's New Order: Nazi Rule in Occupied Europe*. London: Allen Lane, pp. 207, 247. The idea of a 'Nordic Bloc' was suggested by the head of the RSHA, Reinhard Heydrich, in a speech in Prague in 1942, shortly before his assassination.
53 Trevor-Roper (1973), pp. 512–13, 612, entries for 5 June 1942 and 5 August 1942.
54 Ibid., p. 22, entry for 2 August 1941.
55 On German planning, see Alan S. Milward (1972), *The Fascist Economy in Norway*. Oxford: OUP, pp. 61ff.
56 On economic exploitation and Scandinavian dependency, see Fritz, Martin (1991), 'Neutrality and Swedish Economic Interests', and Petrick, Fritz (1991), 'Die Bedeutung der Rohstoffe Nordeuropas für die deutsche Kriegswirtschaft', both in Bohn et al. (eds), pp. 296–9, 312–14, 323–34. On POWs, see Ottoson, Kristian (1991), 'Arbeits- und Konzentrationslager in Norwegen 1940-45', in ibid., pp. 358–9.
57 Lutzhöft (1981), *Deutsche Militärpolitik*, pp. 201–4, for a discussion of the options facing Germany in Sweden.
58 See the discussion in Nuechterlein, Donald E. (1961), *Iceland: Reluctant Ally*. Ithaca: Cornell UP, pp. 23–36.
59 Stafford, David (1983), *Britain and European Resistance: A Survey of the Special Operations Executive*. Toronto: University of Toronto Press, pp. 77, 255.
60 Howard, Michael (1990), *Strategic Deception in the Second World War*. London: HMSO, pp. 110–11, 115–18.
61 For details of the regular bombing of Denmark, see Kristensen, Henrik Skov, Kofoed, Claus, Weber, Frank (1988), *Vestallierede Luftangreb I Danmark under 2. Verdenskrig*. 2 vols, Aarhus: Aarhus Universitetsforlag.
62 Stenius, Österberg, Östling (2011), pp. 11–18.
63 See, for example, Weibull, Jörgen (1991), 'The Politics of the Scandinavian States under the Threat of Hitler', in Bohn et al. (eds), *Neutralität und totalitäre Aggression*, pp. 5–8; Wylie (2002), pp. 9–10.
64 Hardarson, Solrun Jensdottir (1974), 'The "Republic of Iceland" 1940-44: Anglo-American Attitude and Influence', *Journal of Contemporary History* 9: 33–6, 39–41, 43–57.
65 Bohn, Robert (1991), 'Die Errichtung des Reichskommissariats Norwegen', in Bohn et al. (eds), pp. 137–42, 146.
66 Dahl (1999), pp. 214–15, 226.
67 Stafford (1983), pp. 130, 156; Mazower (2008), p. 478.
68 Salmon (2002), pp. 68–70.
69 Trevor-Roper, (1973), p. 462, entry for May 1942; Dahl (1999), pp. 264–70; Halvorsen, Terje (1991), 'Zwischen London und Berlin: Widerstand und Kollaboration in Norwegen 1940–1945', in Bohn et al. (eds), pp. 342–3, 347–50.

70 Kirchhoff, Hans (2002), 'Denmark, September 1939–April 1940', in Wylie (ed.), pp. 49–51.
71 Christensen, Claus Bundgård, Lund, Joachim, Olesen, Niels Wium, Sørensen, Jakob (2005), *Danmark besat: krig og hverdag 1940–45*. København: Høst, pp. 431–5.
72 Poulsen, Henning (1991), 'Die Deutsche Besatzungspolitik in Dänemark', in Bohn et al. (eds), pp. 373–6.
73 Mazower (2008), pp. 103–4, 323, 365; Kirchhoff (2002), p. 51.
74 Ottoson (1991), p. 357.
75 Lutzhöft (1981), pp. 198–9.
76 Ibid., p. 201. See also the discussion Levine (2002), pp. 305–6, 313.
77 Magnusson (1991), pp. 210–11.
78 Aalders, Gerard, Weebes, Cees (1996), *The Art of Cloaking Ownership. The Secret Collaboration and Protection of the German War Industry by the Neutrals: The Case of Sweden*. Amsterdam: Amsterdam UP, pp. 50–1; 61–2.
79 Jones, Reginald V. (1978), *Most Secret War: British Scientific Intelligence 1939–1945*. London: Hamish Hamilton, p. 443.
80 Ekberg, Henrik (1999), 'Finlands Flyktningproblem', in Ekberg, Henrik (ed.), *Finlands Historia Vol 4*. Helsinki, p. 270.
81 Lutzhöft (1981), p. 202.
82 Meinander, Henrik (2011), pp. 57, 61–3.
83 Östling, Johan (2011), 'The Rise and Fall of Small-State Realism: Sweden and the Second World War', in Stenius, Österberg, Östling, (eds) *Nordic Narratives*, pp. 127–9; Branner, Hans, Kelstrup, Morten (eds) (2000), *Denmark's Policy towards Europe after 1945: History, Theory, Options*. Odense: UP of Southern Denmark, pp. 9–40. For a full discussion of Scandinavia and issues of security or neutrality after 1945, see Lundestad, Geir (1980), *America, Scandinavia and the Cold war 1945–1949*. New York: Columbia UP, pp. 338–58 and Wahlbäck, Krister (1982), 'The Nordic Region in Twentieth-Century European Politics', in Sundelius, Bengt (ed.), *Foreign Policies of Northern Europe*. Boulder, Co.: Westview Press, pp. 25–8.
84 Wahlbäck (1982), pp. 21–2.

3

The Nordic Countries and the Second World War

A British Perspective

Patrick Salmon

It is kind of the editors of this book to invite me to provide this introduction. At the same time, I feel in a rather awkward position, squeezed between the wide-ranging insights of Richard Overy's essay on the one hand and, on the other, the stimulating interpretations of the Nordic experience of World War II in the papers that make up the rest of this volume. It is nevertheless a great pleasure to congratulate Jill Stephenson and John Gilmour of Edinburgh University on their initiative in editing a publication on 'Hitler's Scandinavian Legacy'. It is particularly appropriate that this should be taking place just over 70 years after the German invasion of Denmark and Norway on 9 April 1940. It is also a pleasure to contribute to this volume with so many distinguished historians from the Nordic countries. Some I have known for years as mentors or contemporaries, as co-examiners or, in one case, as an examinee; others I have got to know much more recently.

Bloomsbury is, as far as I know, the first British publisher to publish a book of this kind. Not that there have been all that many such works in the Nordic countries themselves. It is nearly 30 years since Nordic historians last published an English-language overview of Scandinavia in World War II.[1] An important conference was held in Oslo in 1976, another in Helsinki two years later, and another in Stockholm in 1995, but only the first of these was devoted to the Nordic countries alone.[2] Placing Norden's war experiences and impact in a wider context may have its merits, but there is also advantage in a narrower focus. And it may sometimes be easier to gain an overview of the Nordic experience from a more distant vantage point than from close-up.

One reason for taking a look at Scandinavia from a British perspective is that British historians have made important contributions to the history of World War II in Scandinavia. One historian in particular, Anthony Upton, caused controversy and even outrage in Finland when he published *Finland in Crisis 1940–41*, as long ago as 1964.[3] This book radically challenged the then-prevailing Finnish orthodoxy that Finland had joined the German assault on the Soviet Union in 1941 solely as a matter of self-defence. At the time, such a book could have been written only by an 'outsider' – though one who knew Finland and the Finnish language intimately. Another pioneering study, the late Alan Milward's *The Fascist Economy in Norway* (1972), described the attempts to force Norway's small, open economy into the straitjacket of Hitler's Greater German Reich, while at the same time identifying a certain kind of rationality in 'fascist' economics.[4] At much the same time Paul Hayes took seriously another variant of Scandinavian fascism in his biography of Vidkun Quisling.[5] The opening of the British official archives for the 1939–45 period in the early 1970s offered new opportunities for research. One of the first outcomes was Thomas Munch-Petersen's study of the iron ore question in relations between Britain and Sweden in 1939–40;[6] some of my early articles, based in part on my unpublished 1979 PhD thesis, also deal with this period.[7] Other PhD theses, also unpublished, include those of Ian Herrington and Christopher Mann.[8]

Such contributions, while they may be distinguished, represent a much smaller investment of British historical talent than in such countries as France, Germany, Italy, Russia, Poland or Spain. In these countries, British historians form part of the historiographical mainstream and their work has to be taken notice of (think of Cobb on the French Revolution or Blackbourn and Eley on the German *Sonderweg*). With the notable exception of Upton, this has not generally been the case, at least for the modern history of the Nordic countries. For earlier periods, of course, it is a different matter, as such figures as Peter Sawyer (for the Viking era) and Michael Roberts (for seventeenth- and eighteenth-century Sweden) amply testify. Introspection and self-sufficiency on the part of Nordic historians may provide part of the answer. In the past, some have not always wished to enter into dialogue with their Nordic neighbours, let alone to look more widely afield. It is true, however, that no British student of recent Nordic history has come up with a work as magisterial as Roberts's biography of Gustavus Adolphus or as groundbreaking a thesis as his 'military revolution'.[9] But recent Nordic history has also failed to attract large numbers of British historians perhaps because it seems to lack drama by comparison with that of other parts of Europe or perhaps because Nordic languages are less familiar (though mostly no more challenging) than many others. Whatever the reason – and marriage may be the single most important starting point – British historians have ventured into Nordic history as individual pioneers. In consequence, they have always lacked critical mass.

The big contrast here is with Germany: a country whose historical links with Scandinavia are comparable with those of the United Kingdom, but where Scandinavian studies have a much more solid institutional base. That base has, moreover, grown stronger in the 20 years since unification. To Greifswald and Kiel, respectively, the two main centres in the former GDR and in the Federal Republic, has been added since 1994 the *Nordeuropa Institut* at the Humboldt University in Berlin.[10] Each of these centres, but Berlin in particular, has acted as a forcing-house for research on Nordic history through the supervision of PhD students and the publication of their research in monographs and scholarly journals. In Britain, on the other hand, Scandinavian Studies departments rarely employed more than a single modern historian (e.g. University College London, East Anglia), while historians with Scandinavian interests were scattered randomly across the university sector, sometimes having little contact even with Scandinavianists in their own institution (Newcastle's two historians with Nordic interests, neither having much to do with the Scandinavian Studies Department, are a case in point).[11] Traditional Scandinavian studies in the United Kingdom have now dwindled almost to vanishing point, though the Scandinavian Studies Department at UCL has managed to capitalize on the growing public interest in Scandinavian culture – notably cinema and crime fiction. Scandinavian history, on the other hand, seems in its modest way to be doing rather well. The Nordic History Group, since 1977 the main forum for those with an interest in Scandinavian history in the United Kingdom, as well as an important link with Nordic historians, had become almost moribund but has revived in recent years with a welcome influx of new members, including a number of younger historians.

If there have been factors limiting the contribution of British historians to Nordic history, there have also been barriers to the dissemination of Nordic historical research in the wider world. Much the most important of these is language. That is one reason conferences like the one at Edinburgh in 2010 are so important, for they bring the work of younger Nordic researchers to a wider audience. English-language journals such as the *Scandinavian Economic History Review* and the *Scandinavian Journal of History* have also provided an invaluable outlet. Moreover, an increasing number of younger Nordic historians choose English as their language of preference when publishing their findings. But much outstanding research remains closed to an English-speaking readership. With the events that took place 70 years ago today in mind, it is worth noting that in recent years, three major studies of the German invasion of Denmark and Norway have been published: by Tom Kristiansen, Geirr Haarr (in two volumes) and Michael Clemmesen.[12] Only one of the three has appeared in English; the others remain – literally – a closed book to those who cannot read Norwegian or Danish. So I conclude this introduction with a request: that there should be more translation of Nordic historical research. And I have one further plea: that there should be more *good* translation from the Nordic languages – a rarer phenomenon than one might think.

Notes

1 Nissen, Henrik S., (ed.) (1983), *Scandinavia during the Second World War*. Oslo, Bergen and Tromsø: Universitetsforlaget; Minneapolis: The University of Minnesota Press.
2 The proceedings of the Oslo conference on 'The Great Powers and the Nordic Countries 1939–1940' were published as a special issue of *Scandinavian Journal of History* 2 (1977), Nos. 1–2. For the Stockholm conference, see Ekman, Stig, and Edling, Nils (eds) (1997), *War, Experience, Self Image and National Identity: The Second World War as Myth and History*. Stockholm: The Bank of Sweden Tercentenary Foundation & Gidlunds Förlag.
3 Upton, Antony F. (1964), *Finland in Crisis 1940–41*. London: Faber & Faber.
4 Milward, Alan (1972), *The Fascist Economy in Norway*. Oxford: Oxford University Press.
5 Hayes, Paul M. (1971), *Quisling: The Career and Political Ideas of Vidkun Quisling 1887–1945*. Newton Abbott: David & Charles.
6 Munch-Petersen, Thomas (1981), *The Strategy of Phoney War: Britain, Sweden and the Iron Ore Question 1939–1940*. Stockholm: Militärhistoriska Förlaget.
7 Salmon, Patrick (1979), 'Churchill, the Admiralty and the Narvik Traffic, September-November 1939', *Scandinavian Journal of History* 4: 305–36; Salmon, Patrick (1981), 'British Plans for Economic Warfare against Germany 1937–1939: The Problem of Swedish Iron Ore', *Journal of Contemporary History* 16: 53–72. My thesis is now published, with additional material, as *Deadlock and Diversion: Scandinavia in British Strategy during the Twilight War 1939–1940*. Bremerhaven: Deutsches Schiffahrtsmuseum, 2012.
8 Herrington, Ian (2004), 'The Special Operations Executive in Norway 1940–1945: Policy and Operations in the Strategic and Political Context', PhD thesis,

De Montfort University, Leicester https://www.dora.dmu.ac.uk/bitstream/handle/2086/2421/Ian%20Herrington%20PhD.pdf?sequence=1 (accessed 11 March 2011); Mann, Christopher (1999), 'British Strategy and Policy towards Norway, 1941–45', PhD thesis, University College London.

9   Roberts, Michael (1953), *Gustavus Adolphus: A History of Sweden 1611–1632*. 2 vols. London: Longmans; Roberts, Michael (1956), *The Military Revolution, 1560–1660*. Belfast: Queen's University.

10 In the case of Berlin, the driving force was Prof Bernd Henningsen. See Götz, Norbert, Hecker-Stampehl, Jan, and Schröder, Stephan Michael (eds) (2010), *Vom alten Norden zum neuen Europa: Politische Kultur in Ostseeraum. Festschrift für Bernd Henningsen*. Berlin: Berliner Wissenschafts-Verlag, pp. 19–33.

11 The late Dr David Aldridge and myself.

12 Kristiansen, Tom (2008), *Tysk trussel mot Norge? Forsvarsledelse, trusselverderinger og militære tiltak før 1940*. Bergen: Fagbokforlaget; Geirr Haarr (2009), *The German Invasion of Norway: April 1940*. Barnsley: Seaforth Books; Geirr Haarr (2010), *The Battle for Norway: April-June 1940*. Barnsley: Seaforth Books; Clemmesen, Michael H. (2010), *Den lange vej mod 9. April. Historien om de fyrre år før den tyske operation mod Norge og Danmark i 1940*. Odense: Syddansk Universitetsforlag.

4

The Obsession with Sovereignty

Cohabitation and Resistance in Denmark 1940–45

Niels Wium Olesen

During World War II, Denmark experienced an occupation that was much more peaceful than that in the rest of occupied Europe. This resulted in remarkable political and institutional continuity in Denmark from the interwar years, through the war, to the post-war years. There are numerous reasons for this. Some of the reasons are exclusively consequences of the German influence on the situation in Denmark, such as Nazi race ideology that regarded Danes as Aryans. Others can be attributed to purely local factors, such as the comparatively stable and nationally homogeneous condition of Danish democracy in the interwar years. But the single most important factor was a matter of *dynamics* between the occupier and the occupied – namely the consequences stemming from the fact that, from the beginning of the occupation, Germany granted Denmark the status of a sovereign state, which on the other hand was utilized to its utmost by the Danish decision makers. For the duration of the war, Denmark's status as an independent country endowed the relationship between the occupier and the occupied with a semblance of parity. This was visible in the way that communication between the two states was conducted, that is, between the two foreign ministries and with the characteristics of a political negotiation. Compromise agreements, rather than violence and repression, were the rule.

Of course, Denmark's allegedly sovereign status and the notion of parity between the two states were largely an illusion. Germany's military presence on Danish soil gave the occupier the upper hand. Parity was only a formal gloss, and Danish sovereignty was curtailed. Almost nothing was left of Denmark's *external* sovereignty, that is, her independence in foreign affairs. On the other hand, *internal* sovereignty – the executive power's relationship with the citizens of Denmark – was left almost entirely intact. Despite the illusory aspects of Danish sovereignty, both the Danish government and German decision makers in both Copenhagen and Berlin had an interest in keeping up appearances and acting according to a façade of parity and Danish sovereignty. As a consequence, the political and constitutional institutions of Denmark continued their functions after the German military seizure of Danish territory on 9 April 1940. The King, the parliament, the government, the judiciary, the police and local government could carry on exercising their tasks and responsibilities in a country that was now occupied.

Essentially, the Danish government could exercise its internal sovereignty as long as it did not conflict with the interests of the occupying power. These interests were typically confined to military affairs. Political and ideological demands were raised only rarely by the Germans in Denmark – and, when raised in the negotiations, were usually met with objections and sometimes even outright rejection by the Danish side. Obviously, Danish decision makers considered it a huge advantage for Danish society that the Germans did not install a new government, be that a Nazi puppet regime, a military government or a *Reichskommissariat*, as happened elsewhere. Safeguarding Danish sovereignty – or what was left of it – and the political and constitutional system as a whole became a prime motive for the Danish government and the governing political parties.[1]

This chapter will focus on the concept of sovereignty and show how the safeguarding of sovereignty was a vital objective for Danish policy during the occupation. The endeavours to maximize sovereignty were to a large extent the reason for the humanitarian, political and economic benefits that Danish society – compared with other occupied countries – enjoyed during the occupation. This has been widely argued by scholars on Danish occupation history – and therefore this chapter can claim no originality on this point. But it will furthermore be argued that the endeavours to safeguard and maximize sovereignty also sometimes led to the most painful moral and political dilemmas of the occupation. In this respect, the chapter is indebted to studies on the German occupation of other European countries during World War II. For instance, in his famous study of the Vichy regime, Robert Paxton illustrated how French politicians and officials often were more interested in 'the outward show of Vichy sovereignty', and thus hastened to accommodate the Germans by taking unpleasant steps on French initiative before such issues were raised as a German demand or even executed by the Germans themselves.[2] The persecution of Jews in France is one example. In a similar vein, Julian Jackson terms it 'the French obsession with sovereignty' in order to explain this mechanism. In the Protectorate of Bohemia and Moravia and in the Netherlands, similar traits are discernible.[3]

The argument here will be built around illustrative cases, but first the events of April 1940 that formed the special occupation situation in Denmark will be explored.

The creation of *modus vivendi*: 9 April 1940

In the early morning of 9 April 1940, the German Ambassador to Denmark, Cecil von Renthe-Fink, informed the Danish Foreign Secretary, Peter Munch, that the German *Wehrmacht* was invading Denmark at that very moment. Simultaneously, the Ambassador handed the Foreign Secretary two documents. One of these expressed the German arguments for the occupation and the determined will to crush any Danish resistance at whatever cost. Taking a Danish capitulation for granted, the other document presented demands to the Danish authorities on how to arrange the occupation on a practical level. The first document unfolded an argument pointing to the British and French escalation of the naval war and the allegation that they were about to invade Scandinavia. Thus, the invasion was not unfriendly, but only a measure to protect the neutrality of Denmark and Norway against Anglo-French aggression. The first document concluded that Germany did not 'intend by her actions, either now or in future, to violate the Kingdom of Denmark's territorial integrity or political independence'. The plain text interpretation of 'territorial integrity' was that Germany did not intend to revise the Versailles Treaty border, despite very vocal claims on the part of the Nazified German minority in South Jutland. Furthermore, 'political independence' could be read as an acceptance of continued democracy in Denmark. These assurances were given on condition that Denmark obeyed the demands made in the second document formulated in 13 points. Among other things, Germany demanded that the Danish government issue a statement urging the Danish military and the Danish people to stop any resistance. If the Danish government, people and military complied with the demands, they could go about their daily business as usual. Even the Danish military was allowed to exist as long as it did not work against the *Wehrmacht*. The Ambassador demanded an immediate response to the German ultimatum and urged Munch to hasten the cessation of Danish military resistance; otherwise, the *Luftwaffe* would bomb Copenhagen.

Munch reacted with a denial of the alleged British and French plans and expressed his protest against the violation of Denmark's neutrality. In addition, he asked for more time since he had no mandate to make such a far-reaching decision on his own as to order the capitulation of the Danish armed forces, to which Renthe-Fink conceded. A meeting with Munch, the King, the Prime Minister, the Minister of Defence and military commanders was quickly arranged. The only issues in the discussion were whether to prolong the armed struggle for a short while in order to show the world that Denmark had defended her neutrality. No one championed the idea that the Danish military could fend off a German occupation. After half an hour of negotiation, it was decided to cease resistance and issue a statement that called for public order and obedience to all officials and urged the people to stay clear of the German military. Denmark was occupied after a few hours of armed struggle and the loss of 16 Danish soldiers' lives.[4] Later in the afternoon of 9 April, the Foreign Ministry drafted a formal response to the German invasion. In the response, great care was taken in repeating – and thereby in fact making *promises* of – German assurances of having no intention of violating Denmark's territorial integrity and political sovereignty. Even more care was assigned to avoiding any hints of Danish recognition of the occupation or any kind of mutual agreement. The Danish government announced that it would 'make arrangements that dealt with the occupation', as this was now a given fact.[5] Surely, in reality it was a *quid pro quo*. Danish sovereignty – or at least some level of it – and continued territorial integrity were bought at the price of capitulating. But this was something that the Danish government would never explicitly acknowledge. To underline that no deal was struck and that the German promises were given unilaterally, a strong protest was expressed as the conclusion.

In the evening of the day of the invasion, the parliament convened. Prime Minister Stauning informed the members about the events of the day. The government, he said, had taken its actions for the sake of the country and the people in order to avoid 'the consequences of a state of war on Danish soil'.

Over the next few days, the German ambassador handed over more demands in addition to the ones already issued. These defined the responsibilities of the Danish government more explicitly: all enemy embassies were to be expelled. Furthermore, it was the duty of the Danish government to secure the safety and the supply of the German military on Danish soil and to prevent any attempts to damage the German presence. The Danish press should, the ambassador advised, encourage the population to stay calm and carry on with daily life, and – now explicitly demanding – the government should stop any forms of anti-German propaganda and behaviour. What the latter meant was rather vague and therefore open to (German) interpretation.

The picture was now clear: the survival of the political system and the executive powers rested on the government's ability and willingness to guarantee the safety of the German military and to crack down on its own citizens if they physically or spiritually resisted the German presence. Otherwise, the Germans would demand some other kind of government. The examples of this in Poland, Norway and the dissolved Czechoslovakia were intimidating. Thus, the survival of Danish democracy was now dependent on the government's ability and willingness to prevent its citizens – endowed by the constitution with the right of freedom of speech – from protesting against a dictatorship's occupation in violation of international law. The paradox could hardly have been more striking.

However, protests or resistance were not on the agenda in April 1940. The overwhelming majority of the population was saddened, shocked and confused. The country was occupied even before most Danes were out of bed. Overall, it was a profound national humiliation – perhaps, for many a Dane, mixed with some sense of relief that no bombing or severe fighting had occurred. Most people retreated into their daily life and made adjustments therein to the new situation.

Even in the political sphere, the abstract paradoxes of cohabiting with a dictatorial military power did not play a major role in the immediate aftermath of the invasion. Practical problems regarding the economy and communication with the occupying power were the centre of attention. One extremely fundamental issue, though, needed to be addressed: the matter of legal jurisdiction in (potential) cases involving sabotage and insults or violence against German military personnel. On 15 April 1940, the Ministry of Justice set up an office named State Advocacy for Special Affairs which would deal with those sorts of offence. The intention was to cut off any German attempts to set up a court martial in Denmark. For all practical purposes, the occupying power accepted the Advocacy, but deliberately gave no promises of not taking over special cases in the future.[6]

The *modus vivendi* established during the diplomatic exchanges in the days following the invasion turned out to be of crucial importance throughout the entire 5-year occupation. Essentially, the format of communication was, as mentioned, one of a political negotiation between allegedly equal partners.

In reality, the balance of power at the negotiating table was, of course, very uneven, since the German side had its military as a potential threat. But one should not underestimate the implications of the formal setting. Since both parties acted under the rules of bilateral negotiations, the Danes were not pushed around by the Germans. In negotiations, there are valid arguments and non-valid arguments. Denmark accepted German military interests as a valid argument. In general, Nazi ideology had no status as valid argument.[7] And only on a very few occasions did Germany try to force the Danish government to comply with Nazi ideological interests. This mode of interaction between the state apparatus of the occupied and the occupying power continued until the Danish government, parliament and King ceased to function on 29 August 1943, when the Danish side refused to succumb to certain German demands.

National unity

On 9 April 1940, the Danish government was a majority coalition consisting of the larger Social Democratic Party and the smaller Social Liberal Party. The Social Democratic Prime Minister, Thorvald Stauning, and the Social Liberal Foreign Secretary, Peter Munch, were its leading personalities. Immediately after the capitulation, the Prime Minister invited members of the Conservative Party and of the Liberal Agrarians to join in forming a government of national unity, which they accepted. This created a situation where more than 90 per cent of the parliament was behind the government. From the outset, the government branded itself 'a coalition of the democratic parties', thereby excluding a group of 'one-to-two per cent parties' such as the Danish Nazi Party, the Danish Communist Party, the Agrarian Party (Agrarian Fascists), Danish Unity (an anti-parliamentary, Christian, right wing party) and the Schleswig Party, representing the German minority.

The government's first aim was to stabilize the country after the shock of occupation. Economically, the challenges were enormous. Denmark was dependent on exports of agricultural produce to Great Britain and imports of fuel and raw materials from different, mostly European, countries. After 9 April, all trade with Great Britain was of course cut off. If no new trade arrangements were made, economic decline, widespread unemployment and perhaps even starvation were to be expected – and, following that, the disruption of the social order with the possible danger that the safety of the German military could not be upheld, potentially leading to a removal of the government by the Germans. However, very soon trade agreements were made with Germany. In return for the delivery of agricultural produce, Germany agreed to supply Denmark with fuel and raw materials. During the 5 years of occupation there was a noticeable decline in the standard of living in Denmark, but the Danes fared better than any other country in occupied Europe. With an average daily intake of about 3,000 calories, a Dane was better fed throughout the war than a German or a Briton – not to mention a Norwegian or a Pole.

Politically, the challenge for the government was to convince the Germans that the government was better suited for the job – especially on the Germans' first priority: peace and order and the safety of the military – than any other alternative. First of all, the fear was that the Germans would install the Danish Nazi Party at the head of government. Indeed, the Danish Nazis did not lack ambition. From April 1940, the party was sponsored by Berlin and it missed no opportunity in calling for an immediate takeover of power. The Danish government was scared out of its wits at the prospect that the Danish Nazis actually could be brought into office by German bayonets. In the first 3 months after 9 April 1940, the Danish Nazis were discussed during 26 government meetings.[8] It has been a matter of considerable discussion in Danish historiography whether Berlin actually at any time during the occupation seriously considered installing the Danish Nazis as a governing party.[9] But it is above controversy that Berlin and the German Embassy in Copenhagen used the threat of the Danish Nazi Party to soften the incumbent government – and did so to some effect. The very notion of a Danish National Socialist government constituted a nightmare for all four government parties. Especially to the Danish Social Democrats and the affiliated labour movement, the thought was frightening. They knew from German party colleagues who lived as emigrants in Denmark in the 1930s how Hitler's regime had persecuted and finally annihilated the Social Democratic labour movement. In July 1940, the Social Democrats in the Netherlands were banned, and in September all parties and the trade unions were banned in Norway. The sense of being in an especially precarious position made the Danish Social Democrats more prone to meet German demands. To the Danish Social Democrats, being in government became a way of not only saving Danish democracy and protecting the Danish people from Nazi rule but also a way of surviving as a party, as a political movement and as individual persons.

Essentially, the spring and summer of 1940 constituted in Denmark as in all of Europe a dramatic swing to the right. As Hitler's *Blitzkrieg* swept over Europe, democracies and parliaments gave way to authoritarianism and dictatorship, either in the form of Nazi puppet regimes or, as in France, in the form of an indigenous right wing revolution that swept away the Third Republic.[10] In Denmark, democracy – though curtailed – survived, but the centre of gravity moved discernibly to the right, favouring farmers and industrialists at the expense of the working class. This swing to the right also showed in other ways. In the summer and fall of 1940, a right-wing network among industrialists and businessmen, who in the interwar years had been highly critical of the centre-left government, advocated and tried to persuade the King to install a government of experts and technocrats. The network did not have its way, but nonetheless it managed to have a say in the formation of a new government in July 1940. Especially at the King's request, but also as promoted by the network, Foreign Secretary Peter Munch was replaced by former diplomat and previous Foreign Secretary during World War I, Erik Scavenius. Two more ministers without affiliation with the political parties were appointed. They were soon to be called 'the three non-political ministers'.[11]

Activism – a new approach to Danish foreign policy

The new government marked a shift in the government's policy towards Germany. In the wake of the fall of France and orchestrated by the new strong man in the government, Foreign Secretary Scavenius, Denmark embarked on a much more activist policy of adaptation. In order to promote Danish interests, Denmark had actively to cooperate with the Germans, said Scavenius. Instead of waiting for German demands to be voiced, the Danish government should, on its own initiative, propose projects for cooperation with Germany. Three notions were crucial to his idea of how to conduct Danish policy towards Germany. First, by actively proposing projects Denmark could have her say in deciding the direction of the bilateral relationship. Second, by displaying loyalty and commitment in cooperation with Germany, goodwill and trust would be established in both Berlin and the German Embassy in Copenhagen. Third, by continuously being engaged at the negotiating table, the Danes would have a stronger sense of where the Germans were heading, and why.

It was Scavenius' view that it was of vital importance for the Danish government to show Berlin that Germany would not gain anything by setting up a Nazi puppet regime. The implicit Danish threat was: if the Germans by means of force installed a government of Danish Nazis, the country would slide into economic and political chaos. The reasoning was twofold: the Danish people would not obey the Danish Nazi Party and it was considered politically, economically and governmentally incompetent. Why not, then, have a group of political professionals, trusted by the people, to run the country and secure the social order in it? Presumably, German officials in Denmark bought into this idea. In 1941, for instance, less than 100 German civil officials were deemed sufficient to administer the occupation of a country of more than 4 million inhabitants.[12]

On the day of the government's inauguration, 8 July 1940, Scavenius stated:

> By the great German victories that have struck the world with astonishment and admiration, a new era has occurred in Europe, which in political and economic matters will lead to a new order under German leadership. It will be Denmark's task to find her place in a proper and mutually active cooperation with Germany. The Danish people are confident that in this new order it will uphold its independence, and hope to find understanding for its uniqueness and its traditional, peaceful, political and social development.

Presented with a draft of this statement, some government members objected. Was 'astonishment and admiration' really necessary? Scavenius made it clear that if he were to remain Foreign Secretary, they had to trust him and his policy. This would later prove to be the normal pattern for government meetings. Members of the political parties in the government would raise objections to Scavenius' activist proposals, Prime Minister Stauning and the non-politicals would mediate – and in the end, Scavenius would have his way, after threatening to resign. In this way, Scavenius proved to be fairly influential in deciding the government's policy. One reason for this was that the Germans soon came to trust the Foreign Secretary and consequently indicated that any possibility of his resignation would be perceived as a severe deterioration in the Danish-German relationship by the occupying power. This was an outcome the Danish government could not afford. Another reason was that the other politicians in the government were not able to formulate a viable alternative to Scavenius' line.[13]

The inauguration statement of 8 July 1940 was not, however, for domestic consumption. It was aimed at Berlin. And despite the bow to the German victories – a bow that has haunted Danes ever since – the last part of the citation contained the central aim of Scavenius' policy: he wanted to protect Danish independence and the political system.

The idea that active cooperation – or collaboration – would lead to German acceptance of this domestic uniqueness was voiced all over occupied Europe. For instance, on *Maréchal* Philippe Pétain's return from his meeting with Hitler at Montoire in October 1940, he declared 'it is in honour and to maintain French unity, a unity of ten centuries, within the framework of constructive action for a new European order, that I enter today down the road of collaboration'. Pétain would learn that not much was left for the weaker partner in such co-operation. So would Scavenius.

Censorship

On 9 April, Germany had stated that it required that the Danish press be censored regarding military matters. The next day the prohibition of anti-German propaganda was issued. In accordance with the established *modus vivendi* of the occupation, it was the responsibility of the Danish authorities to execute this censorship of the press. The task was given to the so-called Press Bureau of the Ministry of Foreign Affairs which saw it as its foremost task to prevent German interference – and thus also to stabilize Danish-German relations – and to ensure that an independent Danish press was still able to work. This meant, however, that the Press Bureau had to negotiate the German demands in a give and take manner and had, in letters sent to the editors, to give guidance to Danish newspapers on what was permissible and what was not. The aim was to avoid any situation that could give the press attaché at the German Embassy in Copenhagen reason to act against the press and possibly shut down papers.[14] In other words, and as another striking paradox of occupied Denmark, the press was subject to censorship in order to continue being 'free'. Evidently, the spirit of Danish democracy was tarnished by this system. Apart from the noble objective of helping the press, it was also a matter of not giving away sovereignty. Direct German measures against the newspapers would have exposed the underlying illusion of Danish sovereignty. On the other hand, doing the dirty job for the occupier was only formally a sovereign act. *De facto* it was the exact negation of sovereignty.

It is remarkable that the Danish press generally accepted censorship and regarded the actions of the Bureau as a helping hand. As the occupation went on, however, ever-increasing German demands for action against the press occurred. Gradually, the demands were more and more targeted at the political bias of the press. The press found the interventions increasingly intolerable, but responded to them, however reluctantly, for fear of being completely swept away. The most far-reaching German demands entailed the removal of editors of specific papers. After 29 August 1943, the Press Bureau and hence the editors came under direct German control with increased restrictions on press freedom as a result. Despite the censorship, there was still considerable scope for the press. Domestic politics could be discussed freely, as long as this did not involve criticism of the Danish state's relations with Germany or give positive coverage to the underground resistance. Also, the Danish Nazi party could be criticized, as long as it was not obvious that it played the role as a proxy for the Third Reich.

For newspapers and book publishers expressing views on the Danish relationship with Germany in opposition to the general national consensus surrounding the governing parties, it was a different matter. The press attaché at the German Embassy zealously monitored the publications that were suspected of containing 'anti-German propaganda'. If the press attaché was seriously offended by publications, he demanded that the Danish judiciary interfere. If the demand were non-negotiable, the Danish authorities would confiscate the remaining copies of the edition and issue a warning to the editor. But when an editor was responsible for repeated offences, the press attaché would go to the Danish Ministry of Foreign Affairs and demand sharper measures. The most illuminating example involved the right-wing writer and historian Vilhelm la Cour. He was a former member of the Conservative Party who resigned his membership in July 1940 as a protest against the party's participation in the government. He later became sympathetic to the Danish Unity party. On several occasions his publications were confiscated. In 1941, he published a pamphlet on the German philosopher Fichte and nationalism. The content was not directly agitating against Germany or the occupation, but presumably the Germans thought that it could nourish a Danish will to resist. In July 1941, under pressure from the German Embassy, a Danish court sentenced la Cour to 80 days of imprisonment.[15] A free man again in the autumn of 1941, la Cour continued writing and publishing. In February 1942, he gave a lecture on the topic of 'Neutrality'. This time German officials demanded that la Cour be brought before a German court martial for charges of 'subversive activities' and sabotage. The Danish judiciary objected to that, but at first to no avail. In this game, where the rules were defined by the Germans, the only chip the Danish side could bring to the table was an assurance that, if brought before a Danish judge, la Cour would be severely punished – in reality for actions endorsed by the Danish Constitution. For the Danish government and judiciary, there was more to the case than the personal destiny of la Cour. For the sake of the protection of Danish citizens and for the sake of safeguarding sovereignty, they wanted to avoid a precedent. In order to convince the German side of the Danish will to maintain legal jurisdiction on this issue, Danish police started investigating other lectures given by la Cour and came up with evidence that he had more problematic activities on his record. In the end, the German side allowed the Danish judiciary to take over the case. La Cour was sentenced to 7 months of imprisonment by the Danish court.[16] In this case, German pressure had set the limits of Danish sovereignty. Only 'the outward show of sovereignty' was safeguarded – and at a price. Freedom of speech was compromised. So was the principle of equality before the law.

Expulsion of politicians

In the autumn of 1940 and during the first 2 months of 1941, four leading politicians were expelled from political life at the insistence of the German Embassy in Copenhagen. The first victim was the Minister of Trade, the leading conservative politician John Christmas Møller. A former chairman of the Conservative party and still *de facto* its leader, Møller was worried about what he considered the government's tendency always to obey German demands for fear of the greater evil. In addition, he was sceptical of Scavenius' activist adaptation to German demands. It was his fear that the population would misunderstand the government's actions and fall victim to despondency. In order to counterbalance this, and motivated by a wish to nourish the national spirit, he embarked on a public speaking tour across the country. His speeches defended the government, but made almost no mention of the German occupier. Instead, the Danish Nazi Party and its *Führer*, Frits Clausen, were strongly criticized and ridiculed. The public knew, the Nazi party knew and the German Ambassador knew that the Danish Nazis in these speeches served as a proxy for the Third Reich. The Ambassador informed the Danish government that he considered Møller harmful to the relationship between the two countries. Loyal to the government, Christmas Møller, therefore, resigned, but only to continue his speeches, which in January 1941 led to German demands that he be expelled from all public activities.[17]

The next in line was the Social Democratic ideologue Hartvig Frisch. Since the 1930s he had been an eloquent anti-Nazi and anti-communist academic and

Member of Parliament. In October and November 1940, the Danish Nazi party mounted a media campaign in which it made ferocious attacks on him for his opposition to Nazi ideology. Since it was Prime Minister Stauning's impression that the German embassy maintained a strong interest in the Danish Nazi Party's campaign, Frisch was asked by Stauning to withdraw from political life in order not to harm the government's position. Frisch, as ever the loyal party soldier, consented and withdrew. Then in February 1941 the young chairman of the Social Democratic party, Hans Hedtoft, and the party secretary, H. C. Hansen, were forced to resign following German demands. They too had fallen victim to campaigns run by the Danish Nazi Party which claimed that they were Marxists and 'fanatical opponents of the new Germany'.[18] Although all four Danish politicians were personally loyal to Prime Minister Stauning and, albeit in various degrees, adhered to the general reasoning behind the government's line, they remained sceptical of Scavenius' adaptive policy. In principle, they had only acted in accordance with the German promise not to violate Denmark's 'political independence'. They were ousted nevertheless.

If they had not been clear before, three things were now evident. First, the so-called German 'promises of 9 April' were honoured only to some extent, and were broken when found to be an obstacle to crucial German interests. Secondly, cohabitation with the German invader meant that the government *de facto* had to violate the very principles that it was trying to defend – the principles of democracy. Thirdly, the situation called for a considerable measure of pragmatic forbearance by leading Danish politicians – as exercised by Christmas Møller, Frisch, Hedtoft and Hansen.

Anti-communist measures

On the day of the German attack on the Soviet Union, 22 June 1941, 'Operation Barbarossa', the permanent undersecretaries of the Danish Ministry of Foreign Affairs and the Ministry of Justice were summoned in the early morning to the German Embassy in Copenhagen. They were informed in writing and verbally that Germany – 'for military reasons' – wanted all harbours sealed off, all Soviet citizens in Denmark and 'all leading Danish communists' interned.[19] In a recollection after the war, the permanent undersecretary at the Ministry of Foreign Affairs, Nils Svenningsen, states that he – for first time during the occupation – thought that the German promises of 9 April, the continued German recognition of the Danish government and Danish democracy, were at stake. The undersecretary phoned the Prime Minister and informed him of the demands. Svenningsen, a trained jurist, did not forget to tell the Prime Minister, that among the leading communists were three members of parliament. In this way, he hinted at the fact that, according to the constitution, MPs were granted special immunity. The Prime Minister, known for his brevity, said, 'There is nothing else we can do. We have to accept it'. He did not advocate that negotiations be started or that limitations to the German demands be suggested. Immediately thereafter, Danish police and coast guards were ordered by the Ministry of Justice to round up the leading communists, including the members of parliament. Around 300 were caught and put in a Danish internment camp. Others went underground.

On that morning, the Danish constitution was violated. The Danish Communist Party was a legal party. The communist members of parliament were elected by the Danish people in free elections, and as Danish citizens the members of the party were endowed with the same civil rights and liberties as everybody else. It could be argued, however, that the violation of the constitution was justified by legal necessity. One legal good was sacrificed for a higher legal good. That is, the Danish communists were sacrificed for the sake of the constitution and the rest of the population.[20] To put it bluntly: the constitution was violated in order to preserve the constitution!

This paradox and the cruel dilemma the Danish decision makers faced were no doubt made easier to deal with because Danish communists were not themselves defenders of the constitution. Additionally, as in many European countries, the majority considered communists to be pariahs or even enemies of the state. And, by cheering for the Soviet Union against the Finns in the Winter War of 1939–40, the communists had offended deeply rooted Nordic sensibilities among the Danes. Still, from a 2013 perspective, one feels obliged to assert that the constitution is supposed to protect all Danish citizens, regardless of their political allegiance.

The issue of sovereignty also played its part in this process. Besides the obvious danger of the Germans sweeping away the entire political and constitutional system, if the Danish government did not comply with German demands, another lesser potential evil no doubt influenced the decision. If the government did not comply, a slice – but an important one – of Danish sovereignty could be cut off, namely by the Germans exporting *Gestapo* personnel to Denmark to round up the communists. It was, then, much preferable to, let the job be done by Denmark's own police force. Yet another consideration played a role.

The communists would be much better off in a Danish camp than in a German one. This concern was, for obvious reasons, voiced vociferously *after* the war by decision makers. In fact, this concern *did* play a role. But it was a long way down the list of priorities.

The pioneers of the resistance

While Danish communists may have been an annoying, yet manageable, element for the government before 22 June 1941, they soon proved much more difficult to handle after they were proscribed and driven underground. Before Barbarossa, harnessed by the Molotov-Ribbentrop Pact, they had criticized the Danish government, especially the Social Democrats, for inflicting social injustice on the working class. After the attack on their communist motherland and the prohibition of their party, and following some time needed to get their underground organization up and running, they combined this critique with a much more potent line of reasoning. Now, they argued, the government was simply selling out to the Nazis. Revealing its true treacherous face, the communists claimed, the government was handing Denmark, the Danish people and Danish democracy on a plate to the occupier. The government, posing as the champion of Danish democracy and sovereignty, even repressed its fellow countrymen for no other reason than that they did not agree with its policy.[21] It did so even to the extent of violating the constitution. Of course, it could be argued that the communists were hypocritical, not themselves being in any way democratic. But during 1942, sentiments were changing and some people, ashamed of the government's adaptation to German demands and its violation of democratic principles, started to gather in what were later to become resistance groups. The Danish Communist Party approached these groups at the beginning of 1942. The contact between the chairman of the Communist Party, Aksel Larsen, and the former chairman of the Conservative Party – now expelled from political life – Christmas Møller, was among the most important. They set up an organization called Free Denmark (*Frit Danmark*), which, as one of its first activities, published a monthly clandestine paper also called *Free Denmark*. Soon, Free Denmark became one of the – if not *the* – leading resistance organization(s) and remained so until the liberation in 1945. Allegedly, Free Denmark was a cross-party organization. But, in fact, the Communist Party dominated the organization because its party members, as trained conspirators, had the ability to control the infrastructure of communication.²² The Popular Front which the Communist Party had failed to form in interwar Denmark now materialized in 1942 and, for the first time in its history, the party was integrated into milieus related to the political mainstream.

Other resistance groups saw the light of day in late 1941 and early 1942. Members of the Danish Unity Party got in contact with the British organization for underground warfare in Europe, the Special Operations Executive (SOE), and facilitated its initial operations in Denmark by receiving and otherwise helping its agents. Another group published the clandestine paper, *The Free Danes* (*De frie Danske*). The group consisted of centre-right, educated and bourgeois men in Copenhagen, many of them working on leading Danish newspapers. And in towns around the country, young men, some of them scarcely more than boys, formed groups that engaged in small-scale sabotage.

In general – with the Free Danes and perhaps the youth groups as an exception – the pioneering resistance groups were characterized by their scepticism of, even opposition to, parliamentary democracy. They did not feel any loyalty to the government and its calls for public order and obedience. Something else was more important to them than saving Danish democracy at any cost. The communists were part of an international organization fighting a war against Nazi Germany and cared nothing for democracy or, indeed, for the government that had outlawed the party. The Danish Unity Party and other right-wing groups of non-democratic conviction felt a national obligation to eject the occupier from the country and were more concerned with national self-esteem than democracy.²³

While the Free Danes in general were democratically minded, they were particularly concerned with Denmark's status abroad. In their view, the government was trying to save Danish democracy by riding on a free ticket while the western democracies fought for the just cause. Therefore, the Free Danes argued, the government compromised the very idea of democracy. The Free Danes wanted to take Denmark onto what they considered to be the right side.

Combating sabotage

Cohabitation with the occupier proved increasingly to be an endeavour to 'avoid the nearest evil', as Foreign Secretary Scavenius once put it in a government meeting. Strategy had to give way to damage control. Organized sabotage against German military interests occurred in a few incidents in the summer of 1942. Some of the attacks were executed by communist volunteers from the Spanish Civil War, while others were executed by youth groups. Special attention was given to the so-called Churchill Club, a group of 15 to 17-year-old boys, all from 'respectable homes' and attending the Cathedral School in the town of Aalborg. The boys were engaged in arson attacks, vandalism of German military installations and weapon theft. In May 1942, they were caught by the Danish police. While in custody, awaiting their sentence, two of them escaped from their cells by sawing through the bars and they continued their activities at night, returning to their cells before dawn. After 19 escapes, German soldiers caught them on the street. The incidents were perceived by the occupying power as an example of Danish negligence in the face of sabotage and, accordingly, the two boys were put before a German court martial and sentenced to 10 and 15 years in German prisons.[24]

The story of the Churchill Club had potential for various interpretations. The authorized press used the story as an example of how dangerous sabotage was and how far-reaching its consequences could be. The clandestine press in general interpreted the story as an example of bravery, of the soundness of Danish youth and of national dignity. And the communist clandestine press, specifically, used the social class of the young boys as a convenient example of the fact that not all resistance or all sabotage was of communist origin. Resistance, the communist press informed the readers, was not subversive action on behalf of a foreign belligerent country, that is, the Soviet Union. It was a way of caring for Denmark and all decent Danes should support it. Even the American boys' publication, *Red Goose Magazine*, conveyed the story in a very heroic cartoon interpretation in 1943.

Studies of public opinion during the occupation of Denmark are in no doubt that sabotage was considered highly dangerous and undesirable by the vast majority of the Danish public in 1942 and certainly well into 1943.[25] Still, the government had reasons to be very concerned by the development. German pressure on the government to harden its combat of sabotage increased, while the court martial and the very severe punishment of the two boys of the Churchill Club were evidence that Germany was ready and willing to infringe Danish legal jurisdiction – this being an essential part of every state's sovereignty. From the government's point of view, the problem had two sides. First, an infringement of Danish sovereignty in a field as crucial as its legal jurisdiction threatened to undermine the government's ability to protect the people, Danish institutions and the core values of Danish society that gave political and moral justification for the policy that was being conducted. Secondly, the very infringement of legal jurisdiction and sovereignty in general threatened to put a stamp of impotence on the government, as a puppet regime in complicity with the German oppressors. And this, in turn, would make the case for the underground opposition so much more well-founded with the danger that it could mobilize more resisters and thereby make the position of the government even more vulnerable. Therefore, Prime Minister Vilhelm Buhl, who in May 1942 had succeeded the deceased Stauning, addressed the Danish people in a radio speech on 2 September 1942. In wartime, the Prime Minister warned, belligerent countries usually sentenced perpetrators of sabotage to the death penalty. It was only because on 9 April 1940 the Danish government and judiciary were granted independence by the occupying power that capital punishment had hitherto been avoided. If the government and the police were not able to put an end to sabotage, Germany would simply take over legal jurisdiction in cases of sabotage, Buhl warned. Therefore, sabotage was an act committed against the interests of the mother country. It was the duty of every citizen, the Prime Minister concluded, to help the police by conveying information that could lead to the exposure of acts of sabotage and saboteurs. Plainly speaking: Danes were encouraged to be informants on other Danes.[26]

When in May 1945 Buhl became Prime Minister again – heading a government consisting of politicians from the four large political parties and resistance leaders, and now with an entirely different and positive attitude to sabotage – Buhl justified the speech by referring to German pressure. From an analytical point of view, though, one misses the point if one focuses on German pressure. Prime Minister Buhl's speech was word for word in strict accordance with the political line of the government since 9 April 1940 – and, from a strictly functional viewpoint, in compliance with basic state interests. He was simply engaged in safeguarding Danish sovereignty in one of its most fundamental aspects: legal jurisdiction over Danish citizens. In the summer of 1945 and in the post-war years, the Prime Minister's speech could be interpreted as that of a collaborating politician encouraging the Danish people to denounce brave 'Freedom Fighters' to the Nazis. (Especially if one, as an act of convenient amnesia, forgot that it was a matter of helping the *Danish* police.) In 1942, it was perceived by the general public as a call for law and order for the sake of the common good.

Safeguarding Danish legal jurisdiction became, indeed, increasingly difficult and marred by political and moral dilemmas as the occupation went on.

Sabotage did not stop, and more saboteurs were seized by the Germans and put before a court martial. Now, Danish police and the executive powers in general were put in a position where they could be accused of complicity in German oppression, since the Danish police force had done the police work that led to the imprisonment of Danes in German prisons.

The Telegram Crisis 1942

The most serious blow to Danish sovereignty – or the illusion of it – so far was the crisis in Danish-German relations in the fall of 1942. The initial impetus for the crisis was rather banal. Hitler was infuriated by a perceived aloof reply to his telegrammed birthday congratulations to the Danish King in September. Hitler called home his ambassador in Copenhagen and the Danish ambassador in Berlin was asked to leave. The underlying reasons for the crisis were a more profound dissatisfaction in Berlin with developments in Denmark. A potential Allied invasion on the west coast of Jutland seemed an increasing possibility and called for a re-evaluation of Denmark's position in German military strategy. The population was said by German officials to be anti-German, the press was uncooperative, the civil service was deprecatory and the government was hesitant and opportunistic. Hitler wanted to get rid of the special *modus vivendi* of 9 April 1940. Away with 'political independence' and away with Prime Minister Buhl and his government that seemed unable and/or unwilling to counter sabotage. Denmark should be treated as enemy territory – and all resistance should be stopped with brute force, if necessary by German hands. In the internal German deliberations in Berlin, Hitler went so far as to demand that Danish Nazi leader Frits Clausen be installed as leader of a new government. This idea was, however, rather quickly abandoned – but a new tougher line was designed for Denmark. Foreign Secretary Scavenius was summoned to Berlin in late October and treated to a 3-hour monologue by Ribbentrop. Berlin wanted a new government that could be trusted. Scavenius had to take over as Prime Minister. Scavenius argued that he was only a diplomat with insufficient experience in domestic politics, and he added that being put in office to meet a German demand was not going to increase the population's trust in his leadership. Although under considerable pressure, when he was presented with a government list including Nazi ministers, Scavenius brushed the list aside as a 'fantasy government' that would lead only to unrest and chaos.[27]

The talks with Ribbentrop were ended without any conclusion on the matter of government formation – but a substantial reshuffle of the situation in Denmark was set in motion by Berlin. A new general for the German *Wehrmacht* in Denmark was appointed and a new political representative was assigned to relieve Ambassador Renthe-Fink. The new leading German representative in Denmark was SS general and former *Gestapo* officer Werner Best. Like Renthe-Fink, Best formally represented the Foreign Office but – in order to obliterate all former notions and illusions of parity between the two nations – he was not appointed with ambassadorial status, but merely as plenipotentiary. Best entered Copenhagen with a mandate to form a new Danish government.

The political leaders of the government parties negotiated for almost a week. There was still some room for manoeuvre. Their impression was that Best wanted a new Prime Minister, preferably Scavenius, and new ministers who signalled a turn in Danish policy. But Nazi ministers could be avoided. By demanding a new government, the Germans abandoned the very basic idea of the *modus vivendi* of 9 April 1940. To some of the leaders, this called for a break with the Germans and a decision to throw away the reins. Others, the majority, were of the opinion that avoiding Nazi participation was sufficient to strike a deal and that they, as elected politicians, still had an obligation to carry on and safeguard – and use for the benefit of the population – what was left of political independence and leverage. It was the politics of the lesser evil. At last, the political parties decided to continue and to meet the wishes of the plenipotentiary. Before that, they had conducted what was close to an interrogation of Scavenius: What would his attitude be to potential German demands for the death penalty, laws against Jews, and an accession to the Axis Tripartite Pact? After declaring his opposition to all three, Scavenius was accepted as Prime Minister and a new list of ministers – more of them 'non-political', but without Nazis – was accepted by the leadership of the four cooperating political parties. Thus, the crisis ended on 9 November 1942.

The so-called Telegram Crisis of 1942 seems like a rupture in the development of the occupation of Denmark. Berlin had dictated who was to be the Danish Prime Minister. This was the very negation of Danish 'political independence' and sovereignty. Yet including Nazi politicians in government was avoided and the government, after all, still had considerable room for independent action. Certainly, Scavenius was not considered by the population to be as legitimate as his predecessors. But still the parliament supported him, making his ruling constitutional.

Surprisingly, no lasting deterioration of bilateral relations occurred. Best proved to be a smooth political operator working quite independently of Berlin.

His aim was to maintain Denmark as a calm area in Europe yielding agricultural produce for the German war effort. He was unsympathetic to the Danish Nazis and established a good working relationship with Scavenius. He understood that in order to keep production in Denmark going, the best way to handle political affairs was to strengthen the Danish government, not to weaken it by undermining its legitimacy. An example of Best's flexibility was that he allowed a parliamentary election to be held in March 1943. The Communist Party was, of course, not allowed to participate, and the crucial topic of Danish politics – the relationship with Germany – could not be discussed freely. Still, public debate on domestic issues was possible. The election had a turnout of more than 89 per cent, the highest ever in Danish history. Ninety per cent voted for the four government parties and a small supporting party, and the Danish Nazi party was humiliated by receiving only 2 per cent. The resistance and the clandestine press had been divided in their recommendations. The left wing advocated a spoiled ballot, abstaining while the centre-right recommended voting for anti-Scavenius politicians in the democratic parties. In the end, half a per cent cast a spoiled ballot.[28] Despite the democratically flawed setting, the election result must be considered a vote of support for the general policy conducted since April 1940.

The summer of 1943

The apparent tranquillity evidenced by the election in March 1943 was, however, fragile, subject to destabilization, and very sensitive to the course of war. This was highlighted in the summer of 1943, when public unrest in larger towns in Denmark put the government under tremendous pressure. Attitudes among people with an activist propensity were influenced by the removal of Mussolini and by a general notion that Germany was losing the war and that the war was about to end soon. Strikes developed into general expressions of anti-German feeling, with street fights between strikers and sympathizers on the one side and German soldiers on the other. Sabotage accompanied the riots and kept the pot boiling by encouraging the unrest and by making the Germans even touchier. The unrest gravitated from town to town.[29]

The mayors, the police, the leading trade unionists, the employers' association – all called for order and a resumption of work. The police were deployed in the streets to restore order. Most importantly, the police had to try to keep the protesters away from German soldiers – and also avoid being caught on the same side as the *Wehrmacht* confronting the Danish public. The latter was the nightmare of both the police and its political superiors. It threatened to de-legitimize the entire police force. The German plenipotentiary, Werner Best, was under pressure from Berlin and Hitler himself to bring an end to the unrest in Denmark. Best transferred this pressure to the Danish government in the form of an ultimatum: Put an end to the unrest, declare a state of emergency and adopt the death penalty for sabotage. Otherwise, the German military will do so and sweep away the Danish government.

Certainly, the organized resistance, especially the communists, had an interest in bringing the government down and thereby stopping cooperation with the German occupier, but most strikers and rioters were motivated not by a desire to undermine the government, but rather to use what was considered perhaps to be the final chance to express their opposition to the Germans.[30] Leading government politicians feared that the strikes and unrest were the prelude to a communist takeover of power that would be launched in the very instant that the occupying power collapsed. If, as perceived, the end of the war was imminent, the safeguarding of sovereignty now was a two-front battle. If the unrest were not stopped, Germany would remove what was left of political independence in Denmark. If, on the other hand, measures to stop the unrest were seen as running the Germans' errands, it would de-legitimize the politicians and the police force in the eyes of the public. This might, in turn, lead to the overthrow of parliamentary democracy, the constitution and the political life of the pre-war years by a communist revolution. In that case, any talk of sovereignty would prove futile. The government was caught between a rock and a hard place. In particular, the death penalty for saboteurs was an impossible pill to swallow. On 28 August 1943, the Danish answer to the German ultimatum was given. It was a 'no'. From the following day, constitutional government with the King and parliament ceased to function.

On 29 August 1943, the German military declared a state of emergency. The Danish army and navy were attacked. The fighting went on for a few hours and cost the lives of 23 Danish and 5 German soldiers before the Danish side finally was disarmed. A number of naval vessels were scuttled before the Germans could seize them.

Towards the liberation

Even without a working government, fundamental traits of the *modus vivendi* of 9 April 1940 continued. The permanent undersecretaries of the ministerial departments carried on administering the country and dealt with the occupying power in a pattern that resembled the cohabitation between April 1940 and August 1943. Until the Liberation, the Ministry of Foreign Affairs kept its prominent role in the Danish-German relationship. Although August 1943 led to a significant tightening of the occupying power's control and repression, the Danish-German relationship maintained its character as a form of political negotiation where the supreme objective on the Danish side remained the same: to protect the Danish people against the consequences of war and to prevent German influence on the Danish society. Behind the scenes, the leading politicians were in contact with the ministries and the leading civil servants. The *Wehrmacht* lifted the state of emergency after only 6 weeks.

An operation to round up Danish Jews was launched by Best in October 1943 – but the vast majority escaped to Sweden. Out of more than 7,000 Jews, 481 were brought to German camps. Of these, 52 died as a result of their internment. The rescue of the Danish Jews is one of the most significant results of the Danish policy during the occupation. Before October 1943, Hitler did not want to risk the functioning cohabitation and, therefore, did not raise the 'Jewish question'. In October 1943, the Swedish government felt strong enough *vis-à-vis* Germany to receive the Jewish refugees. In 1941 and 1942, when persecution of the Norwegian Jews took place, the situation would probably have been different.[31]

The resistance movement developed momentum after August 1943, and increasingly so until the Liberation. The Freedom Council – an umbrella body of resistance organizations – was established in September 1943. The relationship between the *political class* and the resistance movement was continuously problematic, first and foremost because the politicians' notion was that the resistance was dominated by communists. Nevertheless, contact was established between the former adversaries. From the politicians' point of view – especially the Social Democrats' and the Conservatives' – the new strategy was to obtain status as allies of the resistance movement. Therefore, the politicians started secretly to finance the resistance movement with treasury funds. The military services that had been disarmed by the Germans in August 1943 were completely loyal to the politicians. They offered themselves in the name of the Freedom Council, although only making a pretence of it. For the military, the aim was not to fight the Germans, but to control the resistance movement on behalf of the politicians. Around New Year 1944–45, all regional leadership positions within the resistance movement were held by military officers. From late 1944 to April 1945, intense negotiations were held between the old political system and the Freedom Council in order to solve the issue of how to compose a Liberation

Government. In late April 1945, it was decided to form a government consisting of members of the four leading political parties and the resistance movement on a 50:50 ratio. On 5 May 1945, Germany surrendered in north-west Europe and Denmark was liberated.

On 8 May 1945, the Parliament was reopened. Prime Minister Buhl – who in 1942 had called for a common national effort to combat sabotage – gave his opening address on behalf of the new government, celebrating the restoration of democracy and Danish independence. He also promised to hold elections in the near future. Accordingly, parliamentary elections were held in October 1945. Compared with the 2 per cent of the vote that the Communist Party held in 1939, its improvement to 12 per cent of the vote was a clear indication that political sentiments were influenced by the war, especially among working class voters. The communist gain was at the expense of the Social Democrats who lost an equivalent percentage of their vote. Apart from this shift in public opinion, the political landscape both regarding structures and personalities was basically the same. The Communist gains and the Social Democratic losses evened out in the next two elections in 1947 and 1950. Of all the occupied countries in Europe, Denmark displayed remarkable political continuity from the interwar years, through the war to the post-war era. No constitutional change occurred, nor any significant change with regard to who the dominating political parties and personalities were.

Sovereignty and ethics

As a result of a sense of institutional self-preservation, it is inherent in any political system that it will try to safeguard its sovereignty. In a democracy, there are also good and noble reasons for safeguarding state sovereignty – especially in a situation such as that obtaining in Denmark during World War II. The alternatives – rule by the local Nazis or direct German rule – were not attractive. But, as evidenced in this chapter, the attempts to safeguard sovereignty led to acts by the leaders of the political system that were questionable. In certain situations, the executive power, the legislature and the judiciary acted in ways that not only proved to be the very negation of sovereignty – because they were carried out to meet German demands – but also compromised the principles of democracy. The so-called obsession with sovereignty induced the political system to do the dirty work for Nazi Germany.

The paradox was most striking in the confrontation between the political system and the resistance. The resistance would argue that the political system was compromised and de-legitimized by its violations of democratic principles, and, furthermore, it would claim that this gave legitimacy to the acts of the resistance. The leaders of the political system would, on the contrary, argue that the resistance was devoid of any responsibility to the Danish people and, thus, was illegitimate. (Not to mention the suspicion that parts of the resistance, the communists, carried a hidden agenda of revolution.) Furthermore, the political leaders would argue that democratic principles might have been compromised – but that it was for the sake of preserving a higher principle, a higher good. It was the politics of the lesser evil. The clash between these arguments is comparable to a distinction made by the German sociologist Max Weber in a lecture from 1919 called *Politik als Beruf*. Weber distinguishes between two kinds of ethics: the ethic of responsibility and the ethic of conviction. The champion of the ethic of responsibility will let his or her views, positions and acts be guided by their probable consequences. The champion of the ethic of conviction will solely be guided by principles – and if views, positions and acts lead to unwanted consequences, he or she will blame 'the world, other people's stupidity – or God's will because he created them so'.[32]

A common argument posed against the Danish line during the war is: Why did the Danish state (and its political system) abstain from the common fight against Nazi tyranny? Danish politicians would answer that 'We fought Nazism on Danish territory. Through difficult times the banner of democracy was held high, Danish Nazism was totally marginalized – compare that to some other occupied countries!' And as mentioned earlier, the successful rescue of the Danish Jews should also be partly ascribed to the policy of the Danish state. And so should saving hundreds of lives of resistance fighters who avoided deportation to Germany because of the maintenance of Danish legal jurisdiction.

Still, there was a problem. The transactional character of official Danish-German interchanges endowed the relationship with a touch of mutuality and voluntariness. In some ways, the mutuality and voluntariness were as fictional and illusory as the idea of sovereignty during the occupation. But they were not completely insubstantial: nobody forced the Danes to the negotiating table, and it was possible to say no and stop the game. Undoubtedly, there would have been severe consequences for the country and its people, but the choice *was* there. To those who focused critically on the mutuality and the voluntariness rather than on the fatal consequences of saying no, it must have seemed as if Danish concessions to Germany were The deeds of a fellow conspirator, an ally or maybe even an accomplice in the crimes of The Third Reich.

Whether one focused on the element of mutuality and voluntariness or not depended on the person's political views and the perspective from which he or she was observing the policy of negotiation and cooperation. Strong-minded activists did focus on the voluntariness, and – inasmuch as they ever heard about the situation in Denmark – so did large parts of the peoples of the Allied countries, who endured their part of the hardships in connection with the war against Nazi Germany. But the majority of Danes seemed to have the impression that the Danish-German relationship also implied a noticeable element of compulsion, which excused Danish conduct. And the foreign offices in London and Washington also took a reasonable and understanding view of the Danish situation. In Moscow it was, however, difficult to detect any sympathy.

Since 1940 until the present day it is in this field of tension – between the element of compulsion and the threat of a much worse alternative on the one side, and the element of voluntariness and mutuality along with the relative degree of complicity on the other side – that most discussions about the policy of negotiation and cooperation have taken place. It is, and was, a conflict between the ethic of conviction and the ethic of responsibility.

Notes

The author would like to thank Dr Joachim Lund for his helpful comments on an earlier draft.

1. Christensen, C. B., Lund, J., Olesen, N. W., and Sørensen, J. (2009), *Danmark besat. Krig og hverdag 1940–45* (revised edn). Copenhagen: Informations Forlag, p. 472; Poulsen, H. (1997), 'Denmark at War? The Occupation as History', in Ekman, S., Edling, N. (eds) (1997), *War Experience, Self Image and National Identity: The Second World War as Myth and History*. Södertälje: Giglunds Förlag, pp. 98–109.
2. Paxton, R. (1972), *Vichy France: Old Guard and New Order, 1940–45*. New York: Alfred A. Knopf inc., p. 373.
3. Jackson, J. (2001), *France: The Dark Years 1940–44*. Oxford: Oxford University Press, pp. 265; Kitchen, P. (2002), 'From Enthusiasm to Disenchantment: the French Police and the Vichy regime, 1940–1944', *Contemporary European History*, 11:3, pp. 371–90; Mastny, V. (1971), *The Czechs under Nazi Rule. The Failure of National Resistance 1939–1942*. New York: Columbia University Press;

Warmbrunn, W. (1963), *The Dutch under German Occupation 1940–1945*. Stanford: Stanford University Press.
4   Kirchhoff, H. (2002), 'Denmark, September 1939–April 1940', in Wylie, N. (2002), *European Neutrals and Non-Belligerents during the Second World War*. Cambridge: Cambridge University Press, p. 50.
5   Nissen, H. S. (1973), *1940. Studier i forhandlingspolitikken og samarbejdspolitikken*. Copenhagen: Gyldendal, p. 42.
6   Christensen, Olesen, and Sørensen (2009), p. 129.
7   Poulsen, H. (1997).
8   Christensen, Lund, Olesen, and Sørensen, (2009), p. 150.
9   Poulsen, H. (1970), *Besættelsesmagten og de danske nazister*. Copenhagen: Gyldendal; Kirchhoff, H. (1985), 'Konsensus og konflikt i besættelsestidens historie. Forsøg på et rids af forskningsdiskussionen', *Historie & Samtidsorientering*, vol. 24. Copenhagen; Lauridsen, J. T. (2003), 'En storm i et meget lille glas vand. "Problemet" Frits Clausen og Werner Bests eliminering af DNSAP 1943–44', *Historie 2*. Aarhus: Jysk Selskab for Historie.
10 Reynolds, D. (2006), *From World War to Cold War. Churchill, Roosevelt, and the International History of the 1940s*. Oxford: Oxford University Press, p. 23; Olesen, N. W. (2010), '1940 i dansk politik', in Dahl, F., Kirchhoff, H., Lund, J., Vaale, L. (eds) (2010), *Danske tilstande – norske tilstande*. Copenhagen: Gyldendal.
11 Olesen, (2010).
12 Kirchhoff, H. (2001): *Samarbejde og modstand under besættelsen. En politisk historie*. Odense: Syddansk Universitetsforlag, p. 20.
13 Kirchhoff, H. (1996), 'Erik Scavenius – landsforræder eller patriot', in Olesen, N. W. (ed.) (1996), *Mennesker, politik og besættelse*. Esbjerg: Historisk Samling fra Besættelsestiden.
14 Frederiksen, L. B. (1960): *Pressen under besættelsen. Hovedtræk af den danske dagspresses vilkår og virke 1940–45*. Aarhus: Aarhus Universitetsforlag.
15 According to a provisional law of 22 July 1940 'prohibiting publications that have the potential to harm Denmark's relations with foreign countries'.
16 Lundbak, H. (2003), *Danish unity: a political party between Fascism and Resistance 1936–1947*. Copenhagen: Museum Tusculanum Press, pp. 144–55.
17 Olesen, N. W. (2008), 'John Christmas Møller og Hans Hedtoft. To antinazister går hver sin vej', in Kirchhoff, H. (ed.) (2008), *Sådan valgte de*. Copenhagen: Gyldendal.
18 Olesen (2008).
19 Koch, H. (1994), *Demokrati slå til! Statsretslig nødret, ordenspoliti og frihedsrettigheder 1932–1945*, Copenhagen: Gyldendal, p. 258.
20 Christensen, Lund, Olesen and Sørensen (2009), p. 268.
21 Olesen N. W. (2009) Danmarks befrielse 1945 – en mislykket revolution? in *Kontur - Tidsskrift for Kulturstudier*, nr. 18, Aarhus: Aarhus University, p. 31.

22 ibid., p. 32.
23 Christensen, Lund, Olesen and Sørensen (2009), p. 434.
24 Christensen, Lund, Olesen and Sørensen (2009), p. 359.
25 Roslyng-Jensen, P. (2007), *Danskerne og besættelsen. Holdninger og meninger 1939–1945.* Copenhagen: Gads Forlag.
26 Christensen, Lund, Olesen and Sørensen (2009), p. 361.
27 ibid., p. 378.
28 ibid., p. 408.
29 ibid, p. 454.
30 Poulsen H. (2000), 'Hvad mente danskerne', in *Historie 2*, Aarhus: Jysk Selskab for Historie, p. 321.
31 Gilmour, J. (2010), *Sweden, the Swastika and Stalin: The Swedish Experience in the Second World War.* Edinburgh: Edinburgh University Press, p. 192.
32 Weber, M. (1919), '»Gesinnungsethik« versus »Verantwortungsethik«', in *Politik als Beruf.* Vortrag. See also: Kirchhoff (2001), p. 28.

5

Closing a Long Chapter: German-Norwegian Relations 1939–45

Norway and the Third Reich

Tom Kristiansen

Introduction

Vidkun Quisling's seizure of power by way of a broadcast *coup d'état* on the evening of 9 April 1940, only a few hours after the launch of the *Weserübung*, was a defining moment in modern Norwegian history. The country's armed forces had not fired a shot in anger since 1814, and had not been massively assaulted from the sea since the Middle Ages. Norway had, moreover, only been fully independent for 35 years. The German bolt-from-the-blue attack, the five-nation campaign that followed and the *coup* staged by a tiny group of fascists with only an insignificant body of supporters truly put German-Norwegian relations at a historical crossroads and profoundly changed their course for decades to come. The long-standing policy of non-alignment in peace and neutrality in war has never since been regarded as a viable option by any government. And the vastly different war experiences of the Nordic countries made continued efforts to coordinate their security policies exceedingly challenging throughout the Cold War.

The events at the outbreak of war in Scandinavia reflected in a harrowing way the culmination of a steady deterioration in the relationship between Germany and Norway. It had started in earnest during World War I and been exacerbated in the wake of the Labour government's assuming power in March 1935, two years after Hitler was installed as German Chancellor. The savage German attack dealt a ruinous blow to the relations between the two countries. Not surprisingly, both the government's 5 years in exile as a junior partner in the Grand Alliance and the 5 years of increasingly ruthless military occupation also had a fundamental impact on Norway's relations with Britain, and eventually the United States. The repercussions of all these watershed events – not fully grasped at the time – permeated Norway's relations with West Germany during the Cold War and are vaguely felt even to this day, often masquerading as Euro-scepticism or various popular prejudices.

This chapter provides a survey of German-Norwegian historical relations up to the end of World War II with a special focus on the Third Reich. Its overall aim is to present the complexity, the diversity and the longevity of the liaisons between the two countries in order to identify how the events between 1933 and 1945 – Hitler's Norwegian legacy – influenced society and popular sentiments and, furthermore, brought about a fundamental change in Norwegian security and foreign policies which lasted throughout the Cold War. It is fair to say that it is difficult to understand the war legacy without taking into consideration the long history of Norway's relations with Germany both culturally, intellectually, politically and economically.

The long history before the Third Reich

In Norwegian public discourse after the war, the expression pro-German has been levelled against both living and dead in order to stonewall a debate or taint a protagonist. The assumption has been, of course, that relations with anything German would be sinister or suspicious and make a person relentlessly corrupted. As a blanket accusation this was something completely new. The long history of German-Norwegian relations explains why and also reveals the depth of the change that was brought about by fascism and the war.[1]

Without going into any detail, it is nonetheless crucial to identify the core and essence of the historical liaison between Norway and the Germans – the German state from 1871. The history stretches back to the Middle Ages. In the course of that period, Norwegian trade and economy became intrinsically interwoven into the trade system that encompassed the Hanseatic League. From 1360 to 1754, there was an official body organizing its activities. These institutions were later known as the *Kontor* (a major privileged merchant office) in Bergen on the west coast and the so-called *Faktories* (minor trading posts) in the towns of Oslo and Tønsberg in the Oslo Fjord. They exerted almost total control over Norwegian trade in vital commodities such as grain and fish. In traditional Norwegian historiography, this trade monopoly has widely been regarded as an expression of domination and exploitation, while recent historians have been more likely to regard it as a form of internationalization from which all participants benefited.[2] The League was in gradual decline from the late fifteenth century, particularly after Denmark defeated Lübeck in 1536, and much of the trade in eastern Norway was taken over by the Danes and the Dutch. Nevertheless, the Germans continued to have a firm grip on Norwegian fish exports and grain imports in the west and the north, and to exert their influence in a variety of other ways.

Commercial relations became a constant feature down the centuries and they developed considerably from the late nineteenth century. At the outbreak of World War I, exports from Germany represented a good 30 per cent of total Norwegian imports, while only Britain bought more from Norway than Germany.[3] The Norwegian economy has traditionally been open and totally dependent on imports and exports. However, trade was only one part of the economic relations between the two countries. From the sixteenth century, Germans became crucial in developing the prospering Norwegian mining industry and saw mills. When the country underwent its industrial revolution in the nineteenth century, Germany, moreover, became an important supplier of expertise, capital and technology.[4] A corollary to these activities was a substantial German immigration into Norway. Merchants, engineers and craftsmen gradually became naturalized Norwegian citizens. Another notable German influence on Norwegian society from the late nineteenth century concerns social policies. The German model of social security legislation was adapted to a larger extent in Norway than in any of the other Scandinavian countries in the early twentieth century. The system originated from obligatory accident and sickness insurance schemes for workers, which constituted the impetus for the development of the modern welfare state in Norway.[5]

The mercantile and economic relations, in addition to German immigration, prepared the ground for other contacts which came to comprise religion, culture and intellectual life. A few of them need to be mentioned because they had a profound impact on Norwegian society. After the Reformation in 1536–37, the Norwegian church adopted the Lutheran evangelical doctrine as the result of a royal decree. As in north Germany and the other Scandinavian countries, Norway had a state church which eventually dominated religious and cultural life. The German origins and teaching of the church brought about a sense of cultural unity within the whole region. It goes without saying that this had an overwhelming impact in the pre-secular era. North European Protestantism, into which Norway was fully integrated, was heavily marked by German academic theology and institutions and it moulded Norwegian society in a fundamental way.[6]

The strong German influence on intellectual and cultural life is well illustrated by the fact that German was by far the dominant foreign language in Norway until 1940 (albeit that English was clearly on the rise from the early twentieth century). Moreover, the majority of the foreign members of the Norwegian Academy of Science were Germans, and Germany was the preferred destination for Norwegian students going abroad. The University of Oslo – founded in 1811 – was permeated by German academic traditions up to the Nazi era.[7] Likewise, from the early nineteenth century, Norwegian cultural life was truly influenced by the Romantic movement in Germany which inspired the national awakening in Norway throughout the nineteenth century. A vast number of prominent Norwegian artists, authors and musicians were educated in Germany and spent parts of their lives there. The most notable were the composer Edvard Grieg, the Romantic painter J. C. Dahl and the playwright Henrik Ibsen.

From the turn of the century, there was also a marked growth in the number of German tourists, tourism having previously been dominated by British aristocrats.[8] Best known are the Kaiser's annual cruises in Norwegian waters. His somewhat exotic and lavish personality (by Norwegian standards), and his paternalism and generosity on many occasions made him quite a popular figure.[9] Moreover, many Germans, the Kaiser included, nurtured a rather quixotic and nostalgic idea that there was a common Germanic pedigree and that the legacy of the ancient tribes still lingered on in Nordic culture. This was something quite alien to the vast majority of Norwegian politicians and officials.

There was very little popular anti-German sentiment in Norway up to World War I. Nonetheless, there was a suspicion lurking in the higher echelons of society, the reason for which was the trajectory of strategy and great power politics after the establishment of the German Empire in 1871. The Anglo-German antagonism that developed in the decades leading up to World War I left Norway in an increasingly awkward position between the great power blocs. In particular, the naval cruises and manoeuvres in or close to Norwegian territorial waters every summer until 1914 left the impression that the country had moved alarmingly swiftly from being a politically negligible part of Europe to an arena of confrontation. Consequently, Norway's first foreign minister, soon after the dissolution of the Swedish-Norwegian Union in 1905 – Jørgen Løvland – maintained that the town of Kristiansand would be exposed in any Anglo-German conflict. And Admiral John Fisher, the First Sea Lord, confided to the Norwegian Minister in London, Fridtjof Nansen, in 1907 that Britain – for strategic reasons – would have to consider the seizure of a Norwegian port in an armed conflict with Germany if the latter gained control over Denmark and the Danish straits.[10] Thus to become a part of the strategic calculations of the great powers has been characterized as Løvland's 'dire vision' by the historian of Norwegian foreign policy of the period, Roald Berg.[11] But it ought to be added that this 'dire vision' barely influenced the general public and that both British and German diplomats regarded it as inconceivable.

All in all, the overall characteristic of the association between Germany and Norway made it immune to political commotions since it affected the deeper layers of society and human life – not high politics. On the whole, consequently, the relationship was politically uncontroversial. Moreover, it goes without saying that the corollary of these highly diverse and complex contacts was innumerable visible and invisible ties between German-speaking Europe and Norway down the centuries that would take a lot to untie. Just as important as the close cultural, intellectual and economic ties between Germany and Norway is the striking absence of similar relations at the political level. Notwithstanding the fact that official relations on the whole were cordial after the establishment of the German Empire in 1871, German political thought and institutions had little influence on Norway. On the contrary, the elevated position of the Kaiser, the autocratic system and the nationalism and militarism of the Empire provoked suspicion and downright antagonism in Norwegian politics since this was contrary to the democratic and liberal development that characterized Norway after independence in 1814. The labour movement represents an exception. Socialist intellectuals were deeply inspired by German Social Democrats with respect to institutions and ideology, and even the socialist brand of eugenics.[12]

Historical relations between Germany and Norway are all the more interesting when they are compared with British-Norwegian relations. Britain represented a contrast. On the one hand, the religious, cultural and intellectual ties were weak even though there had been close contact throughout history. With the exception of shipping, Germany, between the wars, had become an even more important trading partner for Norway than Britain.[13] On the other hand, British political traditions, thought and institutions had become somewhat of an ideal in Norway.

And, most importantly, Britain was regarded both as the defender of liberalism and democracy and as the ultimate underwriter of Norwegian integrity after the dissolution of the union with Sweden. There was also an assumption that Britain had strong strategic interests attached to Norway and therefore provided what has been termed an 'implicit guarantee' in Norwegian historiography.[14]

World War I temporarily dealt a serious blow to German-Norwegian relations. It was not that the Norwegian public was particularly engaged in the causes and the course of the war. The dominant issue was to deal with the knock-on effects of the war on the Norwegian economy. People tended to regard the war as a conflict between great imperialist powers, but if push came to shove, their sympathies lay increasingly with the *Entente*. The vast majority supported the aim of the government, namely to remain neutral and non-belligerent. There were two aspects of the war experience that had a long-lasting effect. First, the government fully experienced how difficult the position was for Norway in a war between Britain and Germany, and how vulnerable neutrality was in an existential great-power war. The Scandinavian countries did what they could to coordinate their policy, as demonstrated through the meetings of their kings on a couple of occasions. The cumbersome situation was caused by both Norway's geographical position between Germany, the dominant land power, and Britain, the foremost sea power, and by Norwegian control of assets vital for the belligerents, such as raw materials, fish and the merchant fleet. Norway was eventually coerced by Britain into taking a foreign policy stance against Germany. Nonetheless, it remained formally neutral by the skin of its teeth throughout the war, albeit in Olav Riste's classical term as the 'neutral ally' to the *Entente*.[15]

Secondly, what really shattered Norwegian public opinion was the German declaration of unlimited U-boat warfare in January 1917. It was regarded as cowardly and outrageously uncivilized, and, of course, as being in breach of international law. The Norwegian merchant fleet – number four in the world – suffered a devastating blow. Almost 2,000 men and 800–900 ships (1–2 million gross registered tonnage) were lost, or around half the fleet. The losses at sea marked a fundamental change in the attitudes towards Germany and created an undercurrent of anti-German sentiment. This was not wholly forgotten after 1918, but neither Norwegian governments nor the public held the Weimar Republic responsible for the deeds of an imperial Germany in desperation and demise. According to Odd-Bjørn Fure, the historian of Norwegian foreign policy in the interwar years, German influence on Norway was so strong that anti-German sentiment during the war affected non-political relations between the two countries throughout the interwar years in only a limited way.

German foreign policy in the 1920s was dominated by a few prioritized issues. Among them were the efforts to secure support for a revision of the eastern borders decreed in the peace settlement, to renegotiate the reparations imposed by the victors, to put an end to the continued Allied occupation of parts of German territory and to protect people of German extraction who found themselves living outside Germany. The Scandinavian countries became an arena for the Weimar Republic in which it promoted the rehabilitation of Germany's reputation and where it sought support for its objectives. Trade policy was one means of achieving this. The German government was successful in developing commercial relations with Scandinavia in the 1920s. An expression of the importance attached to Scandinavia was the posting of first-rank diplomats, which was not the case with the British.[16] Moreover, the Weimar Republic was to some extent successful in creating sympathy for German foreign policy aims. Notwithstanding these efforts, Germany remained peripheral in Norwegian foreign policy throughout the 1920s basically because it no longer posed a potential military threat. Johan L. Mowinckel, Prime Minister in 1930, forthrightly claimed that the 'likelihood of Norway entering into an armed conflict with countries such as Germany, France, Spain, Portugal, Italy etc. is so remote that it seems justifiable to disregard it totally'.[17] At this point he was in full agreement with the commanding Admiral's staff which had concluded

Figure 2 Gustav Stresemann giving his Nobel Peace Prize lecture in the great hall at the University of Oslo in 1927. [Copyright: Scanpix]

likewise in the previous year.[18] Germany did not reappear in Norwegian threat assessments until well into the 1930s.[19]

The most challenging issue between the two countries after the war was the disagreement over reparations for the Norwegian losses at sea. Following drawn-out negotiations, an arrangement was arrived at only in 1928. Another difficult issue was the abrogation of the so-called Integrity Treaty of November 1907, to which Germany, together with Britain, France and Russia, was a signatory. The treaty was the result of efforts to secure great power acceptance of Norway's independence after the dissolution of the union with Sweden. Norway initiated a diplomatic process after the war with a view to dissolving the treaty because it was regarded as superfluous (and the sort of guarantee not worthy of a fully independent country). Germany was in favour of abrogation. However, it completely dismissed the Norwegian argument that the establishment of the League of Nations had made the treaty redundant because it did not want to agree to anything that would give legitimacy to the Versailles Treaty. In 1924, the Soviet Union (as the last of the signatories) reluctantly conceded abrogation of the treaty. This took effect from 1928. The only remaining unsettled conflict at that point concerned the extent of Norwegian territorial waters. This was a prolonged conflict between Norway, Britain and Germany. From the late nineteenth century, modern British and German trawlers had interfered severely with traditional Norwegian coastal fisheries. Norway imposed regulations in order to restrict these activities and claimed an extension of the sea border to four nautical miles. This led to a bitter conflict with the British, while the Germans were far more likely to accept the Norwegian measures. This was, of course, much appreciated by the Norwegians, who regarded the issue as politically, economically and socially exceedingly important.

What characterizes the conflicts between the two countries during the Weimar Republic is that they were over trivial issues involving resources and money. Indeed, none of them had the potential for serious escalation or, say, becoming a *casus belli*. Another noteworthy aspect of Norwegian attitudes before the Nazi era was the growing sympathy for Germany's policy of normalization and its efforts to revise the terms of the 1919 peace settlement. All in all, there was definitely an ambiguity in Norway's stance. On the one hand, there was the undercurrent of anti-German sentiment caused by the war experience, while on the other there was a recognition, particularly in the labour movement, that the terms of the Versailles Treaty were too harsh to bring about political and economic stability in Europe.

The awarding of the Nobel Peace Prize in 1926 to the French and German Foreign Ministers, Aristide Briand and Gustav Stresemann, for their contribution to the Locarno Treaty of 1925 marked a major step towards normalization between Germany and Norway. When Stresemann visited Norway to give his lecture in the following year, he was treated with the utmost cordiality. The British Minister in Oslo, Sir Cecil Dormer, reported, 'During the whole course of the visit the Norwegians went out of their way to show the German statesman how greatly they appreciated his visit, which contributed not a little to the continued improvement in the relation with Norway which marked that year'.[20] Sympathy for Germany and its post-war predicament continued to grow and ended on a positive note on the eve of the Nazi takeover in 1933 when the Norwegian government tended to support a revision of the Versailles Treaty in Germany's favour.

Norway and the Third Reich before the outbreak of war

Vidkun Quisling's 2-year period as defence minister was drawing to an end when Adolf Hitler was sworn in as Chancellor on 30 January 1933. The Agrarian Party government of Jens Hunseid, of which he was a part, resigned on 3 March and was succeeded by the Liberal government of Johan Ludwig Mowinckel, who also served as Foreign Secretary. The Nazi *Machtübernahme* (takeover of power) had no immediate effect on political and diplomatic relations between Germany and Norway. The disputes over fisheries and the extent of territorial waters lingered on undramatically. Within the armed forces there were some expressions of concern over the potential threat that Germany posed to Norwegian security and neutrality, but at that point only in very limited circles and not as a result of the Nazi takeover. The relegation of Germany to a second-rate power after Versailles, and likewise Russia after the 1917 revolution, had created a more relaxed attitude to any military threats from those countries. National security was still absent from the political agenda of the Norwegian government and in parliament.

In Norwegian society at large, the reactions were more apprehensive. Particularly in the labour movement there was immediate and serious concern over the course on which the Third Reich embarked. Fascist ideology and activism had been loathed and fiercely opposed by the left for years. Hitler's savage persecution of the opposition provoked stern antagonism among both socialists and liberals. The labour movement encouraged the government to set out on a more demonstrative course by way of a trade boycott and an ideological counteroffensive. But to no avail. Both the Liberal government (1933–35) and the Labour government from 1935 disapproved of such measures out of fear of the damage they could cause to the economic recovery in the wake of the depression. Any sort of official activism was, therefore, rejected.

There were very few open supporters of the Nazi regime in Norway. However, some of the bourgeois newspapers in Oslo (to their later embarrassment) did express admiration for Hitler's achievements. By and large, the attraction of fascism was limited, and the supporters were restricted to fringe cliques with no mass appeal. But German fascism, nonetheless, had an offspring in Norway. Only a couple of months after he had left office, Quisling was one of the founders of the Norwegian extreme rightist party, *Nasjonal Samling*. The posture, jingoism, rhetoric, rites and paraphernalia were unmistakably influenced by the European fascist parties, with, however, a streak of *völkisch* Nazism. Even though the party did what it could to stoke the political fire and benefit from the difficult economic situation, it remained an utter failure. The *Nasjonal Samling*'s bid for representation in parliament in the elections of 1933 and 1936 did not yield more than Two per cent of the votes, and hence no members of the National Assembly. After having been a major feature of Norwegian politics for a brief period, it ended in the doldrums after the 1936 election.[21]

As often is the case with extremist parties, the *Nasjonal Samling* suffered a split shortly afterwards. The Norwegian pre-war fascists – few and far between as they were – certainly did not constitute a focal point in history. Their real influence on the Norwegian body politic was exceedingly limited. True, the fascist party contributed to bringing home to Norway the sort of activism and political culture that characterized some of the continental countries. The majority of the public regarded it as somewhat bizarre, but it was mostly supporters of the left and the labour movement who were the active anti-fascists. All in all, the robustness and resilience of the constitutional system under open attack in the 1930s is a far more remarkable feature than those who challenged it. No major restrictions on democratic rights had to be imposed by the authorities to protect the political order.[22]

German policy towards Norway in the years leading up to the invasion was on the whole marked by a lack of genuine interest and any sign of confrontation. For obvious reasons, attention needed to be diverted to more compelling issues. According to Odd-Bjørn Fure, the Third Reich did not try to coerce Norway into certain patterns of action. However, the German government did what it could to influence Norwegian public opinion by way of other organizations.[23] Moreover, German diplomats attempted time and again to encourage the Labour government to take measures against the ardent anti-Nazi campaign of the socialist and liberal press. But again to no avail. In 1936, the German peace activist and editor, Carl von Ossietzky, was awarded the Nobel Peace Prize and that led to tensions between the two countries. At that time, Ossietzky was imprisoned and the German government rightly regarded the prize as a condemnation of the regime. But the controversy resulted only in symbolic measures in both countries. The King was absent from the prize ceremony and both Foreign Minister Koht and the Liberal leader Mowinckel withdrew from the Nobel Committee in an effort to mitigate the initial German reactions. Neither, of course, was the German government represented at the ceremony. The only long-term effect was the rather peculiar decision not to allow Norwegian citizens to receive German honours and vice versa. A British diplomat who commented on the incident was laconic, 'I fear this is rather a case of the irresistible force colliding with the immovable object . . .'.[24]

The Ossietzky incident was only the beginning. The deterioration in relations gathered momentum as Nazi policy became more aggressive, and the gap between Germany and Norway continued to widen in spite of the absence of diplomatic crises. There was, moreover, a reduction in the cultural liaisons between the two countries as the 1930s wore on. Among other things, Norway declined representation when the University of Heidelberg celebrated its 550th anniversary in 1936. The pre-war years were indeed a period without political grandstanding. A case in point is the reluctance of Norwegian governments to accept radical and Jewish refugees from Nazi Germany, which infuriated the left.[25] Promotion of national interests rested firmly on a policy of cunning adjustment and response to the great powers, while the League of Nations was the politicians' arena for the declaration of more virtuous views. The governments of the interwar years were definitely better at walking the walk than talking the talk.

What, then, about German influence on Norway's armed forces? Unsurprisingly, the united Kingdom of Denmark-Norway up to 1814 (parts of Denmark were German-speaking) was a broad avenue for German military influence. The Norwegian army had been founded by a royal decree in 1628. In the following two centuries, the regimental structure, schools, an officer and NCO corps, drill grounds and garrisons were established. It is easy to identify a German footprint, perhaps best illustrated by the vast number of German officers who were commissioned to take part in the build-up of the army (these family names can be traced in the military calendars up to this day). Regulations and field manuals were in German and so was the language of command up to the late eighteenth century. In the nineteenth century, army education and organizational principles were adopted from Prussia (units of the line, *Landwehr* and *Landsturm*). As in a number of other states, there was widespread admiration for the German army in the wake of the wars of unification up to 1871, and in the latter part of the century German weaponry and other routines poured in. This came to an abrupt end during World War I.

But, in the 1920s, General Hans von Seeckt's *Reichswehr* – with its quantitative straitjacket imposed by the Versailles Treaty – became a model for some Norwegian officers who believed that the new *Rahmenheer* was the best way to preserve the core organization and skills that were necessary for a future rearmament. The chief of the general staff in 1933–38, Colonel Otto Ruge, maintained that 'the distress had made it a path-breaker for the future'.[26] By maintaining a highly educated officer corps, by developing new operational concepts and by carrying through technological modernization, the *Reichswehr* had become 'a brilliant core for a great German army in the future', he claimed.[27] But the influence was nevertheless limited in some important respects. Except for the obvious and overwhelming asymmetry in size, the differences between the German and Norwegian armies were far more salient and can be summarized in a few points. In Norway, the conscripts underwent only short training periods during the summer and made up a militia rather than a regular army. There were no permanent forces worthy of the name and, moreover, there were no permanent garrisons. True, Norwegian army officers were traditionally educated and trained, and some attended courses and served for short periods in German units – and vice versa. But this was also the case with a lot of other countries and a part of regular international practice at the time. The cooperation between the navies of the two countries had different characteristics. When Norway introduced submarines in the years leading up to World War I, the boats were of German design, and crews and engineers were trained and educated in Germany. Otherwise, contacts were few and far between. All in all, the contacts between the German and Norwegian armed forces were basically on a service-to-service level and never deeply influenced the defence policy and ideals of any Norwegian government.

Recent historians have examined the conduct of a number of serving officers in the 1930s, and many of them have attracted harsh criticism for their fascist leanings and activities. The core members of the fascist party and other rightist organizations were officers. Quisling and his entourage were even pondering the rather fanciful idea of a *coup d'état* in the early 1930s, as has recently been established by the historians Nils Ivar Agøy and Lars Borgersrud.[28] It flowed from their fear of an unlawful socialist takeover and was meant to forestall such an attempt. The idea is perhaps the most cogent evidence that Quisling and his army followers (he was himself an artillery officer who left active duty after World War I) undoubtedly were in a state of suspended reality. However, these historians are convinced that a coup was feasible, given the number, position and clout of the reactionary officers taking part in the deliberations. Yet the written evidence they have put forward cannot in any way be termed a 'plan' in a military sense but is rather an assorted collection of informal notes and drafts on how to bring about a coup.[29]

I will argue that it was highly unlikely that a tiny group of fascist officers had even the slightest chance of succeeding in a country permeated by liberal ideals. Portugal was the only western democracy to suffer a coup in the interwar years (that in Spain in 1936 failed, leading to civil war), so one may ask why modern historians claim that Norway – in which the revolutionary communist party was close to a *quantité négligeable* – was susceptible. An assessment of the realism in these ideas must rest firmly on an understanding of Norwegian politics and society and, moreover, on the characteristics of the armed forces. There are two forceful arguments against such an assumption. In addition – and now comes the German connection – Quisling and his cohorts attempted a *coup* shortly after the *Weserübung* was launched and failed totally even under such circumstances.

First, the mere configuration of political power in Norway at the time allowed no leeway for a seizure of power by a miniscule grouping. After the Napoleonic Wars, the country had lived through an almost unbroken history of liberal and democratic development punctuated sometimes by fierce struggles. The result was a society where power increasingly was spread and where the literate population was politically and culturally organized in a proliferation of associations. Civil society was strong. Moreover, the political decision-making process distributed power between central and local government and according to the liberal principles of a distinction between legislative, executive and judicial functions. Compared with a number of central and east European countries, or France under the Third Republic, Norwegian society was in a state of relative equilibrium and was not threatened by severe social unrest, or, say, revolution. All in all, this meant that there was no centre of power which potential *coup* plotters could conquer as long as there was exceedingly little public support for fascism. It is barely thinkable that civil servants and the leadership of the armed forces would obey orders which blatantly contravened their constitutional duties and instructions. Such a *coup* could possibly have succeeded in a country divided down the middle. Norway was divided, but the fascists did not represent one of the sides. The labour movement alone would have been in a position to paralyse the culprits within hours by declaring a general strike.

Secondly, the armed forces were hardly capable of carrying out a *coup* because of their organization, training level, distribution and equipment, not to mention the absence of any apparent enthusiasm among the officers outside Quisling's entourage. There were no standing, loyal forces; there was no concentration of units; there was no equipment for riot control; none of the army units was trained for such assignments. The militia-like army – by and large made up of reservist officers and NCOs, and conscripts, was, moreover, permeated by the norms and values of the civil society of which they were a part. Notwithstanding the passionate desire of a few fascist officers, a *coup* was a pipe dream. And, above all, why did they not attempt a *coup* in the 1930s, particularly after what they regarded as a dangerous, unpatriotic socialist government came to power in 1935? The answer is obvious: Norway was simply not '*coup* prone' in the 1930s.

To anticipate the situation on 9 April 1940 for a moment: the idea of a *coup* was actually put to the test only a few hours after the German attack. The fact that the Germans had little confidence in Quisling's controlling and pacifying ability but made him resign the day after, and instead cooperated with the interim Norwegian administrative council and eventually established their own *Reichskommissariat*, provides forceful evidence that even an ideological ally of the Nazis would not be able to hold on to power in a sustainable way. On the contrary, the *coup* probably provoked the King, the government, parliament and the public as much as the German attack. It made Quisling eternally notorious and an entry in dictionaries worldwide. Moreover, according to the latest German account of the *Weserübung*, the planning process took place without any Norwegian taking part or even being consulted.[30] What is thoroughly misleading about these historians' position is that they put the controversy between the armed forces and the left at the centre of the military history of the entire interwar period. And then there is Germany again. Focusing on Germany prevents them from seeing the two dominant Norwegian preoccupations regarding defence leadership in the 1930s: first, putting the defence of neutrality on a higher state of alert, and secondly, greater military preparations contingent on the notion of an increasing German threat to Norway caused by its awkward naval strategic situation in any potential conflict with Britain. The armed forces had almost been in a state of hibernation since the end of World War I, and the overriding task was to arouse them, not to deal with imaginary enemies from within. When the increased defence budgets eventually passed through parliament in 1937 and later, the appropriations went exclusively to war-preparation measures.

What really came to place Norway between the devil and the deep blue sea in the last two years leading up to the war was the question of neutrality. Together with Sweden, Denmark and Finland and some other formerly small neutral countries (known as the Oslo states), the Norwegian government withdrew from the concept of collective security under the League of Nations in 1938 – aptly characterized by the historian Nils Ørvik as 'the flight from Geneva' – and officially declared its intention of returning to traditional neutrality in the event of a great power war.[31] Germany represented a huge challenge in that respect. On the one hand, it was assumed that Germany was in support of Norwegian neutrality, since the Germans would benefit from it in a protracted conflict with Britain. The case in point was the possibility of protected passage through Norwegian territorial waters that was provided by international law, and was the only way to break a British blockade in the Channel and North Sea. On the other hand, it was also assumed that Britain would hesitate to respect Norwegian neutrality if that undermined a maritime blockade of Germany. The British intention of doing what they deemed necessary to secure their interests – even hostilities in Norwegian territorial waters – was actually communicated to the Norwegian government a few days before the German invasion.[32] Germany offered the Nordic countries a non-aggression pact in May 1939. Unlike Denmark, Norway (together with Finland and Sweden) declined because a pact would have no effect on Norway's security in a great power conflict; in addition, it could easily create the impression that the Nordic region was gravitating politically towards the Axis.[33]

In the late 1930s, some influential Norwegian officers firmly believed that the German navy would seize a naval base in Denmark or Norway. The assessment was based on an interpretation of Vice Admiral Wolfgang Wegener's book *Die Seestrategie des Weltkrieges* of 1929.[34] Germany was, in other words, regarded as a potential military enemy well before the outbreak of war in 1939. But these were the thoughts of a limited part of the defence leadership and were blatantly rejected by the government and the Commanding Admiral. One aspect of this perceived threat needs to be emphasized. The officers believed that Germany would only seize a forward naval base for the duration of a war, which is not at all comparable with what materialized on 9 April. No one had ever imagined the possibility of Germany staging a massive combined operation with the aim of conquering the whole country in one decisive blow. That was thought utterly improbable because of Britain's naval superiority in northern waters. Rearmament from 1937 was first of all intended to shore up neutrality but, in addition, some measures were taken to prepare for a limited German attack.

The government was trapped in an impossible situation: its political sympathies were with the British who at the same time were a major challenger to neutrality. Whereas Germany – the political and to a certain extent military adversary – to all intents and purposes was in support of Norwegian neutrality. In the event of an armed conflict, however, it was quite clear that the government would consider siding not with Germany but with Britain. This would make the operations of the armed neutrality guard exceedingly challenging. How could it possibly protect Norway's neutral rights and at the same time refrain from intercepting British infringements? The results could be observed when the guard was mobilized after the outbreak of war in September 1939. It soon lost its credibility because of its partial mode of operation which was ordered by the government and demonstrated during the *City of Flint*, the *Westerwald* and the *Altmark* incidents. It was almost obvious at the dawn of the German attack that Norway once again had become a 'neutral ally'.

The distinguished historian, Professor Halvdan Koht, Foreign Minister from March 1935 to November 1940, had to learn to navigate in these troubled waters. From the outset, he kept such a tight grip on Norwegian foreign policy that the other cabinet ministers and his party did not dare to oppose openly what they regarded as his 'enlightened absolutism'. Koht was nevertheless profoundly democratic and progressive. Moreover, he firmly believed in the rights of small nations and in the development of international law and institutions as a bulwark against war. His great political mission was to merge the liberalism of the Norwegian national movement with the democratic labour movement. Koht was, of course, intimately familiar with German language, history and culture. The British Legation in Oslo gave him the highest recommendation after 4 years in office: 'he has given proof of outstanding abilities. Honest and frank in his opinions and easy to get on with. The most respected figure in the Government, though his colleagues tend to find him dull and heavy.'[35] Nonetheless, in Norwegian history he has become something of a scapegoat for all that went wrong even though no one had a viable alternative.

The Foreign Minister had an even harder time in striking a balance between the labour movement's wish to confront the Nazi regime politically and his responsibility to maintain normal diplomatic relations in order to promote national interests and prepare for neutrality. He found little understanding for his balancing act among the public. He appeared resigned when at one point he confided to the British representative in Oslo 'that Norwegians in general, including the press, knew nothing whatever of foreign affairs. He had found it quite useless to say anything to them because there was no bottom to their ignorance'.[36] In a way, Norway was at check mate. The deterioration of relations with Germany did flow from both the ideological controversy and the strategic predicament caused by a great power conflict. To combine neutrality with a pro-western policy was absolutely impossible in the great power conflict that evolved in the late 1930s.

The legacy of the war

A few examples from the sombre war-time statistics provide compelling evidence of why the intimate relations between Germany and Norway were smashed to smithereens in April 1940. Also at this time, the cultural and intellectual sphere was shaken to its foundation. The war-time relationship was pervaded by destruction, violence, suppression and exploitation, and was suffused with ideological ideals alien to the majority of the population. Around 10,000 Norwegians lost their lives. The merchant fleet took the heaviest toll with nearly 3,700 Norwegian dead and a further 1,000 seamen from other countries. The armed forces lost nearly 880 during the 1940 campaign and another 1,123 servicemen in the exile forces. Altogether 366 Norwegians were executed during the war, among them three women. Thirty-nine were tortured to death. More than 40,000 were arrested, and 638 died in captivity in Norway. At the end of the war, there were some 9,000 Norwegians in German concentration camps, of whom 1,433 lost their lives there. The exact number of other casualties is impossible to calculate, but the victims represented a tangible and sorrowful reminder of the war toll for decades. The network of labour camps in Norway was populated with about 100,000 Soviet prisoners of war, as well as an additional 13,000 forced labourers from other countries. Their contribution to the German war economy is impossible to calculate exactly, as is the value of their toil to Norwegian society. But roads, railways, quays, air fields, mills, fortifications and garrisons were built in vast numbers. Around 30,000 foreign citizens lost their lives in Norway during the war, half of them from the Soviet Union; almost 3,000 Yugoslavs died there. A total of 120,000 Norwegians suffered domestic internment, while 92,000 Norwegian citizens were in exile by May 1945, half of them in Sweden.

What probably made the deepest impression was the senseless destruction of the remote and poor counties of Finnmark and Troms in the far north in 1944–45. When the Twentieth *Gebirgsarmée* under General Lothar Rendulic retreated from Finland via north Norway, it applied – in accordance with a *Führerbefehl* (order by Hitler) – a scorched earth strategy. The result was devastating and the strain put on the population was overwhelming. Virtually the whole of Finnmark and the north of Troms were levelled to the ground. The rebuilding of the counties after the war was an enormous task. It added tremendously to popular resentment that Rendulic was acquitted of war crimes at the Nuremberg tribunal. True, these numbers are not comparable with the distress in occupied areas of east and central Europe and the Balkans, but they were all the more harrowing in a country that had not experienced war since 1814 and had not suffered substantial war damage since the early eighteenth century. The material damage was also distressing. Small towns, villages, farms and infrastructure were destroyed. Industry was run down and hundreds of ships were sunk. The Norwegian Statistics Office has calculated that around 6 per cent of Norway's national wealth was lost. It goes without saying that these numbers had a profound impact on the population's attitude to Germany. I shall, therefore, present only briefly five aspects of the war experience that were formative for German-Norwegian relations for years, namely: the campaign of 1940, the government and armed forces in exile, the resistance movement, the Quisling government and the *Reichskommissariat Norwegen*.

The German attack on Denmark and Norway on 9 April came as a total surprise to the governments of Scandinavia and Britain. The Norwegian armed forces were mobilized only for neutrality duties with no standing orders to escalate a violation into armed conflict. Consequently, they were totally unprepared for hostilities. Nonetheless, they were able to put up some resistance. By yielding territory to gain time, they created room for manoeuvre which the government used to prepare for the Allied assistance that had been promised immediately after an attack. The armed forces were at least able to prevent the King and the government from being captured. As a knock-on effect of the resistance and Quisling's intervention, the King and the government were strengthened in their determination to continue the struggle. The Allied troops that came to assist made little difference in south Norway, which was surrendered at the end of April.

The King and the government fled to the north where the Allies had the upper hand, above all, in terms of air superiority. The fighting continued and by the end of May, the Germans were defeated in the five-nation battle of Narvik. However, with their resources exhausted from fighting both in the north and in western Europe, Britain and France were forced to withdraw from Norway. That was decided only a few days after the audacious re-conquest of Narvik through a joint operation conducted by British, French, Polish and Norwegian forces. In order to buttress their more vital war efforts on the continent, it had become imperative for the western powers to redistribute their troops. At one blow this made it impossible for Norway to continue the fight on her own. The overall effect of the campaign was mixed. In the short term, Norway was conquered and the western Allies were beaten. However, the battle of Narvik showed for the first time that the *Wehrmacht* was not invincible. In Norway, notwithstanding the losses and hardships, it was widely felt that the country had somehow rescued its national honour by putting up a fight and sustaining the 2-month campaign. But Germany won at a high price. Half the surface vessels of the *Kriegsmarine* (German navy) were lost, and a vast number of troops – soon to be needed more in other operational theatres – were tied to the defence of Norway. The long-term effect of the victory was, therefore, exhausting for German resources. For most Norwegians, their perceptions of Germany had altered profoundly.

The crushing effect of the German attack on the government's perception of the great powers was succinctly expressed by Prime Minister Johan Nygaardsvold on the eve of the Narvik campaign in early June. He spoke in exasperation at a meeting with Allied representatives, and when he put pen to paper in his diary, he had obviously realized that the security policy of his government had been illusory: 'I was boiling with fury but tried to control myself to the best of my abilities. I said that we had trusted that the British in their own interest would do everything in their power to dislodge the Germans from Norway. However, so far we had been bitterly disappointed'.[37] During and after the war, this insight was the basis for a policy revision, which basically was all about formalizing the ties to Britain in order to promote national security. This was the dominant political legacy of the war, apart from a lasting resentment of everything the Nazi regime stood for.

The royal family, the government and sections of the armed forces and the civil service were temporarily turned into itinerants when it was decided that they should go into exile and continue the struggle. Deeply shocked and confused, they were driven out of their own country. But they did not by any means arrive empty-handed in London on 10 June. Seen with hindsight, two assets gave a faint hope for the future. First, the exile government was legal in accordance with the constitution and the emergency provision passed by parliament which bestowed on it the right to govern without the National Assembly for the duration of the war. It was recognized by the western powers. Secondly, the vast merchant fleet was rescued from German capture and could immediately be put at the service of the Allies. Moreover, it provided vast revenues for the government-in-exile which could cover the costs of both the administration and the build-up of the armed forces. These assets were the precondition for Norway becoming part of the Grand Alliance and being able to contribute to the war effort up to 1945. The government and the armed forces established themselves in Britain and Canada during the summer of 1940, and eventually in the United States. The future looked desperately uncertain. Against all odds the government did not waver but defiantly reiterated its decision to continue the fight. The merchant fleet was already serving the Allied cause and played an important role throughout the war, particularly up to 1942. The navy-in-exile also saw immediate action. For the first time in Norwegian history, the navy was given priority over the other services and became the senior service with an impressive war record. The air force and the army-in-exile took longer to establish themselves. Both the navy and the air force were operationally integrated into the Royal Navy and the Royal Air Force, respectively, while the army – the so-called Scotland Brigade – was held in reserve in order to secure an orderly transition of power after the defeat of Germany. Norwegian servicemen were also engaged in special operations under British command. All in all, the cooperation within the alliance against the common enemy, Germany, removed a reluctance in the government and the armed forces towards becoming involved with the great powers and thus prepared the ground for a fundamental revision of Norwegian security policy.

The organization of the resistance movement in Norway was slow in taking off. For obvious reasons this was not something anyone had thought about before 1940. In addition, both the political and military situation was in limbo for both the government-in-exile and the administration at home throughout the autumn of 1940. The term Home Front eventually became the common term for both the military and civil resistance, the so-called '*Milorg*' and '*Sivorg*'. The movement comprised both the active partisans and the array of those who marked their disapproval of German rule through symbolic actions and civil disobedience. The overall objective of the resistance movement was to preserve the guiding principles of Norwegian democracy and to contribute to western war efforts. The Home Front was loyal to the government-in-exile and developed close relations with it. *Milorg* was endorsed by the Defence Council in exile in 1941 and placed under the Army High Command in London. The Home Front was formally organized in 1943 with its own supreme leadership. This, of course, gave the Home Front profound credibility.[38]

The starting point for the Home Front was the campaign to promote a patriotic stance against the German intruders, and this was a more central task at the outset than armed resistance. The aim was to mobilize against collaboration and the Nazification of society. This was accomplished by the distribution of information and by issuing guidelines to the public. Another important task was to provide support for those who were persecuted by the regime and to assist their escape to Britain or Sweden. The preparations for the transition of power after the German defeat became an important undertaking later in the war. The government and the central leadership decided early on in the war to keep a low level of armed resistance, mainly restricted to sabotage actions to disrupt German efforts to mobilize Norwegian personnel and resources for war purposes. They feared that German retaliation would represent too high a price for civil society compared with the benefits of armed activism. Intelligence and information gathering became increasingly important tasks throughout the war, as did the protection of values from destruction. Notwithstanding widespread collaboration and profiteering during the German occupation, on an overall level, the Home Front was successful in creating popular cohesion, in uniting the nation and in providing an unwelcoming and hesitant atmosphere for the German masters. There was little doubt that the government-in-exile and the Home Front were at one. Moreover, the comparatively swift transition to normality after the war provides compelling evidence for the success of the Home Front.

The contribution to the Allied war effort in exile, the merits of the partisans and saboteurs, the covert support to the inmates of the labour camps and the endurance of the prisoners in German concentration camps are still widely regarded as heroic deeds. Other sides of the domestic war experience belong to a more dreary grey zone between collaboration and civil disobedience that rarely resulted in activism. But there are also parts of Norway's war record that represent an eternal embarrassment. First of all, the deportation of the Jews in the autumn of 1942. The majority of them were herded on to the freighter *Donau* on 26 November and sent to Germany. The Norwegian police carried out the operation. Of a total Jewish population of 760, only 25 survived. Another such embarrassment is the relatively large number of Norwegians who volunteered for the *Waffen-SS* to fight on the eastern front. A recent estimate shows that around 12,000 volunteered, 5,500 saw active duty and more than 800 lost their lives.[39] A more exotic off-shoot of the Nazi preoccupation with Scandinavia is the activities of the SS association *Ahnenerbe (Ancestral Inheritance)* in Norway from the 1930s. The pan-German belief that the Germanic race had originated in Scandinavia reappeared in Nazi lore and the *Ahnenerbe* conducted ideological research on the history of the Aryan race. It is, therefore, not surprising that Norway could boast the first institutions – nine in total – under the *Lebensborn* (fount of life) programme, more than in any other country outside Germany.[40] In the *Wehrmacht*'s instructions about how to behave towards the Norwegians during the attack, German personnel were informed, among other things, that 'Der Norweger hat ein ausgesprochenes Nationalbewusstsein . . . Der Norweger ist äusserst freiheitsliebend und selbstbewusst . . . . Er lehnt jeden Zwang und jede Unterordnung ab . . . Der Norweger hat kein Verständnis für den Krieg'. ('The Norwegian has a marked national consciousness . . . The Norwegian is deeply freedom-loving and self-confident . . . . He rejects force and domination . . . The Norwegian has no sympathy for war.')[41] Indeed, these were prophetic words and anticipated indirectly what might happen. Nothing went totally according to plan in the initial phase of the attack.

The first German priority was to exert indirect rule through a formal Norwegian government – along the lines of what they had achieved in Denmark. However, the events following the initial military failure in Oslo made this impossible. Quisling's first attempt to seize power on 9 April was not coordinated with the Germans. They realized shortly after that he provoked fierce antagonism and did not provide them with any of the benefits of indirect rule. The government and the King fiercely rejected any cooperation with the occupiers or the *coup*'s leader. Quisling was, therefore, forced to resign on 15 April. The Supreme Court appointed an interim administrative council made up of Norwegian officials as a caretaker government. After a forced exile in Germany during the summer, Quisling gained the support of influential Nazi leaders such as Alfred Rosenberg and Admiral Erich Raeder. Joseph Terboven was appointed *Reichskommissar* on 24 April and in September a *Reichskommissariat* was established. The majority of members were from Quisling's party, while Quisling himself was not included until 1942 when he became *Ministerpräsident* (Prime Minister).[42]

Figure 3 *Ministerpräsident* Vidkun Quisling (right) inspecting the First Police Company of the Norwegian *Waffen-SS* embarking on its first tour to the Leningrad front in September 1942. [Copyright: Norwegian Resistance Museum]

The *Reichskommissariat* was meant to support German efforts to control and centralize the vast European empire.[43] The Nazis' ambition was to create a *Volksgemeinschaft* (ethnic national community) in the occupied areas with Germany as the leading nation. The Norwegian population was totally unprepared for such a grandiose ideological undertaking which had never been a part of any political debate. The whole idea, therefore, provoked opposition. At the outset, it was undecided whether the occupied countries in western Europe should be politically incorporated into the Reich. The salient issue was to integrate their economies into the German *Grossraumwirtschaft* (great economic bloc) in order to strengthen the war effort.[44] Norwegian economic life, thus, became trapped in the German war economy, and, moreover, created opportunities for an array of collaborators. This situation offered few possibilities for ordinary workers to protest other than by resisting the efforts to Nazify and Germanize society. But the enforced integration into a European economic community resulted in some deep-rooted resentment against such grandiose enterprises. Notwithstanding the initial confusion, the collaborators and the profiteers, the attempted Germanization and Nazification of Norway was a total failure, as was the case in many other occupied countries. It goes without saying that increasingly brutal Nazi rule made both Germany and its Norwegian cohorts into defined enemies in the minds of the vast majority of the population, in a totally new way that would take decades to mitigate.

Conclusion

Hitler's Norwegian legacy can be summed up in a few points. The intimate ties between Germany and Norway accounted for in this chapter were either broken or severely weakened in most areas during the years 1933–45. Germany and the Germans were for the first time regarded as the enemies of the Norwegians and indeed of humanity. Political normalization gained momentum in the 1950s, but there was still deep popular resentment, albeit diminishing, for decades. The vastly different war experiences of Denmark, Finland, Sweden and Norway became a stumbling block for Nordic security cooperation after the war. The Norwegian government and armed forces in exile had learnt to cooperate with the great powers. In spite of recurring conflicts of interest, cooperation had been surprisingly smooth, and that paved the way for Norway's integration into western security arrangements. National security and strategy became the dominant elements in Norwegian foreign policy shortly after the war. Moreover, the German occupation brought about a new kind of national unity, and the deep political strife that characterized the interwar period was overcome. The official rapprochement between Norway and Germany began in the 1950s, but was only grudgingly accepted by the public.

Notes

1 For a broad survey, see Simensen, Jarle (ed.) (1999), unter Mitwirkung von Ole Kristian Grimnes, Rolf Hobson und Einhardt Lorenz, *Deutschland-Norwegen: die lange Geschichte*. Oslo: Tano Aschehoug.
2 See, for example, Nedkvitne, Arnved (1999) 'Die Hanse und Norwegen – neue Perspektiven', in Simensen (1999).
3 Fure, Odd-Bjørn (1996), *Mellomkrigstid. 1920–1940*. Vol. 3 of the History of Norwegian Foreign Affairs. Oslo: Norwegian University Press, p. 274.
4 See Berg, Bjørn Ivar (1999), 'Die frühen norwegische Bergwerke'; Nerheim, Gunnar, 'Deutschlands Rolle bei der Industrialisierung Norwegens bis zum Zweiten Weltkrieg', both in Simensen (1999).
5 See Kuhnle, Stein (1999), 'Deutschland und der Durchbruch der Sozialversicherung in Norwegen', in Simensen (1999).
6 See Inge Lønning (1999), 'Das Erbe Martin Luthers. Kirchliche und religiöse Verbindungslinien zwischen Norwegen und Deutschland von der Reformation bis heute', in Simensen (1999).

7   See Collett, John Peter (1999), 'Der deutsche Einfluss auf die norwegische Wissenschaft und Universitätsausbildung', in Simensen (1999).
8   Fure, Odd-Bjørn (1996), *Mellomkrigstid. 1920–1940*. Vol. 3 of the History of Norwegian Foreign Affairs. Oslo: Norwegian University Press, p. 274.
9   See, for example, Marschall, Birgit (1991), *Reisen und Regieren. Die Nordlandsfahrten Kaiser Wilhelms II*, Skandinavistische Arbeiten 9. Heidelberg: C. Winter, and Roll-Hansen, Hege (1993), *'Der Zug nach dem Norden': Wilhelmiske Norgesforestillinger og tysk nasjonal ideologi*. University of Oslo: Thesis in history.
10 Reidar Omang (1957), *Norge og Stormaktene 1906–1914. Aktstykker i det Kgl. Utenriksdepartements arkiv*. Vol. 1. Oslo: Gyldendal, document 134, letter from Fridtjof Nansen to Jørgen Løvland, 13 March 1907.
11 Berg, Roald (1995), *Norge på egen hånd. 1905–1920*. Vol. 2 of the History of Norwegian Foreign Affairs. Oslo: Norwegian University Press.
12 Schwartz, Michael (2000), *Sozialistische Eugenik. Eugenische Sozialtechnologien in Debatten und Politik der deutschen Sozialdemokratie 1890–1933*. Bonn: Dietz Verlag.
13 Salmon, Patrick (1997), *Scandinavia and the Great Powers 1890–1940*. Cambridge: Cambridge University Press.
14 Riste, Olav (2001), *Norway's Foreign Relations: a history*. Oslo: Norwegian University Press.
15 Riste, Olav (1965), *The Neutral Ally. Norway's Relations with Belligerent Powers*. Oslo: Norwegian University Press.
16 Salmon (1997), p. 349.
17 Norwegian National Archives, Halvdan Koht: political papers 1936–40. Box 3: Mowinckel's 'P.M. ang. Norges forsvarspolitiske stilling', 20 February 1930, p. 15.
18 Norwegian National Archives, The Amiral. Staff. Box 234, 'P.M. De stater som har særlig interesse for oss i krigspolitisk henseende', 16 September 1929.
19 Fure (1996), p. 274.
20 Annual Report 1927 from the British Legation in Oslo, cited in Fure (1996), p. 276.
21 For a broad account, Dahl, Hans Fredrik (1991 and 1992), *Vidkun Quisling. En fører blir til*, Vol. 1, and *En fører for fall*, Vol. 2. Oslo: Aschehoug.
22 For the British parallel, see Overy, Richard (2010), *The Morbid Age. Britain and the Crisis of Civilization, 1919–1939*. London: Penguin, p. 369.
23 Fure (1996), p. 242.
24 The National Archives, Kew, FO 371, 22283, N2195, Minister Cecil Dormer to Foreign Office, 26 April 1939. See also Thue, Elisabeth (1994), 'Nobels fredspris – og diplomatisk forviklinger: tysk-norske forbindelser i kjølvannet av Ossietzky-saken'. *Defence Studies*, no. 5.

25 See Lorentz, Einhard, 'Deutsche Flüchtlinge in Norwegen und ihre Bedeutung in Deutschland nach 1945', in Simensen (1999).
26 Ruge, Otto (1933), 'Noen betraktninger omkring vår nye hærordning' [Some reflections on the new army organization], *Vår Hær* no. 20, Oslo, p. 154 [author's translation].
27 Ruge (1933).
28 Agøy, Nils Ivar (1997), *Militæretaten og 'den indre fiende' fra 1905 til 1940. Hemmelige sikkerhetsstyrker i Norge sett i et skandinavisk perspektiv*. Oslo: Scandinavian University Press; Borgersrud, Lars (2000), *Konspirasjon og kapitulasjon. Nytt lys på forsvarshistorien fra 1814 til 1940*. Oslo: Oktober.
29 Agøy (1997), p. 311
30 Ottmer, Hans-Martin (1994), *Weserübung. Der deutsche Angriff auf Dänemark und Norwegen im April 1940*. In the series 'Operationen des Zweiten Weltkrieges. Herausgegeben vom Militärgeschichtliches Forschungsamt. Band 1'. München: Oldenbourg.
31 Ørvik, Nils (1960), *Sikkerhetspolitikken 1920–1939. Fra forhistorien til 9. april 1940. Bind I. Solidaritet eller nøytralitet?* Oslo: Tanum. Part 3. For the question of the neutrality policy of the small North European states, see van Roon, Ger (1989), *Small states in Years of Depression: the Oslo Alliance 1930–1940*. Assen/Maastricht: Van Gorchum.
32 Kristiansen, Tom (2008), *Tysk trussel mot Norge? Forsvarsledelse, trusselvurderinger og militære tiltak før 1940*. Bergen: Fagbokforlaget, p. 63.
33 Fure (1996), p. 282.
34 Wegener, Wolfgang (1941), *Die Seestrategie des Weltkrieges. Zweite durchgesehene und erweiterte Auflage*. Berlin: Mittler.
35 The National Archives, Kew, FO 371, 22281, N282, Minister Cecil Dormer to Foreign Office, Oslo, 1 January 1939, 'Report on the leading Personalities in Norway'.
36 The National Archives, Kew, FO 371, 23656, N3481, Minister Cecil Dormer to Foreign Office, 14 July 1939.
37 Nygaardsvold, Johan (1982), *Norge i krig 9. april–7. juni 1940*. Oslo: Tiden Norsk Forlag, p. 166 [author's translation].
38 For the organization of the Home Front, see Grimnes, Ole Kristian (1977), *Hjemmefrontens ledelse*. Oslo: Universitetsforlaget.
39 Veum, Eirik and Brenden, Geir (2009), *De som falt: nordmenn som døde i tysk krigstjeneste*. Oslo: NRK Aktivum.
40 See, for example, Fure, Jorunn Sem and Emberland Terje (eds) (2009), *Jakten på Germania: fra nordensvermeri til SS-arkeologi*. Oslo: Humanist.
41 The Armed Forces Museum, Oslo, 'Richtlinien für das Verhalten in persönlichen Verkehr mit der norwegischen Bevölkerung'.

42 Skodvin, Magne (1956), *Striden om okkupasjonsstyret i Norge: fram til 25. september 1940*. Oslo: Det norske samlaget.
43 Bohn, Robert (2000), *Reichskommissariat Norwegen. Nationalsozialistische Neuordnung und Kriegswirtschaft*. Munich: R. Oldenbourg Verlag.
44 Mazower, Mark (2008), *Hitler's Empire. Nazi Rule in Occupied Europe*, London: Penguin, pp. 103f, 122.

6

The Case of Sweden

Kent Zetterberg

Sweden, positioned on the Baltic Sea, is a close neighbour of Russia and Germany. This strategic position has shaped Sweden's security policies and destiny for centuries, not least during the two world wars. In the twentieth century, the western powers of Britain, France and the United States, by contrast, have often seemed to be remote from Sweden. During World War I, Sweden like Denmark and Norway, remained neutral but had great difficulties with sea trade and in feeding its population. During the years 1917–21, a democratic constitution with a parliamentary system and universal suffrage was established in Sweden, somewhat later than in Denmark and Norway. The Nordic countries, where Finland became an independent nation in 1917–18, remained stable democracies during the interwar period, when most countries in central, southern and eastern Europe returned to authoritarian regimes. The shadow of fascism, Nazism and communism eclipsed the future for democracy in Europe in the 1930s. Peace in Europe was preserved temporarily by the Munich Agreement in September 1938, but one year later, Great Britain and France declared war on Germany after Hitler's attack on Poland. A new great war had started.

The possibility that Sweden could be attacked or forced into war had been discussed secretly by the Swedish Social Democrats' parliamentary group in 1938 during the Munich Crisis. At this time, all members were united behind Per Albin Hansson, the Prime Minister and party leader from 1933 to 1946, whose view was that Sweden should remain neutral. However, if Sweden were to be forced into war, it was decided that this should be on the 'right' side in the war, meaning the side of the western democracies.[1] This was the starting point and the main Swedish aim for the rest of the war.

The preferred option, then, was to remain neutral but, if attacked, Sweden would have to join the western democracies in the war. However, this ambition and goal, inherited by the coalition government in December 1939, was not easy to pursue in the dark years that followed when Stalin attacked Finland and then Hitler invaded and occupied Denmark and Norway. Only Sweden succeeded in remaining neutral to protect her peace and independence, by using a grand strategy with five great assets. First, Sweden was stubbornly nonaligned and neutral in the war between the great powers; concessions to Germany in 1940–42 and to the Allies in 1943–45 did not change Sweden's status as a 'non-belligerent' state. Second, Sweden had the strongest defence forces among the Nordic countries and a favourable strategic position. Third, Sweden was strategically encircled by Hitler from summer 1940 to summer 1944 but could use trade and other means to counterbalance the power of both Germany and the Allies. Sweden, thus, continued to trade where possible. Trade with Germany, renewed by annual agreements, became necessary for Sweden to survive between 1940 and 1943 by receiving fuel, accomplishing a military build-up and maintaining its agrarian output. London understood Sweden's vulnerable position after Hitler's victories in 1940, and the British government had made agreements with Sweden in December 1939 about the volume of iron ore to be exported to Britain and Germany. Sweden adhered to those agreements between 1939 and 1944 even when Germany wanted it to increase iron ore exports. Finally, political pressure from the Allies made Sweden cease trading with Germany, including the controversial iron ore exports, in August 1944. By then, Sweden could withstand an economic blockade and hold out for one year. Fourth, Sweden, 'a great power in diplomacy', according to Finland's leader Mannerheim, had very able diplomats and trade negotiators who succeeded to a certain extent in neutralizing pressure and influence on Sweden by all the great powers.

By playing London, Washington, Berlin and Moscow off against one another, Sweden could secure advantages and ease the pressure on Stockholm. That was *Realpolitik* in diplomacy and trade. Fifth, the result was that all the great powers respected Sweden's armed neutrality in northern Europe throughout the war. As in World War I, Sweden maintained her status as a non-belligerent by her own strength, *Realpolitik*, flexible security policies, defence and trade relations tracking the course of the war in northern Europe. Because Germany first dominated the Baltic Sea region in both world wars, that meant that Sweden's security policies, within the neutral framework, favoured Germany during the first years of the war, but subsequently favoured the Allies, especially the western powers. This was an expression of 'small-state realism' from the Swedish side in both world wars. Thus, Sweden's armed neutrality functioned rather well during the two world wars. However, Sweden's strategic position, close to Germany and Russia, was not enviable.² Geopolitically, Sweden was in a very unfavourable strategic situation from summer 1940 to summer 1944, first encircled by Germany and the Soviet Union, then by Germany from summer 1941 to summer 1944. But Sweden had strong strategic assets in the government's hands and could play them with great skill. In political, economic and military terms, Sweden was the strongest of the Nordic countries. This position could be used in a grand strategy to keep Sweden out of the war and maintain its independence, hoping for victory on the part of the western democracies in the long run.

In the secret parts of the Hitler-Stalin Pact of August 1939, prior to the war, only Sweden was respected as a neutral state between the two totalitarian regimes. Sweden was not easy to attack and occupy, and had never been so in the past. As Clausewitz considered in his famous book *On War (Vom Kriege)*, only Russia and Sweden held this special strategic position in Europe, with vast 'defence territory' and the Baltic Sea as a bulwark. Added to this, Sweden's sea power had been strong in the twentieth century, which was not easy for an invader to overcome. Sweden's strategic importance and strength grew from 1938, and as long as Sweden was strongly determined to rearm, defend her borders and stay neutral, it was definitely not going to be easy for any great power to attack it. The strategic conclusion to be drawn from these considerations – drawn also by Hitler and Stalin, the ruthless dictators – was that, for the time being, it was best to leave Sweden alone with its armed neutrality.

Sweden's policies: Deterrence and confidence-building through defence and diplomacy

In this chapter, I shall to try to show that all the great powers, from different positions, respected Sweden's armed neutrality during World War II. It was difficult for either Germany or the Soviet Union to attack Sweden with her favourable strategic position and strong national unity promoting neutrality and defence. The western powers hoped to attract Sweden to their side and into the war in the periods 1939–40 and 1943–45, but had very little to offer Sweden if fighting Germany on Swedish territory. Germany considered it too expensive to attack Sweden in April 1940, since that would cost (including occupation) around 20 to 30 army divisions, which Hitler could not afford. By 1942, it was estimated that it would take 30 to 40 German divisions to attack and occupy Sweden which Germany certainly could not afford at that time.

In retrospect, Sweden, mostly by her own strength, managed to stay neutral and out of the war. This interpretation is not well known internationally. A strong national unity and coalition government strengthened Sweden's firm position around peace and neutrality. However, the government in Stockholm was suspicious of Hitler's intentions and thought it best to continue the strictly regulated war trade and transit traffic with Germany until 1943–44 in order to get necessary imports for rearmament, industry and agriculture. When planning during 1940–41 for Operation Barbarossa, Germany hoped to win Sweden and Finland to its side in the war against the Soviet Union, not least since Russia was the traditional 'arch enemy' of both countries, with Finland having been part of the Kingdom of Sweden until 1809. However, Sweden refused to jump on this bandwagon and kept her neutral position in the war. The Soviet Union was eager not to have Sweden as an opponent during the Winter War of 1939–40 and was relieved that Sweden opted for continued neutrality in summer 1941. Sweden now acted as the 'protecting power' for the interests of the Soviet Union in the Axis territories. This was a diplomatic signal to Berlin and to the world.

In 1939–40, many Swedes saw the new war as yet another conflict between the rival great powers in Europe; in addition, they detested the 'red-brown' regimes of the Soviet Union and Nazi Germany. In 1941–42, they understood that this had become a real world war; in 1942–43, they recognized the change of the tide in the war and, by 1943–45, the unfolding defeat of the Axis powers. The evil of Nazi tyranny and occupation became more evident year on year for the Swedes, but they also feared Soviet communism and tyranny as practised and demonstrated in eastern Europe.[3] The Holocaust was not a focus for Swedish policies until the last war year, 1944–45. This can be said for most countries during the war years, since it was difficult to believe rumours and obtain verified reports about Nazi atrocities and the Holocaust. Events and conditions in Stalin's 'communist paradise' in the Soviet Union were also appalling, but equally difficult to verify.

Sweden's peace and survival were the main goals. Neutrality and the outcome of the war and how to handle daily events were the focus, not least how to provide for the population and the military build-up. Swedish diplomats and the government, however, were transformed from indifference to activism in 1943–45, trying to help Jews, refugees and concentration camp prisoners. Sweden saved many Jews and other prisoners from Nazi and Soviet tyranny, including

Raoul Wallenberg's mission in 1944 to Hungary, and was second to none in its endeavours. More than 150,000 refugees were received and saved by Sweden, including many children from Finland during its three wars between 1939 and 1944. The refugees were mostly from the Nordic countries, but some were from the Baltic states, fleeing from the Red Army in 1944–45. In the last year of the war, 1944–45, Sweden was planning to receive large numbers of refugees from Finland and, even in April 1945, to intern in Sweden all the defeated German troops from Norway. However, this was not required because the Germans capitulated in Norway and the Finns remained in their country.

The Molotov-Ribbentrop pact

The pact between Hitler and Stalin in August 1939 exposed the small north European countries to potential intervention by Germany and the Soviet Union. In the secret part of the pact, only Sweden was considered and respected as a middle range state and a neutral zone between Berlin and Moscow. That saved Sweden and her neutrality during the pact years, 1939–41. The Baltic States and Poland were now attacked by Stalin and Hitler; Poland was quickly defeated in a *Blitzkrieg* and the Soviet Union participated in its occupation and partition while next came the basing of Soviet forces in the Baltic States; later, they would fall under Soviet occupation. There followed the attack on Finland by the Red Army and the heroic Winter War from November 1939 to March 1940, when, after hard fighting, Finland managed to survive as an independent nation, with loss of territory in Karelia, including Vyborg. Finally, Germany attacked and occupied Denmark and Norway beginning on 9 April 1940.

The dangerous Winter War

During the Winter War, Franco-British support was offered to Finland on condition that their troops were given free passage through neutral Norway and Sweden. Oslo and Stockholm refused passage since it would be likely to lead to a war with Germany. Churchill and the British government wanted to help Finland, but also aimed at stopping Swedish iron ore exports to Germany. If the British and French allies had succeeded in their war plans in the far north in the period January 1940 to June 1940, it would have meant Sweden and Norway being forced into the war. Sweden could even have ended up on the German side while defending her borders against an Allied expedition in the North.

However, the Allied plans were unrealistic and failed. Thomas Munch-Petersen, in his book *The Strategy of Phoney War: Britain, Sweden and the Iron Ore Question 1939–1940*, is very clear in his interpretation: 'It proved difficult to translate the enthusiasm for intervention in northern Europe which gripped Whitehall in December 1939 into action because British plans depended on Swedish and Norwegian cooperation and the latter was not forthcoming.'[4]

The importance of Sweden's iron ore

The importance of Sweden's iron ore exports to Germany has been discussed for decades. The War Cabinet in London overestimated its importance in December 1939 for tactical reasons, but this judgement still lingers on in research and literature. Added to that, both Hitler and Churchill were obsessed by what they thought was the great strategic importance of Swedish iron ore for the war. The myth still survives. Iron ore exports from Sweden were at about the same volume as during World War I, but no one had then regarded them as crucial in 'deciding the outcome of the war'. In short, one can say that iron ore exports from 1939 followed fixed volumes set out in Swedish trade agreements with London and Berlin. These imports were most important for Germany before the fall of France in June 1940, but comprised only around 10 to 20 per cent of German requirements in the years 1940–44. Compared with World War I, the figures were around the same, but then Sweden's exports to the west had been accompanied by heavy shipping losses in the North Sea.[5] However, the Allied capability for cutting off Swedish iron ore exports to Germany was weak in both world wars. Exports continued for five long war years, but in August 1944, the time had come to end the trade.[6]

Sweden's extensive aid for Finland in the Winter War

Sweden gave huge humanitarian aid and military assistance to Finland in the Winter War, from December 1939 to March 1940, but, similar to all other nations, did not intervene with regular troops. However, a Swedish volunteer corps of 10,000 soldiers was sent and took over the defence of Finnish Lapponia at the end of the war. Sweden sent to Finland most of its heavy artillery, all of its anti-tank weapons and many anti-aircraft guns. Sweden also sent 135,000 rifles, 302,000 grenades, 216 artillery guns and one third of its deployable air force. As a result, on 9 April 1940, Sweden lacked a lot of its modern war matériel, it having been consumed in Finland during the Winter War.[7]

9 April 1940

The German attack on Denmark and Norway on 9 April 1940 dramatically changed the balance of power in northern Europe. Denmark was occupied in one day by the Germans while fighting in Norway continued for over two months. The outcome was that Germany occupied both states. Sweden and Finland became strategically surrounded by the 'pact brothers' of Germany and the Soviet Union. Together with the Allied defeat in France in June 1940, it meant that Sweden had little expectation of any help from the west in the eventuality of a war with either Germany or the Soviet Union. The situation started to ease only one year later with the German invasion of the Soviet Union and the American entry into the war in December 1941. Until the war started to move against the Axis in 1942–43, Sweden had to manage her relations with Germany alone, awaiting the outcome of the world war that would decide the fate of the Nordic countries for a long time ahead.[8] Sweden mobilized almost all her armed forces in April and May 1940, the only time that this happened during the twentieth century. Three army corps were organized and deployed to defend the country, with the main effort in the south, north and along the border with Norway. The navy and air force were fully mobilized and engaged around the coast and borders, with the navy also engaged in protecting the extended sea lanes. A long and exhausting period of high military preparedness began for many units. Sweden's defence costs rose rapidly and reached half of the state budget. The nation, government and parliament were now totally united behind this effort to rearm and protect peace and neutrality.

Strict neutrality and continued war trade

Two main German requirements were intimated to the Foreign Ministry in Stockholm on 9 April 1940: first, Sweden was to observe strict neutrality and desist from mobilization directed against Germany; second, Swedish iron ore supplies were to continue and 'British acts of sabotage' were to be prevented. A cessation of iron ore exports would result in war with Germany. Sweden now started a form of military mobilization termed 'a planned strengthening of Sweden's armed neutrality'. This was the appropriate political message for all capitals of Europe, including Moscow. The Soviet Union swiftly reminded Berlin that Sweden's neutrality should be respected in line with the pact of August 1939. After the war, Soviet propaganda asserted that 'Stalin saved Sweden' when Hitler attacked Scandinavia on 9 April 1940, but this of course does not reflect the realities of the situation.⁹ After the German invasion of Norway and Denmark, Sweden was cut off from its normal trade with western Europe and overseas by the German Skagerrak blockade, although this was not total in its effect. Isolation was eased somewhat by the so-called 'Safe-Conduct Traffic' (also known as 'Gothenburg traffic') which ran to America with some interruptions between 1940 and 1944. Of around 100 ships from America with oil, food and other goods, nine were sunk. The 'Gothenburg traffic' was an agreement requiring the consent of both London and Berlin in order to provide Sweden with oil and some other essential imported products.¹⁰ Even this arrangement demonstrated a respect for Sweden's neutrality and position as a middle-ranking power in the eyes of both Berlin and London. The same goes for the Soviet Union, which in several ways expressed the same judgement. Evidently, Stalin respected only force in international relations: Finland's strong defence in the Winter War and Sweden's political, economic and military strength and support for Finland in the war made an impression on the dictator. A war trade agreement was reached in 1940, and Moscow now emphasized its hope of continued good diplomatic relations with Sweden. Stalin and Molotov even told the Swedish delegates and diplomats in Moscow in 1940, 'This was your war' (i.e. Finland's Winter War), meaning that Sweden had supported Finland by all means short of military intervention in that war.¹¹

A rather strong defence

Sweden had the strongest defence forces of the Nordic countries when war broke out, as well as a favourable strategic position. The navy and coastal defence (*Marinen*) was the strongest in the Baltic after Germany and the Soviet Union and was considered a strategic asset by the great powers in both world wars.¹² In this time of crisis, Sweden had the luck to find its strongest Defence Minister ever in modern history, the Social Democrat Per Edvin Sköld, a very talented and gifted politician but possessed of a very hot temper. In peacetime he was unpopular in every camp, often insulting political friends and foes alike. Now he was the right man to lead Swedish rearmament in brilliant co-operation with the Swedish military leadership, war industry, government and parliament. The admirals and generals were said to 'tremble' when meeting Sköld, with his superb knowledge, strength of will, and his colleagues from the Defence Ministry, 'hand-picked' and often with the best minds in the country, as well as civil servants, industrialists and technical experts. As a result, military planning and organization were redrafted, several military chiefs had to leave and industrial experts made production more effective. The result was amazing – in the last war year, 1944–45, Swedish rearmament peaked and most military units now were trained and modernized with better fire power, protection and mobility. The navy was modernized with much better firepower, a three-fold increase in tonnage and very few losses. It was a strategic asset of great importance for Sweden. In May 1940, parliament accepted a bill for the construction of small ships that could quickly add strength to the navy: four destroyers, nine submarines, six motor torpedo boats and thirty-six minesweepers. In December 1940, parliament allocated funds for another four destroyers, three submarines and two battle cruisers. The Swedish air force was rather weak in 1939–40 but nevertheless was stronger than the air forces of the other Nordic countries. It modernized and began to catch up in the years 1941–45. From 1940, the Swedish state and *SAAB* cooperated intensively, and in the long run they shaped the strongest air force in the world after the great powers during the Cold War, between 1947 and 1990. The foundation for this was laid in the period 1940–45. However, it took many years to catch up, following the Defence Plan of 1936. It was only late in 1943–1944 that the Germans considered the Swedish air force as a new threat in the north, especially in cooperation with the western powers. Early on, Berlin considered Sweden's airfield system and training to be excellent (following the German model) and both Berlin and Washington independently thought that the new fighter and bomber planes from *SAAB* (J21, J22, B17 and B18) were catching up with international standards but were not yet being produced in substantial numbers. Added to this, production of the famous Swedish Bofors air-defence system rose tenfold in various years after war broke out in 1939. The Swedish arms industry was a great asset in protecting the neutrality and freedom of Sweden in the years 1939–45. It produced arms in great numbers for the Swedish defence forces.

The Swedish army was increased from four to sixteen divisions between 1940 and 1944 and was supplemented with modern brigades and battalions. It was well suited for defence in the broken terrain of forests and highlands just like the Finnish army, but it was weak in armoured forces and heavy artillery and could not hold ground in open country against joint operations by modern forces. This was a weakness, but the German view of the Swedish army remained rather positive, regarding it as a potentially difficult opponent, especially in winter warfare, should Germany have to attack Sweden in a preventive action.[13]

Sweden's armed neutrality policies, backed up by strong national unity and the 1939 coalition government, was now a strong defensive bulwark. Only an attack on Sweden from an aggressor would pressure Sweden into the war. As long as the enemy did not pressure Sweden into their camp, it was considered the best strategy for all the great powers to respect Sweden's neutrality and try to make the best of it. In the 'dark years' of 1940–42, Germany pressurized Sweden and gained concessions in terms of trade and transit traffic. Overall, Hitler and the Nazi leadership were disappointed with Sweden for not joining the German camp, as Finland had done. Characterized by Hitler as 'anti-Nazi and with democracy in their blood', and always with good diplomatic contacts in London, Washington and Moscow, in the eyes of the Nazi leaders Sweden did not understand Nazi Germany but rather sympathized with the western democracies.

Defending Sweden

Swedish troops arrived at the Norwegian border long before the Germans in April 1940, but had to stop there and became neutral observers of the war. Ski units (*skidlöparbataljonen* from I 19 in Boden) reached the Norwegian border on 9 April and thereafter formed the so-called *Abisko* group, consisting of four elite army battalions, deployed as a security group around the iron ore fields in Kiruna-Malmberget. The strong Swedish will to defend the country was nourished by the fate of the brother countries. Later in the war, defence readiness in the far north was increased when tensions rose or when rumours of an Allied invasion arose. If Sweden had joined the Allies in 1940, both Hitler and Stalin would have had more problems in the Nordic arena, but the probable outcome would have been hard to predict. The German Military Attaché in Stockholm, General Bruno von Uthmann, in his reports to Berlin during 1939–44, reiterated his advice not to underestimate the Swedish army and navy and the strong will of the whole Swedish nation to defend the country. As a diversion, Sweden often told the Germans that Swedish defence preparations were directed against Allied efforts to gain a foothold in Scandinavia.

Spring and early summer 1940

In their military planning, the Germans estimated that one division would be sufficient to occupy Denmark, 6 divisions were needed for Norway, but 20 to

30 divisions would be required to defeat and occupy Sweden. They regarded Sweden as a middle-range military power with a tradition of good relations with Germany. It was seen as a country that would be more valuable for Germany as a trading partner than as an occupied country. Within the framework of German planning for the offensive against the Low Countries and France, which began on 10 May 1940, a war with Sweden would be a bad, counterproductive outcome. Hitler, therefore, demanded strict neutrality, and continued trade by Sweden and achieved this result. Berlin had no expectation that Sweden would join in the war on the western front with Britain and France.

In spring 1940, two top Swedish diplomats, Erik Boheman and Gunnar Hägglöf, were in Paris and London negotiating with the western powers. Both had excellent contacts and were discussing wartime trade agreements when news broke of the German attack on Denmark and Norway. Boheman met Halifax, Churchill and Cadogan on 11 April and sent a cable to Stockholm about the views of the British government. Great Britain was determined to crush the German navy around Norway and to support the Norwegians by landing at several points in Norway. By taking Narvik they hoped to be able to cut off the iron ore transports from Sweden to Germany. That would, as during the Finnish Winter War, expose Sweden to a German counter-attack. London wanted open communications with Sweden, but warned that Sweden had to choose either to join the British in the war or to become a German puppet state.

London also warned that even if Sweden technically stayed neutral in the war, the Allied treatment of a Sweden almost totally dependent on Germany would be harsh. That was a clear summary of British intentions towards Sweden. However, London did not want to press Sweden further at this time and violate Swedish neutrality, but it was hinted that it would be useful if secret military negotiations could take place. In fact, an Anglo-French military delegation landed at Bromma airport in Stockholm on 9 April in order to contact the Swedish government about the Allies' planned mine-laying in Swedish and Norwegian waters. They waited in Stockholm for some days until the Swedish Foreign Office discreetly despatched them home with the message to keep in contact and follow the events of the war in Norway. However, because of Allied military failures in Norway, the British position in the relationship with Sweden was soon modified. On 16 April, London softened and intimated that Great Britain was 'very satisfied with the Swedish position', declaring that it was even better for the Allies that Sweden stayed outside the war. That was a remarkable shift in British policy towards Sweden in only a week.[14]

National unity in focus

Some days later, King Gustav V, with the consent of the Swedish government, sent a letter to Hitler confirming Sweden's commitment to defend its neutrality universally by all military means. Hitler promptly answered that this was a message of great importance. The Swedish government at this time worked to boost and support the Swedish will to resist involvement in the war. One expression of this was a famous radio speech on national unity by Prime Minister Per Albin Hansson on the evening of 12 April 1940. He expressed great sympathy for Norway and Denmark and the determination of Sweden to remain neutral in the war and to defend herself at any cost.

On 20 April 1940, the Foreign Ministry in Stockholm received a memorandum from the Swedish Minister in Berlin in which Reich Minister Hermann Göring gave Sweden some advice for the future: Sweden should declare her strong will to defend her borders. If she did so, Germany would have no intention of attacking Sweden. Göring also said that he appreciated and respected the Swedish armed forces, especially the army and the navy. The Swedish air force, however, he considered to be weak. In his view, it could be defeated within a few days. This could be interpreted as a warning. The main thing, he added, was that Sweden should defend herself against the English and fight them if necessary.[15] The Chief of Staff of the German navy, Schulte-Mönting, another old friend of Sweden, informed Sweden, on behalf of Grand Admiral Raeder, that the service had no plans directed against that country.[16] On 26 April, Lieutenant General Bodenschatz, head of Göring's office, stressed that Germany respected Sweden's political standpoint in principle against the transit of German troops and armaments as a 'position of honour' ('*Ehrenstandpunkt*') as long as fighting continued in Norway. Bodenschatz now warned that Sweden had little chance of remaining outside the war if the western powers advanced in northern Norway in order to halt the iron ore traffic. However, Germany would be reluctant to fight a war with Sweden for many reasons, not least the estimated 20 to 30 divisions required. Now, the main priority was German military preparation for the great offensive in the west. Bodenschatz concluded that Hitler now trusted Sweden to remain neutral and wanted to take advantage of Sweden as a major trading partner.

New German demands on Sweden June 1940 and new risks

A number of German demands on Sweden were rejected by the Swedish government as long as the fighting in Norway continued. Some 'humanitarian' transits had been granted during the Norwegian campaign in April–May 1940, but thereafter the Germans demanded new transits through Sweden that included non-combatant personnel and military equipment. Negotiations ended in an agreement signed in July 1940 while the Swedish government was under the impression that London would make peace with Hitler. Prime Minister Per Albin Hansson realized the desperate situation when the transit agreement with Germany was concluded. On 18 June 1940, he noted the following pessimistic lines in his diary: 'This broke our loved and strictly maintained neutrality in awareness of the absurdity of the current situation to take the risk of a war.'[17] During the crises, the Swedish Foreign Minister, Christian Günther, directed foreign policy in a way that minimized the risk of a conflict with Germany that both he and the rest of the government sought to avoid. He recognized that Germany's strategic goal was continued trade with Sweden and a greater political 'control' of the country behind the Skagerrak blockade against the West. This proved to be a realistic analysis.

Norway not a strong but a weak war theatre for Hitler

Hitler's attack on Norway in spring 1940 was militarily hazardous and could easily have gone wrong. The Germans lost one third of their navy and the iron ore traffic from Narvik to Germany was cut off and lay in abeyance for a long time. The Germans also had to fight for two months to defeat the Norwegians and the Allies. This was a setback, although they finally won a military victory. Germany now had new sea and air bases for an attack on the western powers, but it also had a heavy burden of occupation and fortification of the long Norwegian coastline. For Great Britain, Hitler's occupation of Norway proved to be a strategic asset. It gave the British time to consolidate defence of their homeland when France fell in June 1940. Now, Germany's sea power was weakened, and it was weakened even further by the sinking of the *Bismarck* in May 1941.

For the rest of the war, Hitler and the Germans worried over their military position in, and the protection of iron ore imports from, Sweden. Hitler invested great resources in military units and arms to fortify and defend Norway against an invasion by the Allies. Hitler saw Norway as 'a zone of destiny for the war' ('*eine Schicksalszone*'). This obsession could be used by the Allies in many ways. The British devised deception campaigns, for example, 'The Scottish Army under General Thorpe' threatening to invade Norway in 1942–44, and in these was supported by the United States.

Sweden as a growing strategic problem for Hitler

But the main problem for Hitler on this front was not the Allies but the growing strength of Sweden. Hitler did not trust Sweden and thought that Sweden and the Allies from 1941–42 onwards were a combined threat to the German position in Norway. Thus, if Sweden joined the Allied side at any time, Hitler would expect to have a major problem in holding Norway. According to new German research, Hitler was not able to build up swift, mobile military units and resources in Norway in order to be able to launch a preventive attack or counterattack on Sweden from Norway. Hitler feared a combined attack from the Allies and the Swedish armed forces and a total cessation of Swedish iron ore exports to Germany.[18] The German defence in Norway was locked down in defence positions along the coast and its leaders soon realized that they would have great difficulties in meeting an invasion from across the Swedish frontier. At German war games in Norway in 1943–1945, this was considered a crucial point about which one could not do much. Eighty per cent of Germany's forces was now heavily engaged on the eastern front and being pushed backwards. Accordingly, German forces in Norway could not have any new resources or any priority at this stage of the war. The heavy German warships had to hide in the fjords and were sunk, one after another. *Luftwaffe* units suffered many losses and were not replaced in full numbers. The Germans had dug themselves into heavily fortified positions in Norway where they had no flexibility, received only second-rate reserve troops and had no hope of substantial aid from the *Vaterland* if attacked. They simply had to fight with the resources available in Norway.[19] All in all, Hitler's invasion of Norway, in my interpretation, was a strategic mistake that mostly favoured the Allies and also Sweden in the long run. It gave Hitler another front to protect for the rest of the war, with great difficulty, and he had to split his resources in the far North into *AOK Norwegen* and *AOK Lappland*. At the end of the war, around half a million Germans, including those from the *Organisation Todt* and other organizations, were standing in Norway just watching the war drawing to its end. That was also an asset for the Allied cause.

Nazi Germany dominated Europe from the summer of 1940. After the harsh events of the war in Finland and Norway in 1939–40, Sweden's military build-up proceeded quickly and made Sweden in each succeeding year less vulnerable to a German attack. That made Hitler's calculations in the far north more difficult and left him with a constant strategic threat in the north from the Allies, Sweden and his iron ore supply. Sweden now came to serve as a 'neutral island' – similar to

Switzerland – in German-dominated Europe during the years 1940–43. German political and economic pressure on Sweden was strong during the years 1940–42, but was never overwhelming. Sweden still had a good position, using armed neutrality, trade and counterbalancing diplomacy. Sweden's neutrality was in the interests of the western powers who were very weak in the Baltic area, and it also proved to be of immense value to the neighbouring Nordic countries. There, Finland was at war with the Allies, Norway was an ally-in-exile and Denmark was occupied under protest by Germany, but with king and government remaining in Copenhagen. Swedish neutrality also had positive humanitarian effects during the war years. More than 150,000 refugees, including many Jews, were received by Sweden in 1939–45, while Germany rejected further Swedish efforts to save additional Jewish families and children.

Sweden's policy towards Nazi Germany in the dark years of 1940–42 was a combination of concessions, resistance and diplomatic manoeuvring that worked surprisingly well. After hard German pressure in the period from summer 1940 to summer 1942, the demands eased. By the winter of 1942–43, Sweden was transforming its policies to become increasingly pro-Allied. Throughout the war, the Swedish government was guided by one overriding interest: wanting to protect the Swedish people from the horrors of war by an adaptive neutrality policy. In order to survive, Sweden became heavily dependent on trade with Germany. Dr Klaus Wittmann, a future Secretary-General of NATO, wrote in his doctoral dissertation – about trade between Sweden and Germany between 1933 and 1945 – that trade was balanced and complex, with negotiations and war trade agreements each year from 1939 to 1944. The agreed export level set at the 1939 tonnage of iron ore exports was respected, but of course Swedish trade with the West almost disappeared after the German occupation of Denmark and Norway in 1940. In the crucial years between 1940 and 1943, 40 million tons of iron ore exports were agreed between Berlin and Stockholm, but only 35 million tons were delivered due to a shortage of ships and other factors.

However, Berlin gave priority to Swedish trade as being of great importance to the war effort. For Sweden, encircled by Germany, there was not much choice other than to continue to trade, since no other big trading partner was in sight and Sweden wanted to stay neutral and survive on its own terms.[20] Wittmann finds that Sweden was able to implement a successful war trade policy of neutrality ('*Handelsneutralität*') using the 'room for manoeuvre' ('*Handelsspielraum*') and a degree of autonomy while setting the power blocs and great powers against each other. Sweden succeeded in evading the German grip and never became a part of the German area of control.

The German transit traffic

The Swedish-German Transit Agreement of 1940–43 included the transit to and from Norway of unarmed troops, war matériel and arms but set within the clear limits of a negotiated agreement.[21] It was criticized by the Allies but was not of great military importance since most of the German traffic went by sea.[22] It was typical of the Swedish diplomatic and military position towards Germany in these negotiations that weapons-systems that could be used against Sweden were not allowed to transit, but fixed installations such as coastal artillery could be permissible.

For the Allies in 1941–1944, it was a war aim to deprive Germany of Swedish iron ore, but they did not succeed by military means. The exception was that Soviet submarines sank some Swedish, German and Finnish iron ore ships in the Baltic during 1941–44. Then Sweden, after heavy diplomatic pressure from Washington, and with the support of London and Moscow, in August 1944 stopped almost all trade with Germany, including iron ore exports. Swedish security policies now definitely favoured the Allied side, and it was a relief for the Swedish government and the Swedish people to be able to do so. However, Sweden did not break her diplomatic relations with Germany in 1944–45 in order to give help and assistance to her neighbours and give shelter to groups such as refugees, Jews and interned soldiers.

Nazi Germany did not present Sweden with a formal ultimatum during the war years, although the Swedish government sometimes feared this would come. According to a report by Herschel Johnson, the US Minister in Stockholm, Prime Minister Per Albin Hansson had said in May 1942 that for two years he had feared that Hitler would present Sweden with an ultimatum containing such harsh conditions that Swedish independence would be forfeited. But at the time of the report, Albin Hansson was more optimistic and the military and political strength of Sweden was increasing: 'He is no longer afraid of German demands or the Swedish ability to defend herself should demands be made on her which cannot be granted'. The Swedes were also well informed from Berlin. According to Erik Boheman, the deputy head of the Foreign Ministry, the Germans now estimated that 30 to 40 divisions were considered to be the minimum number required for a successful invasion and occupation of Sweden.[23] As Sweden became heavily dependent on Germany as a trading partner from summer 1940 until summer 1944, Germany's share increased to around 70 to 80 per cent of all Sweden's trade. This was a direct result of wartime events in northern Europe, and there was nothing much that Sweden's government could do about it. The alternative, to cut trade with Germany, was not discussed, not even by the critics of the government's policies until the last year of the war, 1944–45.

Swedish intelligence from all quarters contributed to keeping Sweden out of the war

Research contributions by Wilhelm Carlgren and C. G. Mackay about Swedish intelligence during World War II are important contributions that show its importance for Sweden's security policies. In an essay, 'To what extent did intelligence contribute to Sweden maintaining its non-belligerence throughout World War Two?', three master's students from the Department of War Studies, King's College, London, succeed in showing that 'Sweden, far from being a pawn in the strategic development of the war, was capable of safeguarding her non-belligerence. This was to a certain extent the result of accurate intelligence combined with shrewd foreign policy assessment'.[24] Signal intelligence which was the best source during the 'dark years of 1940–1942' gave the government and the military information about Germany's plans, moves and military positions around Sweden. The Swedish government used intelligence as a strategic instrument to allow closer cooperation with the Western Powers in the last years of the war, 1943–45. Both SOE and OSS operated in Sweden, thus supporting the bomber war on Germany and other activities. Sweden's military intelligence section, *C-Bureau*, acted in all Nordic countries operating, 'almost wholly without government consensus, though always acting to secure what it believed to be in Sweden's interest'. All in all, Swedish intelligence was effective and operated on all sides in the war, including cooperation with Germany and Finland on intelligence from the Soviet Union, thus giving the government more room for manoeuvre and often providing very accurate information in advance about Germany's intentions and policy towards Sweden. That was another asset for the government's strategy of keeping Sweden out of the war.

The top diplomat Erik Boheman was frank with the US Minister, Johnson, in 1942. He remarked that Sweden was made neutral by sheer force of circumstances, that it would be quite impossible to induce the Swedish people to fight either Norway or Finland. . . . He emphatically stated that it was the determination of the Swedes to resist by force any attack on their territory from whatever quarters it came.

Another US report from Stockholm on 2 July 1942 was also positive: 'Swedes have successfully resisted the German "war of nerves" which seems to have been abounded and it is doubtful if any further effort along this line will be effective.'[25] In retrospect, one can characterize the policy that Sweden followed as a combination of concessions and resistance. The concessions to Germany dominated in the years 1940–41, an intermediate position was reached in 1942, and from 1942 to 1943, Sweden was able gradually to use the growing freedom of action to place herself closer to the side that she had always considered the right one, following an ever more pro-western line during the last war years. In 1940–42, the main objective of the Swedish government had been to prevent the catastrophe of a war with Germany, by staying neutral and maintaining good diplomatic and trade relations with the potential aggressor. There were, however, many politicians, including Social Democrats and Liberals, and also diplomats like Gunnar Hägglöf, who felt that this gave only a limited and artificial breathing space. They did not believe that Sweden could maintain good relations with a victorious Nazi Germany in the long run. Others, such as Foreign Minister Günther, considered this to be an open question. There was a fundamental difference of opinion on Germany in Sweden at this time. Within the security policy elite, that is the Cabinet, party leaders, diplomats and military leaders, most preferred a 'wait-and-see policy' and not to discuss Germany's uncomfortable shadow over Sweden. This view dominated also in public debate and opinion. The thesis of national unity and neutrality was firm and not for discussion. However, even if neutralist opinion dominated, some expressed pro-western and others pro-German sympathies.

German blockade of Sweden in 1943?

Germany considered imposing a trade embargo against Sweden in 1943, in the event of the government in Stockholm trying to cooperate with the Allied powers. The commercial experts in Berlin and at the German legation in Stockholm studied Swedish war economic strength in depth. This gave a gloomy answer to the Germans. Sweden now had built up an ever more efficient war economy. State, government, industry, commerce and agriculture had in cooperation with the Swedish people effectively built a strong war economy. Sweden could withstand a trade embargo for more than one year, concluded the Germans.[26]

Violations of Swedish territory

Sweden often protested about violations of her territory by the Allied powers and Germany. In April–May 1944, as an example, Sweden protested in London about bombers over southern Sweden, in Berlin regarding shots fired at a Swedish submarine and German mines in Swedish waters, and in Moscow concerning bombers at several places.[27]

In total, there were reportedly 4,701 cases of violations of Swedish territory by around 18,000 aircraft, mostly in southern Sweden and by British and American bombers and fighter planes in the years 1942–45. Around 2,620 German aircraft violated Swedish territory, mostly in the period 1940–43. Around 40 per cent were not identified by nationality, but most of them evidently belonged to the Allied bomber armadas taking the route over southern Sweden at high altitude, then attacking Germany from the north and often flying back over Sweden in order to avoid German anti-aircraft fire and fighter attacks.[28]

Table 1 Violations of Swedish territory by foreign aircraft April 1940–May 1945

In total, 4,701 cases
Observed aircraft between 17,701 and 17,880
40% not identified by nationality
8,142 Allied aircraft
2,620 German aircraft

(*Source:* Tommy Pettersson, *Överflygningar av Sverige 1939–1945*, MILITÄRHÖGSKOLAN. MILITÄRHISTORISKA AVDELNINGEN, SNDC, 1996).

Table 2 Forced and emergency landings by foreign aircraft in Sweden 1939–45

Nation	1939	1940	1941	1942	1943	1944	1945	Total
GER	1	17	11	6	8	16	52	111
UK	–	3	–	4	2	14	14	37
US	–	–	–	–	7	109	14	130
Other	1	12	–	–	–	–	1	14
Total	2	32	11	10	17	139	81	292

(*Source:* Tommy Pettersson, 1996, table 2).

Added to this, Swedish air defence shot down or forced down many foreign aircraft in 1940–45, but the figures are unreliable. Germany protested in May 1940: 'Are we at war?', they asked.

United States' positive assessments of Sweden 1943

An analysis of Swedish neutrality and her ability to resist Germany was made in July 1943 in Washington in the War Department by the Intelligence Division (MID). They underlined the national unity on neutrality and the strong Swedish determination to fight if the country was attacked by Germany. 'They will fight, if the need arises, in the streets and everywhere.' The Swedish military build-up had accomplished good results, although it was still only halfway finished. In 1945, the Swedish armed forces would consist of 600,000 well-trained and equipped soldiers, which could be of importance in the final end of the war in Europe. Sweden's neutrality was based on a shared fear of both Germany and the Soviet Union, but public opinion was at 80 to 90 per cent for the western powers and democracy. The German occupation of Norway and Denmark made those Swedes who had sympathized with Germany alter their position. The strong Swedish will to defend the country was proclaimed by King and government in January 1943: 'All messages that the resistance must cease are false.'

The US interest in Sweden increased during autumn 1943. US Defence Staff of the Joint Chiefs of Staff and the Joint Intelligence Committee, with representatives from various ministries, raised the question of how to include Sweden in the war against Nazi Germany. They also continued the evaluation of the Swedish will to engage in defence and resistance. Now, the conclusion was that Swedish troops could be of value in conjunction with the Allies in an operation against Norway, especially to take Trondheim and Narvik. However, the Swedish forces were judged still to have little offensive capability. Of great value for the Allies would be to establish air bases on Swedish territory. This would threaten Germany's strategic positions throughout the Baltic region and would give the Allies air bases very close to Germany for 'close-range air attacks'.

Sweden, thus, was of great strategic value to the Allies. The Swedish army now numbered thirteen divisions, 350,000 soldiers in the first line field units and 200,000 men in local defence units. The Home Guard had 200,000 members, which was believed to be the core of a potentially effective guerrilla force. Infantry equipment was considered to be good, but the corps and army artillery was too weak. Bofors anti-aircraft guns were excellent and in great numbers. Anti-tank weaponry was weak, while the air force numbered about 600 aircraft of which about half were modern and the rest obsolete. The pilots were considered to be well trained, but, due to outdated equipment and limited resources of fuel, they could not fight for long. The navy was considered not to have offensive tasks, but, together with coastal fortifications, formed a coastal defence. In total, because of a lack of fuel, it was calculated that Sweden could fight for up to two months of warfare.

Sweden's strategic position was poor, encircled by German troops, and Sweden would have had to fight Germany mostly alone in a war. The Allies could have sent only a limited amount of reinforcements by sea and air. Modern fighter planes were much needed and could have been sent via Trondheim and Narvik if these cities had been taken by the Allies. However, given the actual state of the war in 1943, Germany could not afford to weaken its forces in order to attack Sweden. That would require a rather large intervention force from all services in joint operations. The conclusion was that, 'In the present state of equilibrium in Scandinavia, the light, but efficient, Swedish defence forces are an adequate defence, simply as a force in being'.

In the event of a war with Germany, the Swedish army now had the ability to hold out for some time, perhaps until the Allies could provide more substantial assistance. If Germany could collect eleven divisions for an attack on Sweden from Norway and Denmark, with strong air support, it was calculated that southern and central Sweden would fall within one month, while the resistance north of Stockholm was likely to continue for much longer. The United States' assessment of the Swedish defence and military position was mixed but, strategically, Sweden was particularly interesting as a location for Allied air bases. All in all, Sweden could be an asset to the Allies and further weaken the German war potential.

The Joint Chiefs of Staff now wanted to get both Sweden and Turkey into the war against Germany. This issue was discussed both in Washington on October 25, 1943, and during the Moscow Conference. The US Defence Staff thought it was desirable to get the two states into the war, but stated that the western powers had little chance of helping Sweden and Turkey by military means, since this would affect other operational areas in Europe negatively. Operation OVERLORD, the invasion of France in June 1944, now had first priority, and any Scandinavian operation would split the forces. The western powers could not help Sweden and Turkey if they went to war with Germany while the Soviet Union was fully engaged on the eastern front with Germany.

An amphibious operation in Norway would be hazardous, and even more so would be an operation to establish and maintain air bases in Sweden. Such operations furthermore ought to be carried out before the invasion of France, at great risk. In principle, it was considered desirable to get Sweden into the war, but the Allies had little to offer by way of substantial assistance for fighting the

Germans on Swedish soil. This was the military advice given to the US President. President Roosevelt and Secretary Hull now followed the same line as that of the Joint Chiefs of Staff. London and Moscow were told that the United States could not deploy some 600 fighter planes and 4 to 5 army divisions to support Sweden, plus 6 to 7 army divisions to take parts of Norway and establish lines of communication. An operation of this magnitude would seriously affect the planned cross-channel operation.

The US Stockholm legation also discouraged such thinking. In a letter dated 21 November 1943, Minister Johnson and the Military Attachés said it would be almost impossible for the Allies to establish air bases in Sweden since the Germans would probably attack and destroy them.[29] Churchill's attitude to Swedish neutrality moved from critical to supportive. He met Erik Boheman several times in London from 1940 to 1942. In his memoirs, Boheman recalls a long conversation he had with Churchill in 1942 when the two men discussed Sweden's precarious situation after the Winter War and Hitler's occupation of Denmark and Norway. Churchill's analysis was clear:

> I think I understand your attitude and your policy, you must arm and arm and prepare yourself for the worst, do not give way to German demands more than you absolutely must, but on the other hand do not be fool-hardy, we do not want another victim. We do not want another victim, he repeated in his most boisterous tone.[30]

Further, in a telegram to Roosevelt on 23 October, 1943, on Sweden and the war, Churchill wrote from London: 'It would be a great advantage to bring Sweden into the war. We do not think the Germans have the strength to undertake a heavy invasion of Sweden. We should gain a new country and a small but good army.' Churchill's analysis was based mostly on wishful thinking. A pro-Western policy had already dominated Sweden in anticipation of a German collapse. However, without substantial help from the Allies, Sweden was not ready to abandon its neutrality.

The end of the war, 1944–45

During the last wartime years, 1944–45, Sweden strengthened its position politically, economically and militarily. The government openly followed a pro-Allied political line, in anticipation of Germany's defeat. Germany now protested diplomatically against the training of around 20,000 Danish and Norwegian troops in Sweden, but this had no effect. The western powers of the United States and Britain were very satisfied in these last years of the war with Sweden's new security policies and even hoped that Sweden would take part in the war on the Allied side, if necessary, and later on in the reconstruction of war-torn Europe. Finally, the Red Army invaded Norwegian Finnmark in 1944–45 and Norwegian troops trained in neutral Sweden were flown by American transport planes from Kallax airbase in north Sweden into Finnmark. *Operation Balchen* was undertaken in order to establish Norwegian authority (but also in order to 'contain communism').[31] Finland obtained an armistice with the Soviet Union in September 1944 and then expelled the German army from Finnish Lapponia in the Lapland War of 1944–45.

In April 1945, the Commander-in-Chief of the Swedish Defence Staff, General Count Carl August Ehrensvärd, a volunteer in Finland in both 1918 and 1939, declared at a secret press conference in Stockholm that the Swedish defence forces were ready to join the Allies to liberate Denmark and Norway from German occupation if the Germans did not surrender, in Operation Save Denmark and Operation Save Norway. Fortunately, the Germans surrendered in good order. General Ehrensvärd also noted that the course of the war in the far north could not have been predicted and said that if anyone had told him two years previously that Finnish troops would be chasing the Germans out of Finland with the Red Army standing by, just watching, he would have said that this person was mad. And now, Swedish and Allied troops, together with Norwegian and Danish troops, trained in Sweden, were ready to liberate Denmark and Norway if needed. Two years ago, this also was unforeseeable.[32]

And so ended the war in Europe in May 1945. The shadow of Nazi Germany and Hitler was gone and neutral Sweden wanted to do its share to rebuild Europe and give as much humanitarian help as possible to a suffering mankind. This was done within the framework of the United Nations and in other arenas. To sum up, Sweden used her strategic assets, political, economic and military strength and traditional neutral position in the power struggle in Europe with great skill in both world wars. That preserved her peace and independence. As long as any power bloc did not force Sweden into their camp, Sweden could stay neutral and aloof from the conflict in both world wars. And so neutral Sweden could survive by her own strength in 1939–1945, trading and arming, giving humanitarian aid, helping her Nordic neighbours in many ways and by many means, and planning and hoping for the future of a better world after yet another disastrous war.

Bibliography

Andersson, L. and Tydén, M. (2007) (eds), *Sverige och Nazityskland: skuldfrågor och moraldebatt*. Stockholm: Dialogos.

Areschoug, R. (2008), *Dödlig resa: svenska handelsflottans förluster 1939-1945*. Stockholm: Svenskt Militärhistoriskt bibliotek.

Bergquist, M. and Johansson, A. W. and Wahlbäck, K. (1987), *Utrikespolitik och historia*. Stockholm: Militärhistoriska förlaget.

Björkman, L. (1971), *Sverige inför Operation Barbarossa*, SUAV, Stockholm.

The Bofors Gun in the Second World War, (1955), Stockholm: Militärhögskolan. Militärhistoriska avdelningen (MHA).

Böhme, K.-R. (1982), *Svenska vingar växer*. Stockholm: Militärhistoriska förlaget.

Carlgren, W. M. (1973), *Svensk utrikespolitik 1939-1945*. Stockholm: Allmänna Förlaget.

— (1985), *Svensk underrättelsetjänst 1939-1945*. Stockholm: Allmänna Förlaget.

Ehrensvärd, C. A. (2005), *Arméchef i orostid, Dagboksanteckningar 1938-1957*. Stockholm: Svenskt Militärhistoriskt bibliotek.

Hirdman, Y. (1974), *Sveriges Kommunistiska Parti 1939-45*. Stockholm: Allmänna Förlaget (Series on Sweden during the Second World War).

Hugemark, B. (ed.) (1989), *Stormvarning - 1939*. Stockholm: Probus förlag.

— (1990), *Blixt från en klar himmel - 1940*. Stockholm: Probus förlag.

— (1991), *I orkanens öga - 1941*. Stockholm: Probus förlag.

— (1992), *Vindkantring - 1942*. Stockholm: Probus förlag.

— (1993), *Nya fronter - 1943*. Stockholm: Probus förlag.

Böhme, K.-R. and Huldt, B. (eds), (1994), *Vårstormar - 1944*. Stockholm: Probus förlag.

— (1995), *Horisonten klarnar - 1945*. Stockholm: Probus förlag.

Hugemark, B. (ed.) (1986), *Neutralitet och försvar. Perspektiv på svensk säkerhetspolitik 1809-1985*. Stockholm: Militärhistoriska förlaget.

Johansson, A. W. (1984), *Per Albin och kriget*. Stockholm: Tidens förlag.

— (1993), *Den nazistiska utmaningen. Aspekter på andra världskriget*. Stockholm: Tidens förlag.

— (1994), *Europas krig*. Stockholm: Tidens förlag.

Wangel, C.-A. (ed.), (1982), *Sveriges militära beredskap 1939-1945*. Stockholm: Militärhistoriska förlaget.

Zetterberg, K. (2000), 'Det neutrala Sveriges skuld och ansvar: till frågan om den svenska politiken under det andra världskriget och den svenska debatten efter kriget', in Zetterberg, K. and Åselius, G. (eds) (2000), *Historia, krig och statskonst: en vänbok till Klaus-Richard Böhme*. Probus, Stockholm.

— (2000), 'Den mångtydiga neutraliteten och demokratins kriser: till den svenska"neutralitetspolitikens" långa historia: några reflexioner inför den svenska fredens 200-årsjubileum', in Björklund, Fredrika, Johansson, Alf W., Björk, Ragnar, *Människan i historien och samtiden: festskrift till Alf W. Johansson*. Stockholm: Hjalmarson and Högberg.

— (2007), *Konsten att överleva: studier i Sveriges försvar, strategi och säkerhetspolitik under 200 år*. Stockholm: Försvarshögskolan.

— (2001), 'Staffan Söderblom' och 'Sven Grafström', in Artéus, G. and Leifland, L. (eds) (2001), *Svenska diplomatprofiler under 1900-talet*. Stockholm: Probus.

— (1993), '1942: storkriget vänder, Sveriges utsatta läge består', in Hugemark, Bo (ed.) (1993), *Vindkantring: 1942 - politisk kursändring*. Stockholm: Probus.

— (1992), 'Neutralitet till varje pris? till frågan om den svenska säkerhetspolitiken 1940–42 och eftergifterna till Tyskland', in Hugemark, B. (ed.) (1992), *I orkanens öga*. Stockholm: Probus.

— (1995), 'Storkriget går mot sitt slut: Sveriges läge förbättras', in Huldt, Bo, and Böhme, Klaus-Richard (eds) (1995), *Vårstormar: 1944 - krigsslutet skönjes*. Stockholm: Probus.

— (1994), 'Svensk säkerhetspolitik 1943: en balansakt på slak lina mellan de krigförande', in Hugemark, Bo (ed.) (1994), *Nya fronter? 1943 - spänd väntan*. Stockholm: Probus.

Notes

1 Wahlbäck, K. (1987), in *Festskrift till Nils Andrén*. Per Albin Hansson had been a newspaper correspondent in London in World War I and held warm sympathies for Great Britain and fellow Nordic countries and their style of democracy.
2 See Zetterberg (2007).
3 Zetterberg (1992), pp. 85–6, p. 148. Also Carlgren (1973), Chapters 5 and 7.
4 Munch-Petersen, T. (1981), *The Strategy of Phoney War. Britain, Sweden and the Iron Ore Question 1939–1940*. Stockholm: Militärhistoriska Förlaget, p. 252.
5 Zetterberg (1992), (1994), (1995), also Carlgren (1973), Chapter 2.
6 This was done in a diplomatic way in August 1943 by a joint Swedish-German official agreement saying that this was due to the increased insurance costs for the sea routes (!). Zetterberg (1993).
7 Carlgren (1973), Chapter 5.
8 A large proportion of foreign orders for war material was seized by the Swedish government and used for domestic consumption. See also *The Bofors Gun in the Second World War* (1955).
9 Both Sven Linderoth and Hilding Hagberg, communist leaders of SKP, proclaimed this thesis – the Soviet Union had saved Sweden's neutrality in 1939–45. See Hirdman (1974).

10 The merchant fleet lost 206 ships and 1,270 Swedes plus citizens of other nationalities. Twenty-five ships were confiscated. The fishing-fleet lost 31 ships and 89 lives and the navy 8 ships and 92 Swedes. Wikipedia.se. See also Areschoug (2008).
11 Assarsson, V. (1963), *I skuggan av Stalin* (Stockholm). Also Carlgren (1973), Chapter 5.
12 See Zetterberg (2010).
13 Zetterberg (1992), pp. 123–9; Zetterberg (1994), pp. 45–51. The German military view of Sweden was somewhat Wagnerian, calling Sweden 'Heimat den Vikingen und Goten'.
14 Carlgren (1973), Chapter 7; Boheman, E. (1964), *På Vakt. Kabinettssekreterare under andra världskriget*. Stockholm: Norstedt.
15 Åmark, K. (2011), *Att bo granne med ondskan: Sveriges förhållande till nazismen, Nazityskland och förintelsen*. Stockholm: Bonnier, pp. 104–7. Also Carlgren (1973).
16 That the Swedish officer corps (the General Staff and the Navy Staff) did not sever its good relations with the German officers corps (the General Staff and the Navy Staff) during the Weimar Republic (1919–33) proved to be an asset at this time.
17 Per Albin Hansson's diary, 18 June 1940. Stockholm: Arb.A.
18 Radowitz von Krämer, S. (2005), *Schweden und das 'Dritte Reich' 1939–1945: Die deutsch-schwedishen Beziehungen im Schatten des Zweiten Weltkrieges*. Hamburg: Krämer, cited in Åmark (2011), pp. 89–95.
19 Zetterberg (1994).
20 Wittmann K. (1978), *Schwedens Wirschaftsbeziehungen zum Dritten Reich 1933–1945*. Munich: Oldenbourg, Summary, pp. 393–400. Chapters V-VIII deal with the years 1940–45.
21 From summer 1941, it also included some military equipment to Finland and the German troops in the extreme north (*AOK Lappland*). A departure from the agreement was the German armed *Division Engelbrecht* which was allowed to cross from Norway through Sweden to Finland in the summer of 1941. See Carlgren (1973), Chapter 11.
22 Zetterberg, K. (1978), 'Den tyska transiteringstrafiken genom Sverige 1940–43', in Ekman, S. (ed.) (1978), *Motstånd och eftergifter*. Stockholm: SUAV.
23 Telegram Johnson – Washington, (FRUS Europe 21/2 1942), Foreign Relations of the United States.
24 Aklundh, J., Burnett, G., Harison, S. (2011), 'To what extent did intelligence contribute to Sweden maintaining its non-belligerence throughout World War Two?', in *The Royal Swedish Academy of War Sciences Journal*, no. 1/2011, pp. 137–45 (citation p. 137).
25 Hugemark (1991), p. 26.
26 Zetterberg (1994).

27 Fogelström, P. A. (ed.) (1944), *Världspolitiken i karikatyrer, 1943-1945*. Stockholm: Världspressen, p. 40, 'Sweden protests'. For the diplomatic protests, see Carlgren (1973), Chapter 19.
28 Pettersson, T., 'Överflygningar av Sverige 1939-1945', (unpublished), MHA, SNDC, 1996. Also Wegmann, R. and Widfeldt, B. (1991), *Nödlandning Sverige! Nödlandningar i Sverige 1939-1945*. Nässjö: Air Historic Research; Widfeldt, B. (1983), *The Luftwaffe in Sweden 1939-1945*. Massachusetts: Boylston; Wangel, C-A. (ed.) (1982), *Sveriges militära beredskap 1939-1945*. Stockholm: Militärhistoriska förlaget.
29 Zetterberg (1993), p. 22.
30 Ibid.
31 Zetterberg (1995), 'Svensk säkerhetspolitik i krigsslutet' in Böhme, K.-R. and Huldt, B. (eds) (1994), *Vårstormar – 1944*. Stockholm: Probus förlag, pp. 191-5.
32 SIS, Informationsstyrelsen, Förtrolig presskonferens, Försvarsstaben april 1945. Genmj. C. A. Ehrensvärd.

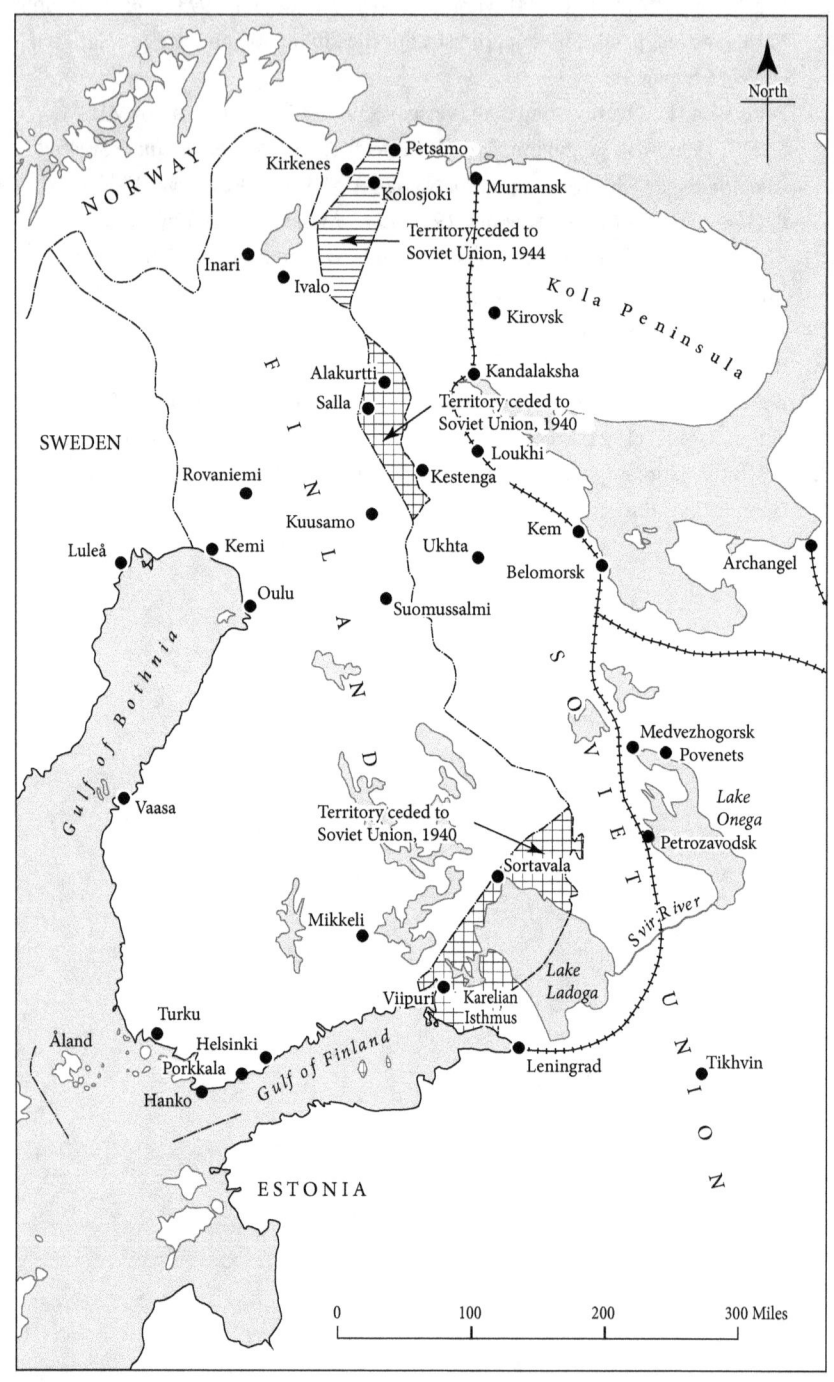

Map 2 Finland, 1939–44.

7

Janus of the North? Finland 1940–44
Finland's road into alliance with Hitler

Oula Silvennoinen

Of the Scandinavian countries, Finland became the only one to ally herself with Nazi Germany in World War II. In the process, she also gained the dubious distinction to be 'the only democracy to fight on the side of Hitler'. Indeed, Finland's participation in the Axis, though lasting only a little over 3 years, has proved an enduring source of embarrassment. For present-day Finns, Finland's partnership with Nazi Germany is still, 60 years after the end of the war, in a seemingly constant need to be somehow qualified, put into perspective, relativized or explained away. Yet, once the possibility of allying with Hitler did become real in 1940, very few in Finland were ready seriously to object, and the country was taken to war by a broad-based coalition government. This was a clear signal of the near-unanimous popular acceptance of a policy which tied Finland's interests and fate to a dictatorship that has become the very symbol for the most appalling horrors of the twentieth century. It, thus, seems pertinent to ask, how did it come to this?

Finland had been part of the Swedish empire from the Middle Ages, until it was annexed as an autonomous Grand Duchy under the Russian crown in 1809. Towards the end of the nineteenth century, rising Finnish nationalism began to clash with the ambitions of an imperial government whose control of the empire was increasingly beginning to slip. As an attempt to stem the tide, the government launched a series of Russification programmes intended to bring the potentially restive parts of the empire into a tighter union with the mother country. The decay of the imperial system was not, however, to be halted. After revolution had engulfed Russia in 1917, Finland, among many other ethnically and culturally non-Russian parts of the empire, broke free and declared independence. Almost immediately in 1918, however, Finland was plunged into an atrocious civil war between the socialist Reds, backed by now-Bolshevik Russia, and the non-socialist Whites, backed by Imperial Germany. The triumph of the Whites, while confirming the rejection of socialist visions, also revealed the deep differences of opinion within the White coalition. The post-civil war political settlement was characterized by the adoption of a Republican, democratic form of government as well as by efforts to bring about a reconciliation with the former Reds.[1] All this left the radical right-wing core of the White movement disappointed and embittered, yearning for a final showdown with socialism and with Bolshevik Russia. And while Finnish society largely succeeded in reconciling the majority of socialists with the post-civil war political framework, the hard core of the radical Reds fled to Soviet Russia to form the Finnish Communist Party. It began a long, clandestine campaign to bring about a new armed uprising in Finland. The interwar period was, thus, characterized by intense enmities arising out of the civil war. While the vast majority of Finns came to be united in their rejection of both revolutionary socialism and Soviet communism, among the right this shared anti-communism tended to be much more confrontational and given to radical visions. Moreover, anti-communism was often accompanied by ethnic hatred of Russians, who were seen as culturally and racially inferior arch-enemies of Finnish national aspirations.[2]

Hatred towards Russia and the Russians was relatively recent in Finland. During the period from the Middle Ages up until Finland's incorporation into the Russian Empire, the popular image of the Russian had naturally enough been one of a traditional enemy. The Orthodox Russians represented a culturally and ethnically alien 'other', against whom first the Catholic and then the Lutheran Swedish empire was at war every now and then. Nevertheless, it was not until the late nineteenth century that a consistently negative image of the Russian as a hereditary, implacable enemy of Finland began to emerge. Such imagery was consciously fostered by Finnish nationalist activists during the period of struggle for independence in order to create a focal point for nationalist and irredentist projects of aggrandizement.[3]

Nationalisms everywhere tend rather effortlessly to give birth to ideas of gathering each and every linguistically and culturally related member of the perceived 'one great nation' under a single, undivided polity. Finnish nationalism was no exception. Linguistic and cultural relatives of the Finns were found from the shores of the Baltic Sea all the way to northern Norway and across the Ural mountains in Siberia. While ideas of including the farthest-flung speakers of Finno-Ugric languages into one and the same empire may have appeared far-fetched even to contemporary visionaries, thoughts of incorporating the closest linguistic relatives into an imagined 'Greater Finland' were far more frequent in appearance, especially among the educated public and students during the 1920s and 1930s. In these schemes, 'Greater Finland' was usually planned to include, as a non-negotiable minimum requirement, Russian Karelia with its Karelian and Finnish-speaking, but mostly Russian Orthodox, population. The area had by this time come to be seen as the cultural heartland of Finland after the compilation and publication of the Finnish folk epic *Kalevala* in the mid-nineteenth century. The orally transmitted tradition forming the basis for this work had mainly been collected from among the inhabitants of Russian Karelia, even though the area had never been politically part of Finland. Another target for claims was Ingermanland, the area around St. Petersburg (later Petrograd then Leningrad), with a population derived from Finnish immigrants settled there by the Swedish crown in the seventeenth century. Further claims included the Kola peninsula with its Sámi population, the Finnmark region of Norway and Västerbotten, the part of Sweden sharing a border with Finland, including a substantial Finnish-speaking minority. While the Estonians, linguistically, culturally and ethnically close to modern Finns, were usually included in these schemes upon a basis of assumed voluntariness, it is easy to see that attempts to redeem these Finnish irredenta would have brought Finland into conflict with practically all of its neighbours.[4]

Imperial dreams born of nationalist visions remained for a long time hopelessly unattainable, but the collapse of the Russian empire seemed suddenly, and tantalizingly, to bring them within reach. The consequence was a series of irredentist interventions in the conflicts following the disintegration of the empire, in a spirit combining anti-Bolshevism with romantic visions of gathering together all the Finnic nationalities. In this spirit, Finnish volunteers participated in the Estonian War of Liberation, fought against the Bolsheviks in 1918–20 and staged an improvised invasion of Ingermanland in 1919 in the hope of drawing in the Finnish government and army, to hasten the demise of the Bolshevik regime. A far more ambitious attempt to intervene in the Russian civil war with a military operation to occupy Petrograd was also contemplated. It was eventually abandoned due to the political risk involved and the unwillingness of the main beneficiary of such an operation, the Russian White forces under Admiral Aleksandr Kolchak, to recognize both Finland's independence and claims to the adjacent territories as the price of assistance. Other expeditions were launched in 1918 and 1920 to take over the Petsamo area, a strip of land from between Norwegian and Russian territory in the far north, giving Finland access to the Barents Sea.[5]

All these undertakings were the projects of the nationalist activists without the official sanction of the Finnish state. To end the continuing instability on the border areas of Soviet Russia, Estonia and Finland, a peace agreement was finally negotiated in Dorpat (Tartu) in Estonia in 1920. While the Peace of Dorpat resulted in the incorporation of the Petsamo area into Finland, the other military ventures proved eventually unfruitful, and the dreams of the irredentists were left unfulfilled. The agreement was, thus, seen as betrayal by those radicals clamouring for a relentless campaign to realize the nationalist visions of the future. As a result, a further private military adventure was launched by sending an expedition of volunteers from Finland to tip the balance of forces hopelessly stacked against the insurgents in the Karelian uprising in 1921–22. The defeat of both the uprising and the expeditionary force marked the end of the period of open armed conflict on Finnish border areas.

As it was, back in Finland the fervour aroused by the experience of the civil war had already largely abated. In the political struggle against the republicans concerning the form of the future polity of Finland, the monarchists had suffered a decisive defeat. A lawyer with a strong constitutional and liberal background, K. J. Ståhlberg, was elected as the first president of the republic. While Ståhlberg became the focal point for the ire of much of the political right, the moment seemed to have passed for all those favouring a violent, military solution to Finland's many domestic and foreign political challenges. Instead, the new republic seemed to settle down to a dull parliamentary routine and rapidly abandoned the martial spirit, as well as the dizzying visions, of 1918. The hour of destiny had turned into a lacklustre, unfulfilling experience for the generation of radical nationalist youth who for a brief moment had seen a great future dangling in front of their very eyes. The early 1920s meant that dreams of warlike aggrandizement had to be laid to rest. They would nevertheless resurface again when the next round in the global conflict, World War II, began, and it seemed that the bell of destiny rang for one more, last time. But for the time being, perhaps nobody better captured the disillusionment and frustration felt by the radicals than their avowed enemy, Raoul Palmgren, an acerbic young writer of the radical left:

> The defeated White guards' troops return from Red Karelia, their heads still filled with the mysticism of war, hearts aching from defeat and the embarrassing

collapse of the expedition, unable to accommodate themselves to the new conditions. The country is busy creating a basis for Ståhlbergian reconciliation, in the university the counter-effect of war is manifested as fatigue and self-indulgence, jazz and Estonian hard stuff enter Finland. The Mosaic "heroes" of Karelia stand spiritually angered among this Sodom...[6]

From virtues to necessities

Modern Finns will tell you without hesitation that theirs is a western society and a western country. They have good reason to say so, but, for understanding Finland's position in World War II, such a perception is not helpful at all. Indeed, it is downright misleading, for Finland was, and is, a western country only in a cultural and political sense. Finland's geographical and geopolitical position made her not a western, not a Scandinavian or even a Nordic, but an eastern European country with eastern European problems. During the years between the world wars, European imagination, the landscape of fears and hopes, was dominated by a single great dictatorship. This regime was widely feared because of its open expansionism, and it was widely detested for its brutal repression of both political opponents and ethnic minorities. It ruled over a country of prison camps, mock justice and summary executions. To make matters even worse, there were good reasons to believe that one day this country would unleash its armies upon the rest of Europe in a bid for world domination. Throughout the interwar years, most Europeans would unhesitatingly have recognized this dictatorship as the Soviet Union.

The proximity of the aggressive Soviet regime created a uniquely intense problem of security for every country it shared a border with. Finland was in no sense an exception to this. No eastern European country was able to find a working solution to this problem between the world wars. In due course the lack of security policy alternatives contributed to the rise of authoritarian regimes in all eastern European countries, just as it made them vulnerable to Soviet aggression and to the growing influence of Nazi Germany. Finland was an exception to this development only in the sense that she eventually did not succumb to the societal and political pressures which elsewhere led to the establishment of fascist or authoritarian regimes. Having survived such a crisis in the early 1930s, the republic was confirmed as a western democracy situated in eastern Europe.[7]

If interwar Europe was, until the 1930's at least, generally convinced of the potential threat of the Soviet Union, the rise of Hitler began rapidly to change perceptions in the west. In time, the Nazis began to appear as a more tangible menace than the Soviet Union which, despite the enduring legacy of the 'Red Scare', appeared rather passive when compared with the restless aggressiveness of the Nazi regime. The Nazi threat led Britain and France in short order to revise their priority list, and public opinion in countries without immediate contact with the Soviet Union followed suit. But in eastern Europe, far fewer things had changed. Thus, the decisive factor dividing Europe into western and eastern halves was whether one could dismiss the Soviet Union as a threat because of Hitler. In this sense, the border between Scandinavia and eastern Europe, between west and east, came to run through the Gulf of Bothnia between Sweden and Finland.[8]

If the west watched the rise of Hitler with growing anxiety, in Finland perceptions of the Nazi regime were already mixed with a considerable dose of hopefulness. The defeat of Imperial Germany in World War I had left Finland without a committed guarantor state. After the desolate years of Weimar Germany's foreign political impotence, there was finally a vigorous regime, in word and deed opposed to communism and therefore also, finally, a potential ally against the Soviet Union.[9] While Finnish public opinion certainly did not embrace Hitler's new state without grave reservations, there was at least the rather realistic hope that the new Germany would form a vital counterweight to the growing Soviet power. Against this background, German rearmament and her aggressive foreign political stance were welcomed by many as a sign that Germany was finally breaking the paralysis imposed upon her by the peace of Versailles. Finland was far enough from Germany not to have to fear her aggression, but close enough to hope for her support against the Soviet Union.[10]

Finnish foreign policy between the world wars had been characterized by a pursuit of security through international co-operation. From the Finnish point of view, this naturally meant the containment of the Soviet Union. By late 1939, however, all the initiatives aimed at this, as well as the hopes initially attached to the League of Nations, had proven to be futile. The Molotov-Ribbentrop Pact in August 1939 was immediately understood to mean a fateful deterioration in Finland's position. Finland was now politically isolated, and in due course she became, in November 1939, a victim of Soviet aggression. The lessons taught by the resulting short but brutal conflict, known in Finland as the Winter War, were simple and difficult to argue with. Finland emerged from the experience of the Winter War in mid-March 1940 territorially reduced, and embittered to the core by Soviet aggression, universally perceived as the basest of injustices. Furthermore, after the Winter War Finland was politically just as isolated as before, and she, therefore, had to fear that the Soviet Union might renew hostilities at any given moment. While during the Winter War there had been widespread and vocal sympathy with Finland's plight throughout Europe and the United States, tangible military help had failed to materialize. Armaments from the west had either been unavailable or arrived too late. On the basis of their pact, Germany adopted a pro-Soviet neutrality policy, which was damaging to Finnish interests. In effect, German unwillingness to co-operate served effectively to isolate Finland from several sources of foreign military support. The Third Reich chose to block, for instance, the shipping of armaments offered to Finland by the sympathetic and rather more consistently anti-communist Mussolini through German territory.

The chequered group of international volunteers pouring into Finland from all over the world, including over 200 British volunteers, proved to be militarily of little value due to the lack of military training, language difficulties and suspicions of political reliability. Only the contingent sent by Sweden, all officially volunteers acting without the sanction of their government, saw military action in the northern part of Finland.[11] The intervention plans of the Western Allies, Britain and France, had the character of last-minute improvisations. The Finnish leadership suspected the plans of being aimed more at taking control of Swedish iron ore than rendering any effective aid to Finland. In early March 1940, the situation on the front was already critical. The refusal of both Norway and Sweden, fearful of German and Soviet retaliatory measures, to grant passage for a Franco-British expeditionary force seemed to remove any realistic basis for hopes of a western intervention. Moreover, any such operation at this late hour would have to be of decisive force in order to prevent the nightmare outcome of Finland being drawn into the larger European conflict while being left without timely aid to prevent military collapse. Finland, thus, sued for peace, which the increasingly embarrassed Soviet Union was for the time being happy to accept.[12]

In Finland, eventual disillusionment with the possibilities of international co-operation was severe. The belief in both the ability and willingness of especially the western powers to help Finland had been profoundly shaken by the experience of Soviet aggression. Harold Macmillan was to lament this in March 1940 in a letter to Gösta Serlachius, a Finnish industrialist who had been closely involved in attempts to raise significant aid for Finland in the United Kingdom:

> There seems to be a fatal inability in modern democratic governments to make up their minds until it is too late, and I am afraid that this is another case of

which there have been many examples before. I do not know how I can write to you or what to say. Sometimes I feel that none of you will wish to think of or hear from your English friends again: but I would like you to feel that I am ready to do, in the future, anything I can for your cause, tragic as the present position is.[13]

From insecurity to radicalization

Soon enough, Finland's options were even further reduced by the commencement of the German offensive in the west in April 1940. As a result of German seizure of Denmark and Norway, Finland's isolation from the west became virtually total, as foreign trade routes through the Skagerrak were closed, and trade with Great Britain cut off. Finland's last remaining opening to the high seas, the low-capacity port of Petsamo in the far north, came within German striking distance when Germany occupied northern Norway in June 1940. It seemed that Finland was in a position where anybody's help would have been welcome, and the options were practically reduced to either Hitler's Germany or Stalin's Soviet Union. Considering that the independent state of Finland was based upon a definite rejection of communism and the Soviet system, the choice was a foregone conclusion. As the speaker of the Finnish parliament, Väino Hakkila, explained in 1941: 'In order to resist the Soviet Union, Finland would ally herself even with the devil.'[14]

Germany also was reconsidering her options. In contrast to the loyally pro-Soviet line she had maintained during the Winter War, in the spring of 1940 Germany began to send more and more sympathetic signals towards Finland. Thereafter development was rapid. In September 1940, the first German troops entered Finland, officially just passing over Finnish territory in transit between Germany and northernmost Norway. German officials had also increasingly begun to drop hints about the possibility of German-Soviet conflict in the immediate future. By the end of the year, the Finnish military was already planning for such a contingency. As the spring of 1941 progressed, the Finns were taken deeper and deeper into German trust.[15] By this time, the point of no return had already been passed. Finland went to war with her eyes open, officially to defend her integrity and freedom, and to reclaim the territories lost in the Winter War. The Finnish leadership, however, was not left in the dark as to the German war aims. If realized, they would mean the total destruction of the Soviet Union and the carving up of the Soviet empire by the victors. It was obvious that in such an event there would be little reason for Finland to limit her gains to regaining previous losses. More, much more, seemed to be within her grasp.[16]

Finland entered into a military partnership with Nazi Germany out of a mixture of genuine anxiety for her security, a determination to seek compensation for the damage caused by the Winter War and a decidedly opportunistic readiness to gamble, when a lucrative combination of low risk and huge gains seemed to present itself. The opportunism behind Finland's decision to go to war, as well as the inherent disagreements among the Finns as to what the war was actually about, become apparent when one considers the studied vagueness of Finland's publicized war aims and the palpable contradictions present in its conduct as a belligerent and as an occupying power.

Officially, Finland defended her involvement in the fighting because of having come under renewed Soviet aggression. To this effect, a series of foreign political documents detailing the Soviet pressure upon Finland was published in the United States as 'The Blue-White Book of Finland'. The pressure had, according to this official explanation, finally led to Soviet military aggression, forcing the Finnish parliament in late June 1941 to find the country again at war with the Soviet Union. This explanation was not entirely devoid of a factual basis, as the Soviet air force had indeed been the first to strike, and staged a large-scale attack against Finnish cities and military targets on 25 June 1941. The Soviet Union dealt in exactly the same way with Hungary, whom it also came to consider a *de facto* enemy power. As in the case of Hungary, however, Finland had naturally enough long ago decided on joining the hostilities and had allowed the German armed forces to use its territory as a staging area for acts of war against the Soviet Union. The Soviet air attacks, while politically playing into Finnish hands, only affirmed an existing state of affairs.[17]

The majority of Finns in 1941 needed little persuasion to go to war against the Soviet Union. The popular understanding of the Finnish war aims centred upon the recouping of the losses of the Winter War. That was also where the unanimity ended. Nevertheless, the triumphant months of victorious war against the Soviet Union in 1941, when anything seemed possible, released and brought to the fore many pent-up forces within Finnish society. To the radical right, never reconciled to the ideas and values of liberal democracy and republican life, there seemed now to be at hand a unique historical opportunity to destroy the Soviet Union and thus solve, by the sword, Finland's long-standing security problem. At the same time, a chance to realize even the most feverish dreams of extending the borders of 'Greater Finland' to the shores of the White Sea beckoned. It is small wonder that the Finnish radical right, nationalist activists and all those disappointed by the way that the Finnish state had turned out after the civil war saw that the moment to fulfil Finland's destiny had struck. Wartime policy-making with regard to Finland's war aims, as well as her conduct during the war, thus became a battleground between nationalism and radical anti-communism with authoritarian leanings on the one hand and with the enduring tradition of Scandinavian legalism on the other.

Once battle had been joined, the dangerous legacy left by the experience of the Winter War also became visible. The Soviet assault upon Finland had seemed to confirm without doubt the very worst fears about the eastern neighbour. The Soviet Union had proven itself to be just as unreliable and dangerous a neighbour as the most extreme right in Finland had always claimed. The result was radicalization, a general narrowing of the field of vision, a willingness to see the conflict in terms of 'either us or them' and a readiness to understand the new war as a final battle in which there could be only one survivor. In other words, an atmosphere conducive to extremism was created out of the bitterness and fear brought about by the experience of the Winter War. Yet, the Finnish public was hardly united by anything more than a common understanding of the necessity and justification of seeking the return of territories lost in the Winter War. This became clearly visible in autumn 1941, when there were several cases of soldiers either hesitating or even refusing to cross the 1939, pre-Winter War borders. Their understanding was that the war was about reclaiming the lost territories, and they had to be cajoled by threats and appeals to strategic necessities to march further into Soviet territory.[18] Many others needed no cajoling, and more confusion with regard to the actual war aims of Finland was to follow, both at home and abroad. The grass-roots conscientious objections overcome and dealt with, Finnish forces advanced in late summer 1941 into Soviet Karelia. Finland, thus, became an occupying power. Signs that the occupiers had no intention of ever leaving were soon visible. In the nationalist vision, the conquest of Karelia was to lead into the establishment of Greater Finland which was to be an ethnically and culturally homogeneous state. Those considered ethnically or politically unfit to participate in the realization of this vision were herded into concentration camps to await deportation.[19]

Within the Finnish prisoner-of-war administration, another ominous development took place, as Soviet prisoners began by late 1941 to die in droves.

The reasons were all too familiar, hunger and disease, but the death toll was embarrassingly high. The overall mortality of Soviet prisoners-of-war in Finnish custody reached almost 30 per cent. The explanation is to be sought in a deliberate policy of neglect, sharpened by the general shortage of foodstuffs and the wildly under-resourced prisoner-of-war administration. A notable racist undercurrent is also detectable in explaining the mortality rates, as ethnic Russian prisoners were to suffer the most of all the Soviet nationalities in Finnish hands. Moreover, the mass deaths occurred during the months of greatest confidence in German and Finnish victory in 1941 and 1942, underscoring both the gravity of the situation in the prisoner-of-war camps and the fact that mass deaths could be prevented once victory began to look less assured.[20]

The Finnish security police and military authorities also came to take a direct part in the Nazi ideological and racial war unleashed on the Soviet Union. In the last days of June 1941, a German security police unit with a long official name, *Einsatzkommando der Sicherheitspolizei und des Sicherheitsdienstes beim Armeeoberkommando Norwegen, Befehlsstelle Finnland*, was set up. The task of the unit was to wage an ideological and racial war against the Soviet Union similar to that waged by the larger *Einsatzgruppen* on the more southerly sectors of the German eastern front. Motivated primarily by radical anti-communism, Finnish authorities not only sanctioned the activities of the *Einsatzkommando* on Finnish territory, but also actually assisted the work by lending it a group of Finnish security police officers and interpreters.[21]

The very existence of the *Einsatzkommando* was successfully buried in the archives after the war. The German forces in the northernmost part of the eastern front could never penetrate Soviet territory far enough for significant numbers of enemy civilians to fall into their hands. The planned German-Finnish police operation to hunt down and execute active communists and Jews after the occupation of the only major urban centre of the area, Murmansk, never took place. As a result, the *Einsatzkommando* was forced mainly to concentrate on the Soviet prisoners-of-war in German hands. The Finnish prisoner-of-war administration also handed over more than 500 prisoners suspected of communist activities. The total count of victims of the *Einsatzkommando Finnland*, as the unit was unofficially known, probably comes down to around 1,000, lying in still unlocated mass graves. Nevertheless, lack of progress in the north caused the SS ultimately to reconsider the position of its northernmost *Einsatz*-unit, and it was disbanded in November 1942. No charges were ever filed in Finland, and a post-war investigation by the authorities of the Federal

Republic of Germany came to naught because the police was unable to identify any suspects on the basis of eye-witness statements.[22]

Throughout the war against the Soviet Union, Finland remained torn between ideological fervour, strategic necessity and political prudence in foreign policy. Majority opinion was solidly behind the reconquest of pre-1939 territories, but not much else. The alliance with Germany was characterized by dependency in foodstuffs, fuel and armaments, as well as by a distinct sense of unease, because the sensibilities of the western Allies had to be taken into account. Britain's alliance with the Soviet Union in 1941 had naturally enough been greeted with outrage in Finland, and Britain also went on to declare war on Finland in December 1941, but the United States never lost its political leverage in Finland. Nevertheless, as the war unfolded, Finland prepared to take whatever would fall into its lap – including large tracts of territory from Soviet Karelia as well as booty from a conquered Leningrad – while maintaining that the country was fighting in a coincidentally parallel, but separate, conflict from that between Germany and the Soviet Union. In November 1941, the president of Finland, Risto Ryti, formulated the official policy line to an American journalist: 'Finland is fighting its own separate war and our army will not march further than to a previously agreed-upon line of defence.'[23]

As a result of Finland's limited strength on the ground – the Army comprised a mere sixteen divisions – the Finnish leadership was often forced to play a waiting game in which no risks would be taken without the main burden being carried, and a prior decisive success achieved, by the Germans. After having by the end of 1941 reached the previously agreed lines on the Karelian Isthmus and Soviet Karelia, Finnish troops went onto the defensive. German entreaties for Finnish participation in a renewed push to cut the Murmansk railway line, or in attacks towards Leningrad from the north, were not accepted due to the anticipated high casualties and heavy political cost involved. Most prominently, the United States took an active role in dissuading the Finns from further aggressive operations against vital Soviet interests. In the absence of further convincing German successes, and in the presence of clearly voiced potential foreign political repercussions, the Finnish political and military leadership showed little enthusiasm towards the German initiatives.

However, during the heady summer and autumn months of 1941, Finland stood to gain much more should the Soviet Union really collapse from the weight of the German onslaught. The same people in Finland who in the years 1918–22 had seen their visions dashed were now occupying several influential positions in Finnish society. To them, it was clear that fate was offering a golden chance once more to realize the vision of an ethnically homogeneous, politically united 'Greater Finland.' It was equally clear that a decisive German victory over the Soviet Union would lead to a German-dominated Europe, in which the influence of Britain and the United States would be heavily curtailed. There would then be no need to take into account their reactions, and Finland would be free to realize its own Finnic empire as it saw fit. Symptomatic of this kind of thinking were the preparations the Finnish occupiers took to put their presence in Soviet Karelia on a permanent footing. Most importantly, preparations for an ethnic cleansing of the area were underway soon after the arrival of the occupiers, with the representatives of Russian and other 'alien' nationalities herded to concentration camps to await eventual deportation and settlement of the area by new Finnic immigrants.[24]

If there was, both at home and abroad, justified confusion as to Finland's actual war aims, Finland was fighting officially for limited objectives. This was the line developed within the political and military leadership well before the commencement of hostilities. And the further the war progressed, the more useful the claim to be waging a separate war became. In September 1943, the Prime Minister Edwin Linkomies expounded to foreign journalists the vital distinctions one ought to keep in mind, despite the heavy presence of German troops in northern Finland and the country's acute dependency on German deliveries of supplies:

> We are not participants in the war between great powers; we are not tied to anybody or dependent on anyone. It is not our fault that Germany is fighting the same enemy, even though it has made us co-belligerents with Germany. One must particularly stress Finland's independent and exceptional position, and its right to act freely.[25]

From disillusionment to disentanglement

By late 1942, disillusionment about the German alliance had begun to grow in military and political circles in Finland. In February 1943, Finnish military intelligence came to a pessimistic appraisal of the situation: Germany would lose the war, and Finland should begin to look for a way out while there still was time. From there began Finland's quest for peace, which finally, in September 1944, led to an armistice with the Soviet Union, the severing of diplomatic relationships with Germany and, by October 1944, to the commencement of military operations against the retreating German troops in Finnish Lapland. This was done at the insistence of the Soviets, and the German retreat and apparent Finnish pursuit were at first conducted under mutually agreed conditions and no clashes of a military nature. The Soviets could nevertheless be fooled for only so long, and eventually their demand for more forceful action resulted in the first shots being fired in anger between the German and Finnish troops in mid-October 1944. The German response was, after an abortive attempt to seize by surprise the Suursaari (Hogland) island in the Gulf of Finland, to put into effect pre-existing plans for the eventuality that Finnish Lapland would have to be evacuated. As a result, the German troops both torched and blew up everything that could be of use to the enemy. The war in Lapland, thus, rapidly turned into a very real conflict, with bitterness for the destruction wrought in Lapland lingering in Finland to this day. After staging a protracted fighting retreat, the last German soldiers vacated Finnish territory by mid-March 1945. For Finland, World War II was finally at an end. The experience of living with the consequences of the war was, however, only just beginning.

After the war, the story of Finland's involvement in the war against the Soviet Union alongside Nazi Germany was most often told in terms of dissociation. At every level, it was claimed, Finland fought her own separate war and never entangled herself in Nazi atrocities. It is this process of post-war selective forgetfulness which makes Finland appear Janus-faced: a country insistent on its western heritage and identity, yet the only democracy to fight on Hitler's side; a country riding on a wave of international sympathy for her defensive struggle in the Winter War, yet seemingly, and, to many contemporaries in the west quite incomprehensibly, ditching all that to ally herself happily with the Nazis; a country supposedly fighting a separate war, yet one with half of the country a German-controlled theatre of war and one with unmistakable expansionist, ethnically exclusive and, as we now know, murderously anti-communist tendencies lurking just behind the public face. The Finnish social and political system was eventually able to contain these influences, but the damage that by then had been done left enduring ambiguities about the way the war was subsequently viewed among the Finns.[26]

In the emerging post-war era, the wisdom of maintaining distance from Nazism was clear enough for everyone to see. The influence of the Soviet Union in Finland was ubiquitous. There were real fears that history might be used to discredit the Finnish wartime leadership and society, perhaps paving the way for a communist coup and making Finland a people's democracy, or a Soviet republic. Now, such fears feel remote and unreal, but the mindset to which they gave rise is still very much with us. To be able to interpret Finland's past in a way meaningful for today, the new generation of Finnish historians has to shed the political wisdom of a bygone era.[27]

Notes

1. For an English-language general work on the Finnish Civil War, see Upton, A. F. (1980), *The Finnish Revolution 1917–1918*. Minneapolis: The University of Minnesota Press; Maude, G. (2010), *Aspects of the Governing of the Finns*. New York: Peter Lang Publishing, p. 35.
2. Vares, V. (2010), 'Pakinoitsija Ollin talvisota: huumorilla moraalia kotirintamalle', in T. Lintunen and L. Clerc (eds), *Kenen sota? Uusia näkökulmia talvisotaan*. Ajankohta 2010. Turku: Helsinki and Turku Universities, p. 155.
3. Ahti, M. (1987), *Salaliiton ääriviivat: Oikeistoradikalismi ja hyökkäävä idänpolitiikka 1918–1919*. Espoo: Weilin+Göös, pp. 258–60.
4. Ahti (1987), 108–10.
5. Ibid., 174–8, 190–3.
6. Palmgren, R. (1980), *Tekstejä nuoruuden vuosikymmeniltä*. Helsinki: Love-kirjat, p. 163.
7. Siltala, J. (1985), *Lapuan liike ja kyyditykset 1930*. Helsinki: Otava, pp. 119–25.
8. Read, A. (2008), *The World on Fire: 1919 and the Battle with Bolshevism*. London: Jonathan Cape, pp. 328–30.
9. Peltovuori, R. (1975), *Saksa ja Suomen talvisota*. Helsinki: Otava, p. 25.
10. Vares, V. (1986), *Hakaristin kuva: Kansallissosialistinen Saksa Suomen johtavassa puoluelehdistössä sisä- ja ulkopoliittisena tekijänä 1933–1939*. Turku: University of Turku, pp. 14–21, 64.
11. Brooke, J. (1984), *Talvisodan kanarialinnut: Brittivapaaehtoiset Suomessa 1940–41*. Porvoo: WSOY, pp. 40–1. A supplemented version of this work exists in English: Brooke, J. (1990), *The Volunteers: The Full Story of the British Volunteers in Finland 1939–1941*. Upton-upon-Severn: Justin Brooke.
12. Jokipii, M. (1987), *Jatkosodan synty: Tutkimuksia Saksan ja Suomen sotilaallisesta yhteistyöstä 1940–41*. Helsinki: Otava, p. 105.
13. Harold Macmillan to Gösta Serlachius, London March 29th, 1940, Gösta Serlachius, Yleistä (4), Div. brev betr. Kriget 1939–40 och brittiska frivilligkåren, Serlachius-museot.
14. Tarkka, J. (1987), *Ei Stalin eikä Hitler: Suomen turvallisuuspolitiikka toisen maailmansodan aikana*. Helsinki: Otava, pp. 22–4; the quote is taken from

Rasila, V., Jutikkala, E. and Kulha, K. K. (1976), *Suomen poliittinen historia 1905–1975*. Porvoo: Werner Söderström Osakeyhtiö, p. 224.
15 Jokipii (1987), p. 117.
16 Ziemke, E. F. (1963), *Saksalaisten sotatoimet Pohjolassa 1940–1945*. Porvoo: Werner Söderström Osakeyhtiö, pp. 280–1. The English-language original of this work is titled *The German Northern Theater of Operations 1940–1945*, published in 1960 in Washington DC by the Office of the Chief of Military History, United States Army.
17 Jokipii (1987), pp. 610–11.
18 Heinilä, H. (2005), 'Vanhan rajan ylitys hyökkäysvaiheessa 1941 jalkaväkimiesten näkökulmasta', in J. Leskinen and A. Juutilainen (eds), *Jatkosodan pikkujättiläinen*. Porvoo: Werner Söderström osakeyhtiö, pp. 286–94.
19 Laine, A. (1982), *Suur-Suomen kahdet kasvot: Itä-Karjalan siviiliväestön asema suomalaisessa miehityshallinnossa 1941–1944*. Helsinki: Otava.
20 Silvennoinen, O. (2012),'Limits of Intentionality: Soviet Prisoners-of-War and Civilian Internees in Finnish Custody', in Kinnunen, T. and Kivimäki, V. (eds): *Finland in World War II: History, Memory, Interpretations*. Leiden: Brill.
21 Silvennoinen, O. (2010), *Geheime Waffenbrüderschaft: Die sicherheitspolizeiliche Zusammenarbeit zwischen Finnland und Deutschland 1933–1944*. Darmstadt: Wissenschaftliche Buchgesellschaft, pp. 164–71.
22 Silvennoinen (2010), pp. 177–227.
23 Vilkuna, K. (1962), *Sanan valvontaa: Sensuuri 1939–1944*. Helsinki: Otava, p. 75.
24 Silvennoinen (2012), pp. 382–90.
25 Vilkuna, *Sanan valvontaa*, p. 79.
26 Silvennoinen, O. (2009), 'Still Under Examination: Coming to Terms with Finland's Alliance with Nazi Germany'. *Yad Vashem Studies*, 37, (2), 67–92. The classic first, and later much criticized, presentation of the so-called 'driftwood theory', describing Finland as a helpless victim of circumstances and as a 'detached co-belligerent' in a German-Soviet war was put forward in 1960 by Prof Arvi Korhonen in Korhonen, A. (1960), *Barbarossa-suunnitelma ja Suomi: Jatkosodan synty*. Porvoo: Werner Söderström Osakeyhtiö.
27 Meinander, H. (2009), *Suomi 1944: Sota, yhteiskunta, tunnemaisema*. Helsinki: Siltala, pp. 188–9, 228–9.

Figure 4 In Denmark, over 50 years after the war, a 1999 article in the leading newspaper, *Berlingske Tidende,* revealed A. P. Møller's business links with Nazi Germany that shook Denmark and led to a bitter dispute between the publisher and one of its major shareholders. [With kind permission of *Berlingske Tidende.*] *Avisreproduktion v. Statens Avissamling – Statsbiblioteket*, Aarhus, Denmark.

8

'The Five Evil Years': National Self-image, Commemoration and Historiography in Denmark 1945–2010

Trends in Historiography and Commemoration

Claus Bundgård Christensen

There is no period in modern Danish history that interests Danes more than the so-called 'Five Evil Years': the German occupation of Denmark from 9 April 1940 to 4 May 1945. One can get an idea about the scale of interest from the number of books and articles about the period, which in the year 2000 had reached almost 10,000 titles.[1] The numbers today are probably around 15,000. It is a considerable amount in a country with a little over five million inhabitants. The interest in the occupation goes beyond articles and books. Temporary exhibitions about the occupation are often a major attraction, and scarcely a month goes by without television or newspapers bringing 'news' of the 'The Five Evil Years'. Thus, it is no coincidence that the largest Danish film success, measured by number of tickets sold, is about the Danish resistance movement.[2]

The purpose of this chapter is to outline the major trends in the commemoration, historiography and interpretation of the German occupation of Denmark. It will present the different phases of historiography, the public debate and the changes in scholarly discourse.

The discussion on how the occupation should be perceived and understood started almost immediately after the announcement by the BBC, in its Danish broadcast from London on the evening of 4 May 1945, that the German forces in Denmark had surrendered. The very first interpretations were mainly to be found in the daily press, but hot on their heels came a series of hastily assembled works.³ These works were almost all written by people who had been decision makers during the occupation, who in this way found a platform to justify their cohabitation or cooperation policy with the German occupiers.⁴ The publications had close links to the major political parties, mainly the Social Democrats and the Conservative Party, and were an expression of what the two historians Claus Bryld and Anette Warring have described as a hegemonic and basic narrative of the occupation. The basic narrative told a story in which almost all Danes – politicians, resistance fighters and ordinary citizens – took part in passive or active resistance against the German invaders. According to this interpretation, only a miserable little group of traitors was not a part of the opposition.

The early post-war publications not only reflected the political positioning of the authors but also represented a clear entertainment and commercial aspect. This commercial side was clearly expressed through a genre called saboteur novels. Between May and December 1945 alone, more than 170 such novels were published. The commercial aspect of the occupation still exists. Saboteur novels have, however, been replaced by history books of a rather variable quality. Good examples of more recent publications with a commercial aspect are titles about the more sinister aspects of the war years, such as the German-Danish Corps and persons associated with the German terror in Denmark. Journalists, especially, seem to have specialized in this genre.⁵

The interpretation of the occupation in the first decades after the war has often been described as a consensual myth according to which the period 1940–45 is understood in the light of a broad national unity that relegated social and political problems to the margins. An important point in the consensual myth is that the politicians and the resistance movement fought together, with the politicians acting as a sort of shield around the illegal resistance. Soon, however, a critical counter-narrative seriously challenged this interpretation. It is remarkable how the interpretation in Denmark in the first decades after the war is in many ways similar to the early French historians' 'shield and dagger' understanding of Vichy, Pétain and his associates' role in France. The Vichy regime was understood as a shield against German diktat and De Gaulle and the resistance as the dagger. This discourse was first challenged by Robert O. Paxton's *Vichy France - Old Guard and New Order* of 1972.⁶ Correspondingly, in Danish historiography, the Danish shield and dagger interpretation was initially challenged by several historians in the 1970s.

In the late 1950s, the first academic study on the occupation was published. It was a dissertation called 'Contact with England' (*Kontakt med England.*) The author, a high school teacher and historian Jørgen Hæstrup, was himself a veteran of the resistance movement. His study concerned the contacts between SOE and the Danish Resistance Movement. 'Contact with England' was a pioneering work. Hæstrup's next book, entitled *Secret Alliance (Hemmelig alliance)*, became an example of how the occupation history could have serious political consequences in the post-war years. In *Secret Alliance*, Hæstrup demonstrated how the communist resistance movement had been undersupplied with weapons from the resistance movement's military leadership which was called the 'Small General Staff'. The man responsible for this was Viggo Hjalf. But problems arose because in 1959 he was Denmark's army chief. Nevertheless, Hjalf admitted openly to the press what had happened.[7] He apparently expected his conduct to be understood in the light of the urgent threats of the Cold War. He was, however, wrong. What Hjalf did not appreciate was that his confession undermined the idea of consensus and the image of a united nation. Shortly after the revelation of his wartime conduct, Hjalf had to resign as Danish army chief.

There can be no doubt that the impact of *Secret Alliance* was important. Even the Parliament began to discuss the occupation and what had actually happened during the war. As a consequence, politicians decided to launch a research project about the occupation years. The project was named the 'Publishing Company of Denmark's Recent History' (*Udgiverselskabet for Danmarks Nyeste Historie*), usually referred to by its abbreviation, DNH. In the DNH, a selected group of young historians received funding and exclusive access to the archives. During the 1970s, this group, under the leadership of Hæstrup, published a number of books and doctoral dissertations that had a considerable influence on the historiography of the occupation. The DNH dissertations were all conceived and written within the framework of traditional political history. The fields of study varied, but all works produced by DNH scholars continue to be considered important studies to this day.

As a consequence of the research on the occupation in the 1970s, the basic post-war narrative was severely challenged. Historians from the DNH demonstrated that there had been a much more variegated situation during the war. However, this research had a relatively limited influence on commemoration. Within the DNH project, two dissertations in particular can be regarded as being seminal to the interpretation of the occupation. The first was Hans Kirchhoff's dissertation, completed in 1979, on 'The August Rebellion in 1943' (*Augustoprøret 1943*), about the great strikes in the summer of 1943. These strikes triggered the resignation of the Danish government in part as a result of German demands for the reintroduction of the death penalty for sabotage. The death penalty was abolished in 1930 but had not been carried out since the late nineteenth century. Kirchhoff's thesis was a very clear break with the consensus myth. In his dissertation, Kirchhoff documented how the breakdown of the cooperation policy did not happen because the Danish politicians wanted such a breakdown, but basically because they lost control of the situation with large-scale riots in several cities. This conclusion was in direct opposition to what the political parties had proclaimed after the war. They had stated that they wanted to abandon the cooperation policy because the time was right.

The second work from the DNH that merits attention here was a doctoral dissertation of 1971. In 'The Railway Sabotage in Denmark during World War II' (*Jernbanesabotagen i Danmark under den Anden Verdenskrig*), historian Aage Trommer demonstrated that the resistance movement's widespread sabotage of the railway network in Jutland did not have any important military significance since the operations had not delayed the transportation of German troops from the military bases in Jutland to the front. The actual defence of the thesis was undoubtedly one of the most dramatic at a Danish university in modern times. Former resistance veterans who had asked to speak were so hurt, sad and angry that they were not able to say anything. A leading character from the resistance movement described Trommer's thesis as pure '*nonsense*' and devoid of any regard for the extent to which the operations also had an influence on the morale of both German soldiers and the Danish public.[8]

Trommer's relations with the veterans did not improve when, a few years later, he published a study that established that resistance fighters were not recruited broadly from the Danish population but mainly came from the outer fringes of Danish politics.[9] Trommer's publication was yet another confrontation with the basic narrative, since his results showed that it was neither an integrated nor a broad part of Danish society that participated in the resistance movement, at least not for the period 1942–44. Scholars like Trommer who identified problems in the consensus approach and the basic narrative did not, however, have any effect on the popular commemoration of the resistance. Their limited impact was in fact evidence of the distance between historians and large parts of the population.

The widespread interest in the occupation, which manifested itself in the summer of 1945, began relatively rapidly to decline. The Cold War and domestic affairs such as the continued rationing and housing shortages in the latter half of the 1940s became more relevant than the events of the war years. Under the influence of the Cold War, the commemoration of the war years achieved a different meaning from that which it had previously had. The occupation assumed a mythological character that pushed the more uncomfortable issues aside and concentrated on national unity. The occupation became a story about democracy versus dictatorship and good versus evil.[10] The basic narrative was, thus, very strong in the early commemoration of the war years. In 1955, 10 years after the liberation, politicians still had a firm grip on the public celebrations and their content.[11] People were taught that politicians represented the element of so-called passive resistance, while the resistance movement took care of active resistance. The overall message was that both kinds were equally important and worked together.

By 1970, the thirtieth anniversary of the start of the occupation, it became clear there had been a generational change. The young men from the resistance movement had grown older and more powerful. The generation of politicians from World War II had died or retired. In 1970, the Royal Theatre in Copenhagen planned to celebrate the liberation with a play about the occupation. It was about an ordinary family during the war. The focus was not on resistance but on everyday problems such as blackouts, shortages and rationing. By April 1970, several former members of the resistance movement had attacked the Royal Theatre and the play. Their criticism was aimed at the fact that the play was not about fighting the Germans but rather expressed what they regarded as grey everyday materialism. Therefore, the play was perceived as an insult to the memory of the resistance movement and the liberation it was supposed to celebrate. In the wake of the criticism, the theatre decided to cancel the play.[12]

The occupation was not, however, discussed in public only in relation to jubilees. The history of the war years has time and time again proven to be very helpful when politicians wanted to send a message to the public. A good example of this is the debate about membership of NATO in the post-war years. The main slogan for supporters of membership was 'Never again a ninth of April'. The reference to the weak defence that neutral Denmark could muster in 1940 was obvious.

Another good example of the political use of occupation history is the vote on joining the EEC in 1972. The communists proclaimed the EEC as a Nazi project of the same kind as that fought by the resistance movement during the war. In general, those who opposed EEC membership, from both left and right, often used references to the occupation and the resistance movement in their propaganda and the political debate.[13]

In recent years, references to the occupation years have been prominent in two types of public debate: on asylum legislation and on foreign policy, especially regarding Denmark's participation in the military operations in Iraq and Afghanistan. The debate about asylum legislation and immigration from Muslim countries became a major topic in Danish politics during the 1980s. It was a decade when the right wing stood strongly in both parliament and public debate. Many of the right-wing intellectuals who criticized the liberal asylum legislation came from the same group that had opposed EEC membership in the 1970s. The use of the 'Five Evil Years' in their rhetoric was also more or less the same. Those who were opposed to liberal immigration often identified themselves with the resistance movement, while the politicians who accepted the liberal asylum legislation were compared with the members in parliament who cooperated with the foreign invaders during the war.[14] The debate about immigration remains quite intense. The same can be said about the frequent use of comparison with the occupation years in this debate. *Dansk Folkeparti*, which is among the largest political parties in Denmark and opposed to liberal asylum and emigration legislation, often uses the war years as a point of reference.

The most recent and prominent example of the use of occupation history for contemporary purposes comes from the former Danish prime minister and NATO Secretary General, Anders Fogh Rasmussen. Similar to the use of the slogan 'Never again a ninth of April' during the Cold War, Fogh Rasmussen used the occupation to justify the current Danish foreign policy that has led to Danish soldiers participating in military operations in Iraq and Afghanistan. In a speech to the Danish Naval Academy in August 2003, on the occasion of the 60th anniversary of the resignation of the Danish government in the summer of 1943, Fogh Rasmussen attacked the policy of cooperation. He repeated this critique several times and in harsh terms labelled the policy of cooperation as a moral betrayal and a naïve understanding of the German Nazi regime.[15] As late as March 2010, Fogh Rasmussen repeated his criticism of the policy in a major Danish newspaper. This was the first time that a Prime Minister had distanced himself from the political line pursued in Denmark from 1940 to 1943. All his predecessors had been deeply rooted in the basic post-war narrative.

The political usefulness of the occupation was also evident at the two liberation jubilees in 1985 and 1995. In 1985, the Prime Minister Poul Schlüter celebrated the anniversary of the liberation of Denmark with an official speech. The speech was held at the prominent Town Hall Square in Copenhagen. But the situation ended in a fiasco as the Prime Minister had to hold his speech sheltered behind police shields, as left-wing activists threw eggs and tomatoes at him. These radical groups stressed that the resistance fighters of today were those who fought against the modern structure of society. This incident during a prime ministerial speech was basically an expression of how increasingly widespread the uses of the occupation to legitimize particular contemporary political beliefs had become, without any real connection to the historical facts of the period.[16]

This was also reflected in the fiftieth anniversary ten years later in 1995.[17] The great anniversary triggered an intense debate about the so-called Peace Sculpture created by artist Elle Mie Ejdrup. She had a created a sculpture that enabled a laser beam, fixed on German Atlantic Wall bunkers on the Danish west coast, to connect Denmark and Germany. The laser beam was to act as a symbol of reconciliation and peace between the two nations. The project was met, however, with sharp protests from a number of prominent veterans from the resistance movement. The criticism pointed to the unclear perception of the sculpture – was it a symbol of reconciliation with Germany or an insult to the victims of the Nazi terror? Some even described the sculpture as Nazi art that could have been created by Hitler's chief architect, Albert Speer. Those who looked more positively on the peace sculpture frequently appeared to be those with moralizing pacifist views. The general trend was that the debate was not firmly based on any real knowledge or reflection about the period. The culmination came with a total fiasco on 4 May 1995 when the laser beam was turned on, because the laser beam was interrupted at several points, allegedly because of sabotage!

It was not only commemoration that had changed since the 1960s and 1970s. Danish historians concluded a series of studies in the years 1990–2011 with the focus on topics and problems that the members of the DNH project did not deal with. This earlier omission was partly because these topics did not interest the previous generation who primarily focused on traditional political history, and partly because these topics had earlier been perceived as taboo. It was significant that, similar to the earlier DNH scholars, the new groups of younger historians, often born in the 1960s, were critical of the basic narrative. This group of younger historians fixed their focus on more marginalized groups. A pioneering work was Anette Warring's dissertation about the girls who engaged in intimate relations with German soldiers – a group of women who were generally hated in Danish society and received harsh treatment after the war.[18] Other new topics include the approximately 6,000 Danish volunteers in the *Waffen-SS*, the Danish Nazi Party, anti-Semites and members of different groups operating in Denmark such as the German-Danish guard, the police and the terror corps. All in all, the works reflected a great interest in what could be called the traitor group – an interest that is still prevalent. One of the latest studies, published in 2010, covers Danish concentration camp guards in the SS.[19]

A tendency in the above-mentioned studies is the more balanced portrayal given to the traitors' groups. They are not demonized compared with the early post-war year publications, where such groups often were described as degenerates and monsters. It is important to stress that these new studies cannot in any way be described as apologetic (e.g. the study of the *Waffen-SS* volunteers established their participation in the Holocaust and war crimes on the eastern front), but they do to some extent express a more empathetic approach that was unheard of in the early post-war years.[20] Focus on the traitors was not limited to scholars. The public also showed a great interest in them. As an example, the book published in 1998 – 'Under Swastika and Danish Flag' (*'Under hagekors og Dannebrog'*) – about *Waffen-SS* volunteers became one of the best-selling books about the occupation in decades. In 2011, it had sold about 40,000 copies. A biography from 2008 about a notorious Danish *Waffen-SS* officer – Christian Frederik von Schalburg, who died on the eastern front – likewise became a bestseller.[21]

Publications about the occupation can still provoke political debate and have consequences in the new century. A good example is found in a book published in 2000 on the Danish arms industry during the war. Here, the authors – who were journalists at the national newspaper *Berlingske Tidende* – demonstrated that the ship-owner, A. P Møller, earned a good return on his shares in an arms factory that sold machine guns to the Germans. This revelation outraged A. P. Møller's son, the powerful businessman Mærsk McKinney Møller. As a result, he decided to sell all his shares in *Berlingske Tidende* in protest, with the consequence that this newspaper, which had been a Danish publication for over 250 years, fell into foreign hands.[22] Symbolically, the publication marked a change in the historiography. An increased focus on economic history gave rise to a number of new and prominent studies. Several younger historians studied economic relationships with Germany, such as agricultural exports and the influence and changes effected in Danish business conditions by German markets.[23]

The studies about traitors, agricultural exports and economic life presented a more detailed and complex picture of the occupation years. In the public and in the press, the results were often regarded as shocking revelations. One example is the above-mentioned study which established that Danish *Waffen-SS* volunteers committed atrocities on the eastern front. Another study demonstrated that

Danish companies used slave labour in the German-occupied territories in eastern Europe.[24] The internationally most celebrated and best-known event in Denmark during World War II is probably the successful escape of the Danish Jews to Sweden in October 1943. It is a well-known fact that this escape was possible only through the help and sacrifice of non-Jewish countrymen. However, this event has in recent years been the object of intense debate since several studies have demonstrated that the fishermen who transported the refugees to Swedish waters were very well paid for their activities.[25]

The reaction in the press and among politicians to studies like the above mentioned testifies to a shift away from the hegemonic and basic narrative towards a moral narrative that is now predominant. This narrative can be observed among scholars, politicians and the press. In the press, new studies are often described as revelations with the claim that the history of the occupation has to be more or less rewritten. More often, such reactions are not based on a solid knowledge but rather are the result of a limited understanding of Denmark's situation during World War II. The same can be said about the political reactions. In several cases, studies have resulted in morally based demands for more research so that the 'truth' about the occupation could finally be revealed.[26]

Will the interest of the Danes in the 'Five Evil Years' eventually dwindle? Scholars who research the Cold War often claim that this period will become the new focus of interest for the historians and public alike. Although it is true that many scholars now study the Cold War, this period has until now failed to overshadow the occupation history in terms of a more general interest. There is no doubt that the basic Second World War narrative after the Cold War has been forced aside and replaced by a more moral narrative. On the one hand, it is a narrative that reflects a more realistic understanding of the period since it allows more unpleasant aspects to be discussed and acknowledged. On the other hand, the new narrative also reflects a more fragmented insight that is expressed in the press and public which allows different groups to use the occupation more or less as they see fit, without any regard for the actual conditions or the problems decision-makers had to deal with at that time.

Notes

1 Lauridsen, John T. (2001), *Samarbejde og modstand. Danmark under den tyske besættelse 1940–45. En bibliografi.* Copenhagen: Det Kongelige Bibliotek-Museum Tusculanums Forlag.

2　The film was released in 2008 and entitled the *Flame and the Lemon* (Flammen og Citronen). It was based on the real story of two men from the resistance who specialized in the liquidation of traitors. In Denmark, the movie sold more than 650,000 tickets.

3　The following is based on Warring, Anette and Bryld, Claus (1998), *Besættelsestiden som kollektiv erindring*. Gylling: Roskilde Universitets Forlag. Warring and Bryld (1998) is the most important study regarding the historiography and commemoration of Denmark and the occupation, 1940–45, in the post-war era.

4　On Danish cohabitation – or cooperation policy during World War II – see Christensen, Claus B., Lund, Joachim, Olesen, Niels Wium, Sørensen, Jacob (2009), *Danmark besat. Krig og hverdag 1940–45* (revised ed). Copenhagen: Informations Forlag.

5　Some of the most criticized is a series of books by journalist Erik Haaest about the infamous HIPO-Corps which helped the Germans in combating the resistance movement. Haaest, Erik (2007), *HIPOFOLK – Lorenzengruppen – danske terrorister i Nazitiden*. Copenhagen: Documentas.

6　Paxton, Robert O. (1972), *Vichy France – Old Guard and New Order 1940–1944*. New York: Columbia University Press.

7　About the case of Hjalf, see Warring and Bryld (1998).

8　Warring and Bryld (1998). About the person from the resistance movement, see Gade, Svend Ove (2011), *Toldstrup-En biografi om en modstandshelt*. Gylling: Gyldendal.

9　Trommer, Aage (1973), *Modstandsarbejde i nærbillede: Det illegale arbejde i Syd – og Sønderjylland under den tyske besættelse af Danmark 1940–45*. Odense: Odense University Studies in History and Social Sciences.

10　See Warring and Bryld (1998).

11　The following is based on Christensen, Lund, Olesen, Sørensen (2009).

12　Warring and Bryld (1998).

13　Sørensen, Niels Arne (2003), 'Danmarkshistoriens vigtigste parentes. Besættelsestidens virkningshistorie', in J. Lund (ed.), *Partierne under pres-demokratiet under besættelsen*. Gylling: Gyldendal.

14　Sørensen, Niels Arne (2003).

15　Christensen, Lund, Olesen and Sørensen (2009).

16　Bryld and Warring (1998).

17　The following is based on Bryld and Warring (1998).

18　Warring, Anette (1994), *Tyskerpiger-under besættelsen og retsopgør*. Copenhagen: Gyldendal.

19　Christensen, Claus Bundgård, Poulsen, Niels Bo, Smith, Peter Scharff (1998), *Under hagekors og Dannebrog. Danskere i Waffen-SS 1940–45*. Gylling:

Høst & Søn; Lauridsen, John T. (2002), *Dansk nazisme 1930-45-og derefter.* Gylling: Gyldendal; Petersen, Andreas Monrad (2002), *Schalburgkorpset og dets medlemmer 1943-45.* Odense: Odense University Studies in History and Social Sciences; Bak, Sofie Lene (2004), *Dansk antisemitisme 1930-45.* Gylling: Aschehoug; Larsen, Dennis (2010), *Fortrængt grusomhed. Danske SS vagter 1941-45.* Gylling: Gyldendal.

20 On participation in war crimes and the Holocaust, see Christensen, Claus Bundgård, Poulsen, Niels Bo, Smith, Peter Scharff (2003), 'The Danish volunteers in the *Waffen SS* and their Contribution to the Holocaust and the Nazi War of Extermination', in Jensen, Mette Bastholm (ed.), *Denmark and the Holocaust.* Odense: Odense Universitetforlag, 2003. For an example of a more emphathetic approach, see Kirkebæk, Mikkel (2008), *Schalburg-En patriotisk landsforædder.* Gylling: Gyldendal.

21 Christensen, Poulsen, Smith (1998); Kirkebæk (2008).

22 Christensen, Lund, Olesen and Sørensen (2009).

23 Lund, Joachim (2005), *Hitlers spisekammer. Danmark og det europæiske storrum 1940-43.* Viborg: Gyldendal; Andersen, Steen (2005), *De gjorde Danmark større. Danske entreprenører i krise og krig 1919-1947.* Copenhagen: Lindhardt og Ringhof; Andersen, Steen (2003), *Danmark i det tyske storrum. Dansk økonomisk tilpasning til Tysklands nyordning af Europa 1940-41.* Copenhagen: Lindhardt og Ringhof; Nissen, Mogens R. (2005), *Til fælles bedste-det danske landbrug under besættelsen.* Copenhagen: Lindhardt og Ringhof.

24 Lund (2005).

25 Bak, Sofie Lene (2011). *Nothing to speak of. Wartime experiences of the Danish Jews 1943-45.* Copenhagen: Danish Jewish Museum; Mogensen, Michael, Rasmus Kreth (1995), *Flugten til Sverige.* Gylling: Gyldendal.

26 See the newspaper *Information*, 5 May 2005. The political party *Dansk Folkeparti* here demanded the appointment of a commission to investigate the war years.

Figure 5 Norway's *Dagbladet* headline from 2012. 'Hitler's secret trains through Sweden.' The article re-examines the controversial transits that remain actively recalled and discussed in both countries. [With kind permission of *Dagbladet*.]

9

Hitler's Norwegian Legacy

Ole Kristian Grimnes

It is a characteristic of Norwegian occupation history that it draws more attention from the general public than any other period in Norwegian history and that the public develops its own ideas and images of the era. These ideas and images are heavily influenced by the mass media, and much of the debate on occupation history is carried out in the media. Academic historians participate in this debate, but their voice is only one among several and not necessarily the most influential. Still, these debates cannot be discarded by serious scholarship partly because they may elicit new research and provide the broader background against which this research should be understood and partly because at times real insights are won in these debates. Also, academic scholars are not the only ones who do serious research. So do also journalists of various kinds and amateur historians, their work ranging from the rather uninteresting from a scholarly point of view to highly valuable contributions to the history of the occupation. An interesting question is whether this intermingling of scholarly, journalistic and amateur research and mass media representation is even more marked in Norway than in other countries and, if so, whether this can be explained by an amalgamation of high and low culture which is perhaps more of a hallmark of Norwegian than, say, of Swedish or Danish society. Be that as it may, scholars specializing in the history of the war years certainly deal with a sprawling field in which they must often go to the media instead of to their scholarly journals and books to find out what is going on in the field.

The interest in the war years has been so widespread and pervasive that, characteristically, it has spawned a new branch of research, that of inquiring into the collective memory of those years. This type of research encompasses in principle all forms which remembrance of the occupation assumes. Collective memory may be seen as a unifying factor in a post-war national context, suited to consolidating the patriotic and cohesive sentiments of society. Or it may be viewed more as a battle field where diverging memories clash and different groups in society participate in a contest for memorial hegemony, with dominant actors or marginal groups trying to influence the basic national narrative. In this process, not only what is being brought forward and hallowed is of interest to the scholars but also what more or less consciously falls into oblivion. The study of collective memory is legitimate in its own right and it may throw light on the war years as such. But it does pose a challenge to those who primarily want to know what the war years were really about. Collective memory is by its very nature highly selective and if it is taken to represent reality, as it once was, a skewed and distorted picture emerges.

The German invasion of Norway in 1940 came as a devastating shock to the Norwegians who had not participated in any war since 1814. One of its most obvious consequences was to set off a fundamental reorientation in Norway's defence and foreign policy. The country had pursued a policy of neutrality during World War I and of non-alignment in the interwar period. This policy was broken in literally a matter of minutes in the early hours of 9 April 1940 when the Norwegian government refused to bow to the German demand for surrender and the next day confirmed its resolve to resist. Through its legal and legitimate authorities, the King and the government, from June 1940 resident in Britain, Norway continued to be a belligerent country for the remainder of the war.

At the same time, war and occupation produced a more profound change in the Norwegian mentality, which meant that there would be no return to the policy of neutrality and non-alignment. The lesson that was drawn from the German invasion was that the position of a small state like Norway would always be precarious. The country, therefore, must be prepared to defend itself and would have to build a much stronger military force than the weak one which confronted the Germans in 1940. Likewise, if the chronic antagonism between the great powers took on a deeper and more critical and permanent character, as it had in the late 1930s, Norway must choose a side and ally itself with one or more of the great powers with which it wanted to be associated. Consequently, after the war, Norway rearmed, by contrast with the disarmament of the interwar period, and in 1949 joined NATO, which has since been a cornerstone of Norwegian foreign policy, again contrasting sharply with the interwar period. A comparison with Sweden shows how significant the war experience was for the reorientation of Norwegian foreign and defence policy. The essence of Sweden's war experience was that neutrality paid off as Sweden had managed to stay out of the war. So, Sweden stuck to neutrality in the post-war years, whereas the experience of invasion and occupation pushed Norway in the opposite direction.

It is less obvious what war and occupation meant for Norway's attitude towards European integration to which the Norwegians have been deeply ambivalent in all the post-war years and which has split the country into two. Today, of the five Nordic countries, Denmark, Sweden and Finland are members of the European Union, whereas Norway, together with Iceland, has chosen to stay outside. In Norway, this has been the result of two referenda, held in 1972 and 1994, respectively, in which a majority, though admittedly a small one, each time voted against joining the European Community/Union. It is possible that the rejection of such integration has little to do with wartime experience, other factors explaining the outcome of the referenda more adequately. It is more likely, however, that the German invasion and occupation in some diffuse and murky fashion did produce a feeling that evil things come from the continent and that Norway had better remain outside an association or union whose core is precisely that continent. At the very least, anti-German feelings manifestly persisted in post-war Norway for a long time and disappeared only during the 1970s. They may have predisposed a number of Norwegians to vote against membership of the European Economic Community (EEC) in the first referendum of 1972, although it is hard to see them as an explanatory factor behind the result of the second referendum in 1994. All in all, the experience of war and occupation should probably not be rated as more than a subsidiary explanation for why Norway has chosen to stay outside the European Union.

The war in certain ways paved the way for the growth and development of the post-war years in the economic and social sphere, solving problems which had beset the economy and the social system in the interwar years. The Germans drew heavily on Norwegian economic resources during the occupation, partly to build barracks and construct airfields, fortifications and strategically important roads and railways, and partly to develop Norwegian industry in the interests of the German war economy, with the aluminium industry occupying a particularly important place in the German scheme of things. The German demand for labour was, therefore, particularly acute and very soon unemployment, which had remained high in the interwar period, vanished. Public and private debt had marred the economy in the same period, but during the war the abundance of money created by the heavy outlays of the occupation force eliminated this problem. Another blessing was that stark poverty disappeared and expenditure on poor relief was reduced to a minimum. Social inequality lessened and farmers, fishermen and agricultural labourers improved their position relative to other strata in society.

On the other hand, the war created new and pressing problems. Northern Norway was ravaged when German troops withdrew in the winter of 1944-45, practising a scorched earth policy, and it needed to be rebuilt from scratch. In other regions, towns and villages had not been rebuilt after the devastations of the military campaign in 1940. Real capital had been reduced, equipment and machinery were run down, there had not been much maintenance or renewal and there was an acute shortage of housing. All kinds of reconstruction projects loomed large. The country lagged behind new developments in science and technology which had taken place in the outside world. The standard of living had deteriorated appreciably for the majority of the population and almost everything was in short supply and subject to rigid rationing.

Norway came out of the war with a command economy, all aspects of the economy being strictly regulated. In this way, it had been possible to control the economy more efficiently than during World War I even though this time the country not only had to adjust to increasingly scarce resources but also had to bear the burden of an occupation force totalling between three and four hundred thousand men. When the war ended, there was general agreement that the command economy could not be dismantled immediately as this would create chaos, but there was also a consensus that over time it would have to be unravelled. However, to what extent this was to be done was a controversial issue since the bourgeois parties were more anxious to return to the market economy than the socialists, who viewed such an economy with considerable hostility.

Attitudes changed as a result of the war. An overwhelming majority had by the end of the war rallied around the King and to a lesser extent around the government-in-exile and around the resistance movement at home. Only a minority had participated in the more or less permanent organizations and networks of the resistance movement, but as a whole, the population identified itself with resistance and saw it as the expression of their feelings of hostility to the occupation regime and of their hopes and aspirations for liberation and the post-war period. Thus, at the end of the war, a sense of national solidarity pervaded the great majority of the population, disposing it less to the class war and labour conflicts of the interwar years and more to a concerted effort to rebuild the country after the devastation and hard wear and tear of the war. Gone was also a certain disenchantment with parliamentarianism and the weakness of democracy in the interwar years, giving way to a new belief in democracy as an outcome of the victory in war. The counterpart to this solidarity and sense of oneness and the strength of 'us' was the castigation of 'them', the quislings, traitors and collaborators of different sorts. Hateful words were used easily during the occupation and the initial post-war period against those who were considered to have betrayed their country and placed themselves outside the ranks of the genuine patriots. It was generally agreed that they had to be taken to court, and the government-in-exile, together with the resistance movement, had drawn up the guidelines for a settlement with the 'traitors' when the war was over.

Related to the sense of national solidarity and a new optimism and hope for the future was a sense that national solidarity ought to be accompanied by social solidarity. The post-war world ought to be a better world to live in. Thus, the mood of the country was in favour of reform after the war. The Labour Party was better prepared to meet the requirements of this mood than were the bourgeois parties. Indeed, the war set the Labour Party on the road to its greatest triumphs in the twentieth century, enabling it to start building the modern welfare state and, more generally, to put its imprint on society, introducing, it is often said, a whole new order, 'a social democratic order'. In one way, the war only accelerated developments which had started in 1935 when the country's first stable Labour government was appointed. However, the war did play a major role, partly by shaping a favourable background for a party of social reform, partly by laying the foundation for the Labour Party's absolute majority in Parliament in the years 1945–61 and partly by changing its political platform. This change was clearly seen when the Party rejected its legacy of anti-militarism altogether and accepted rearmament and an alliance policy in foreign relations. Even more important, the Party finally gave up traditional socialism and concentrated its efforts on economic and social development. It favoured Keynesianism and a planned economy and laid particular emphasis on developing Norway as an industrial country and modernizing sectors of the economy which were considered backward.

In the command economy which the party inherited from the war, it had a ready-made tool for forming the economy and society in the way it wanted. But it was not only a tool, but also a temptation. The Party had to determine how far it wanted to take the planned economy and only did so after a heated debate among the political parties and in society at large at the beginning of the 1950s. In this debate, the experiences of war played their part as many felt that too much direct state intervention in the economy would smack of totalitarianism and run counter to the democratic ideals over which the war had been fought. As a result of this debate, the party came around to favouring more of a mixed economy than it had done originally and to preferring financial and credit policies instead of direct intervention in managing the economy.

Norwegian nationalism was changed by the war. In Norway, nationalism had traditionally been liberal, and liberal nationalism still held its sway in the interwar period when nationalism came to include even right-wing and fascist currents. The war did away with such currents altogether and seems to have inoculated Norwegians almost wholly against the neo-fascism which other countries have experienced in the post-war period. Yet on 22 July 2011 a 32-year-old Norwegian, Anders Behring Breivik, single-handedly carried out 2 terrorist attacks in Norway in which 77 people were killed. The atrocities sent shock waves through Norwegian society and hit the headlines throughout the world. There is no obvious connection, however, between Breivik's stand and the Norwegian Nazi movement during the war. Breivik is primarily against Islamism, Marxism, multiculturalism and the political elite in western Europe which to him is impregnated with these -isms. He does not favour classical fascism or Nazism, nor their antisemitism or racism, which in his view only draw attention away from the Islamic threat. He is not a Norwegian nationalist and is generally not concerned with Norwegian history, only with European history and the Islamic threat to Europe and its values. He may be closest to fascism in his fascination with violence, and his visions of a paramilitary force, the Knights Templar, who will be the vanguard of his anti-Islamic revolution. There is also the similarity between Breivik and the fascists that both have absolute enemies which give their views an apocalyptic dimension. For Breivik, the enemy is Islam and the Muslims, for the fascists, it is communists and Jews.

The strong anti-fascism of the war years did away with the archaic, Old Norse brand of nationalism which had thrived under the liberal nationalism of the nineteenth century and which was still part of the cultural and political scene in the interwar period. The Norwegian fascist party cultivated this kind of nationalism eagerly, making a point of employing Old Norse symbols and salutations and drawing its inspiration from the Viking age and Norwegian hegemony in the high middle ages. Thus, it compromised the Old Norse components of Norwegian nationalism and made for a more sober and low-key approach to them.

At the same time, the war in a general way watered down traditional nationalism for at least two or three decades, replacing it partly with the democratic patriotism which the war had generated so profusely and partly with an indifference to issues of national identity which was more or less taken for granted and therefore provoked little debate because it was now so unquestioningly mingled with the omnipresent belief in democracy. Cultural nationalism had played a major role in nineteenth- and twentieth-century nationalism in Norway and had given rise to two official languages, one taking Danish as its point of departure but 'norwegianizing' it (*bokmål*), the other basing itself on dialects in the countryside (*nynorsk*). The linguistic issue had, since the beginning of the nineteenth century, been a stock-in-trade of the cultural debate in Norway. *Nynorsk* had been on the offensive since the late nineteenth century and profited more strongly from cultural nationalism than *bokmål*, although they both bore its mark. However, *nynorsk* was weakened when traditional nationalism petered out after the war. The war rendered linguistic nationalism less potent as wartime patriotism did not distinguish between adherents of either language as long as they were anti-fascist.

On the other hand, the post-war mood favoured another approach to the linguistic question. The split between *bokmål* and *nynorsk* was felt not to be in tune with the feeling of national solidarity and the need for a common effort in the reconstruction of the country. Instead, the wind of *samnorsk* – pan-Norwegian – blew strongly. There was a feeling that the two languages ought to become fused at some time in the future. They were so close that it was thought that by a more or less strict bending of them towards each other they would eventually merge. The state adopted *samnorsk* as the official goal of its linguistic policy. This was not conducive to linguistic harmony, however, as adherents of *bokmål* felt that the *samnorsk* policy made *bokmål* suffer more than *nynorsk* and therefore protested strongly. Thus, the linguistic debate continued until the *samnorsk* line was given up later in the post-war era and the debate took on new forms and moved in new directions.

The war meant a turn in Norway's cultural relations with the outside world. Those relations had traditionally been strong in two directions, towards the Anglo-American world and towards the German-speaking part of the continent. Germany used to serve as the entrance to much of the European academic and cultural sphere. Science in Norway was heavily influenced by the Germans, a number of Norwegian engineers received their education and training in Germany and the Lutheran church had its roots in the Reformation which started in Germany and made its way to Norway through Denmark. Norwegian cultural nationalism in the nineteenth century took much of its inspiration from its German equivalent. Famous Norwegian artists like Edvard Grieg were educated in Germany or like Edvard Munch, not to mention Knut Hamsun, won much of their reputation in Germany. In Norwegian schools, German was the most important foreign language. The war put an end to all of this. Instead, Norwegians found their cultural, scientific and linguistic bearings in the Anglo-American sphere to an extent that would have been unthinkable before the war, with the emphasis now being much more on the American than on the English constituent of that sphere.

Let me pose a Nordic question: what is the basic issue which more than any other challenges the nation's self-understanding in each of the Nordic countries? Let me be so bold as to answer that in Finland it is the question how far Finland's war was different from Germany's war. In Sweden, it is the wide range of the neutral country's concessions to Germany. In Denmark, it is the character of the occupied country's policy of state collaboration with Germany. In Norway, the awkward question is why so many, that is more than a tiny minority, joined the fascist party and supported the Norwegian fascist government and its Nazification campaign. It was a special feature of the occupation regime in Norway that the Germans let the country's Nazi party, led by Vidkun Quisling, take over the reins of government under close German supervision and let the government start a Nazification campaign which aimed to turn the Norwegians into national socialists and give the party a firm footing in Norwegian society. During the campaign, party membership rose to an all-time high in the autumn of 1943 with 43,000 members. The party also scored other successes in its Nazification drive before the resistance against it and the turn in the fortunes of war produced its utter failure.

The feeling of uneasiness about the Norwegian Nazis' position during the war is closely related to a never-ending debate since 1945 on the legal proceedings against the Nazis and other collaborators. The *landssvikoppgjør* ('The Settlement with the Traitors'), as the proceedings are called, was possibly not harsher than in other countries. It certainly did not encompass all those extra-legal lynchings which were part of the settlement in France. There probably were no more death sentences in proportion to the population than in other countries. But in one way it was more extensive: not only active but also passive rank-and-file members of the fascist party were convicted of treason. Much of the debate on the *landssvikoppgjør* has centred on this fact.

The reason why the settlement was so extensive can be attributed to the special structure of the occupation regime in Norway. Since the Germans let the Norwegian fascist party obtain a grip on the power of the state and left it to the party to Nazify the population, even passive membership might be seen as a legitimization of a 'traitorous' regime, counting as one measure of its success. In a setting in which there were no votes from nationwide elections, even nominal membership in the party could be taken as a kind of vote and provide the party with some of the legitimacy which it so sorely needed. Still, many have not been convinced by this argument, have thought it odd that passivity could qualify for punishment and would have preferred the settlement to catch only the big fish and not the small fry. They have been strengthened in their conviction by a comparison between the settlement with the political and the economic collaborators. The settlement with the latter was far less extensive and much more concentrated on the big fish.

The *landssvikoppgjør* both expressed and cemented the basis on which the collective memory of the occupation period was constructed in Norway. The memory takes for granted that the vast majority of Norwegians were on 'the right side', being anti-fascist, anti-German and supporters of the Allied cause. They were all part of the 'home front' (*hjemmefronten*) which was a wide-ranging concept, including resistance as an organized or collective movement, but being more far-reaching, encompassing all on 'the right side', suggesting a 'nation-in-arms'. Only a small minority, so the collective memory assumed, had excluded themselves from this nation in such a way as to commit a crime against it, which made them liable to punishment and punished they were, deepening the gulf between the two. In other words, the war produced a master narrative, which is the fashionable term these days, presupposing an all-embracing struggle between freedom and dictatorship, resistance and regime, between good and evil, white and black. It is a narrative which is continuously being maintained by the press, radio, films, popular books, school and cultural institutions, and not so much by what there has been of serious scholarship on the war years.

The notion of a nation-in-arms or a nation-in-resistance is certainly not unique to Norway but it probably has been more hegemonic in this country because political collaboration disappeared as a patriotic option at an early date. Political collaboration means an arrangement in which institutions and persons being considered by a majority of the population to be their legitimate representatives, collaborate with the German organs of occupation. In the early years of the occupation, this arrangement prevailed in western countries like France and Denmark, there were elements of it in Belgium, and even in the Netherlands it had quite a few adherents in 1940–41. In Norway, there were negotiations in the summer of 1940 between the Germans and the Presidency of the national assembly on the establishment of a new government which would disavow the King and government-in-exile and collaborate with the occupying power. However, the negotiations broke down and, on 25 September 1940, the Germans instead supported Vidkun Quisling and the Norwegian Nazi party which received most and later all the ministerial posts in the government. After 25 September 1940, political collaboration was ruled out as an alternative in Norway. The politicians who had participated in the negotiations were severely and almost unanimously criticized after the liberation and were easily marginalized. This meant that a resistance-oriented interpretation of the war years did not have any serious competitor and did not have to face the difficult task of trying to reconcile political collaboration and resistance within the framework of an overall national narrative.

The master narrative and its dominance in the collective memory has been challenged over recent decades. Former members of the Nazi party, SS volunteers, economic collaborators and others who were affected by the *landssvikoppgjør* are met with more empathy, understanding or curiosity than before. They gain more easily access to the media and the publishing houses than in the first post-war decades. More scholarly work is done on different aspects of Nazism and collaboration. Stigmatization by the public is less manifest than it used to be, though at family level the shame produced by the *landssvikoppgjør* may still linger on and be felt by new generations. Former national socialists have received more of a hearing when it comes to the motives behind their actions and encounter more of a willingness to listen to their perception of themselves as Norwegian patriots who fought for the interests of their country. Still, there has been a limit to this rapprochement between the two fundamentally opposite views inherited from the war. A book which treated two veterans on an equal footing, one from the resistance and the other a former SS-volunteer, describing their personal reconciliation sparked off a public debate. In it there might be acceptance of the reconciliation between the two at a purely personal level but little support for the view that both sides fought for national ideals, the only difference being that the one was on the German side, the other on the Allied. The idea of patriotism and national identity is too strongly associated with democracy for such an equality to be accepted.

An important trend in recent years has been an increasing uneasiness not so much about the basic features of the master narrative as about its all too pervasive character. It is pointed out that there are grey zones between the black and white, that the white is not always so white as it seems, nor is the black so black, and that much behaviour during and even after the war simply does not square with the narrative. In recent years, there has been a focus on groups who were treated badly during or after the war by *bona fide* patriots. Sons and daughters of Norwegian Nazi parents have suffered much discrimination, understandably so perhaps during the war as a social boycott of Nazi families was one of the civilian resistance's most potent weapons, but indefensibly so when the discrimination and boycott continued after the war. Norwegian girlfriends of German soldiers were dealt with harshly and shamefully although their behaviour was not unlawful according to the *landssvikoppgjør*. Their offspring have met with difficulties in the post-war world. Recent research has shown how collaborators in prisons and camps awaiting trial were maltreated and that there were limits to the criticism which could legitimately be levelled at the *landssvikoppgjør*. Thus, the reintroduction of democracy and *Rechtsstaat* ideals did not run so smoothly as is usually thought. There was for a time much controversy about the liquidation of informers until an in-depth study of it put an end to the debate. Also, there was for some time a call for a study of the Soviet and other east European prisoners of war in Norway, totalling more than 100,000 persons whom the Germans imported to exploit as a labour force. However, this is a field which by now has been largely covered by research.

Whereas the heroic image has always been a major feature of the master narrative, victimization has become a serious competitor which partly challenges the narrative, partly seeks to be integrated into it. It is often accompanied by a new moralization in the public debate. This is surprising because one would think that moral questions, generated by war and not immediately applicable to today's society, would not be able to elicit such moralizing. But they do, possibly because the master narrative in itself is heavily moral. Thus, it calls forth its opposite as new generations detect that the impact area of the narrative is less than they have been made to believe by the narrative itself and by the strong forces which uphold it.

It is part of Hitler's legacy that the debate on the war years still goes on with seemingly undiminished strength. Many in the new generations take an interest in how these years should be understood and interpreted and how they fit into the ever-continuing process of national self-identification. So how, after the many years of debate, is our view of the occupation period different today from what it used to be? It is a huge question and I shall confine my answer to pointing out four areas in which I believe our understanding of the occupation has changed or ought to change. The four concern collaboration, police, Jews and communists.

'Home front' and 'resistance' are positive concepts and represent ideals with which most Norwegians identify themselves, and much has accordingly been written about them. However, cooperation with the occupation regime was a more widespread phenomenon than resistance. In fact, cooperation between the occupier and the occupied was not only inevitable but even desirable. No occupied society can exist without such cooperation. The concept of '*collaboration*' may be suggested as the right one to get a grip on it. True, it has the disadvantage of being originally a disparaging term, which is unfortunate because it is a cardinal point that much of the cooperation between the Germans and Norwegians was considered legitimate. On the other hand, 'cooperation' seems too innocuous and tinged with overtones of a normal society to be employed as an analytical concept. So 'collaboration' it must be.

Four forms of collaboration can be distinguished. The first form is ideological or political-ideological collaboration which is represented by the Norwegian national socialists. Though their party was a nationalist party and therefore in certain ways strove to distance itself from the Germans, it was chiefly the ally of the occupier ideologically and politically. Ideological collaboration was the most unacceptable form of collaboration. The second form has already been mentioned, political collaboration, which by its very nature was considered legitimate. The third kind was administrative collaboration which entailed the cooperation between German and Norwegian non-Nazi authorities, which was vital for the running of the country, and which was, therefore, considered an acceptable form of collaboration. It held a particular place from April 1940 when the Supreme Court appointed a central administrative council (*Administrasjonsrådet*) in charge of the different ministries until the Germans dissolved it on 25 September of the same year. From then on, non-Nazi civil servants continued to collaborate with the occupier, often in an intricate pattern in which they tried to stay aloof from the Nazi ministers but cooperate with their opposite numbers in the German administration. If political collaboration had continued after 25 September 1940, it is not certain that it would have been very different from administrative collaboration as far as actual policies are concerned. The difference would be in the sharply contrasting sources of legitimacy. Political collaboration in the final analysis rests on popular consent, whereas administrative collaboration is legitimized by sheer necessity, by the generally recognized need for keeping the wheels of society going even in a dictatorially ruled country.

The fourth form was economic collaboration which was widespread on two levels. On one level, industrial firms, farmers and fishermen delivered their products in large quantities to the Germans. On another level, workers, not only in tens of thousands but also in hundreds of thousands, laboured on German sites, building barracks, fortifications, strategic railways and roads, airports and aluminium plants for the Germans. Economic collaboration represents a broad and still to a large extent neglected field in which research is only now starting up. Recent investigations have focused on the eagerness of Norwegian industrialists and capitalists to invest in and assist German construction projects and have also touched on the use of prisoners of war for these projects.

The general attitude towards economic collaboration changed during the war. In the first two years of occupation, it was widely accepted. Later, a gradually dimmer view was taken, and there was more passive sabotage and stigmatization of economic collaborators. The dividing line between legitimate and illegitimate economic collaboration was, however, always hard to draw in a society where the occupier controlled so many of the resources needed to employ and feed the population. The courts, therefore, found it difficult to define more precisely what kind of collaboration was liable to prosecution, trying to distinguish between those who had too eagerly and ostentatiously made too much money through their collaboration and those who had only continued to serve German consumers in the same way as they had served their Norwegian clients before the war. The task was not made any easier by the fact that what had passed as acceptable in 1940 was frowned upon in 1945.

The position of the Norwegian police force during the occupation was pivotal. There has been some research on it, but it still constitutes a field where more research is needed. Police activities ranged from conspicuous collaboration to patent resistance, although, one has to add, collaboration was more salient than resistance. New research has shown how Himmler, the SS, and the German police had high ambitions when they entered Norway. They considered Norwegians to be of the purest Germanic stock which they intended to employ for their own racist purposes. Their avenue to Norwegian society partly went through the Norwegian police which was seen not only as an instrument of law and order but also as a vehicle for the building of a Germanic racist elite under SS auspices. A new ministry of police was established and headed by a Norwegian adherent of the SS, and the Norwegian police was subordinated directly to the German SS and police in Norway. A particular intense Nazification drive was directed at the police and was crowned with considerable success as about half of the policemen became members of the Norwegian Nazi Party. The new ministry organized its own state police, *Stapo*, which set upon the enemies of the regime and cooperated closely with the *Gestapo*. In all this, there was cooperation but increasingly also rivalry between the Norwegian Nazi party and the German SS. A good deal of what the police, and especially the state police, did was collaboration of an illegitimate kind. Some of it was legitimate as there was a recognized need for a force which could investigate ordinary crime and maintain law and order, an activity which might also require contact and cooperation with the Germans. Finally, much police work was of a regular pre-war kind which did not call for any relations with the Germans at all. But to disentangle the whole complex of the police and draw the lines between illegitimate and legitimate collaboration and non-collaborative police work is no easy task.

Acts of resistance gradually emerged within the police force. Much of it was in the shape of confidential warnings about coming raids and arrests. Within the state police, a small nucleus of resisters developed who in a more systematic manner issued such warnings. A clandestine police leadership was established which issued secret directives about how the police ought to behave in certain situations but was chiefly engaged in planning and preparing for the liberation when a reliable police had to spring into action. The growing mood of resistance worried the Germans and provoked a crisis in August 1943. When a chief superintendent in the police backed up his subordinates who had refused to arrest three girls for not showing up for compulsory labour service, the Germans wanted to set a warning example and have the superintendent executed. They pressured the Norwegian Nazi Government to establish a new police court which sentenced him to death. On the same day, the Oslo police were forced to sign a special declaration of loyalty while German police arrested several hundred policemen of whom approximately one half was later shipped off to a prison camp in Poland. These measures created an acute situation in which the police might have left the service in protest and gone underground, but the clandestine police leadership issued a more prudent directive. It said that the police should remain on duty to assist the public and prevent injustice even though this meant that they would within certain limits have to execute orders contrary to law.

The fate of the Norwegian Jews also exposes some of the problems of the police. In the first post-war decades, little attention was paid to what had happened to the 2,000 Norwegian Jews during the war. To the extent that there was any concern, the fate of the Jews was seen as another example of the evil of fascism in its German and Norwegian guise. In the last two or three decades, with the growing impact of the Holocaust on the European conscience, the misery of the Norwegian Jews has triggered a soul-searching debate in Norway, too, and new and divergent views have been expressed. First, it should be pointed out that in Norway there was a division of labour between the Germans and the domestic Nazi government and its police. The Germans left it to the Norwegians to carry out the arrest of the Jews in autumn 1942. The Germans only took over in Oslo harbour when the Jews embarked on the ship that would convey them to the continent and Auschwitz. The traditional view has been that the Holocaust in Norway was a purely German and Norwegian Nazi affair. The Quisling government and its heavily Nazified police were responsible.

However, new voices have pointed out that the Holocaust in Norway was a Norwegian affair, stressing not Norwegian Nazi, but just Norwegian, contrasting it with countries where the German and not the local police was responsible. Even if the arrest of the Jews was mainly the work of the state police and other Nazified parts of the police, non-Nazified segments of it also participated. The Quisling regime in its execution of the Holocaust drew on the resources of the state and society at large as when bureaucrats registered the Jews, taxi drivers were employed to take the arrested Jews to prison, or engine drivers in trains transported them to internment camps. Another contentious issue has been how in the *landssvikoppgjør* complicity in the Holocaust was not considered particularly incriminating, other charges usually being deemed more important. There has been much debate about a particular Nazi police officer in the state police who was in charge of the arrests in Oslo but who also did valuable work for the resistance movement. After the war he was acquitted by the courts which considered that the officer's assistance to the resistance movement outweighed his involvement in the arrests of the Jews.

There is no doubt that the debate has broadened our view of how the Holocaust cannot be seen as a purely fascist measure, isolated from all other aspects of life in an occupied society. It also involved strata of society outside the circles of the German and Quisling occupation regime. A more tricky question is to what extent this calls for a redistribution of moral responsibility. Such responsibility clearly weighs heavily on the Norwegian Quisling regime, but was it exclusively responsible? Should other Norwegians be considered morally responsible also? A dispute on this issue must involve the question of which moral standard is to be applied, ours or that of the contemporaries. It should also involve a historian's duty to view the agents in the light of the information that was available to them at the time and the options that were within their radius of action.

Resistance is part of the Holocaust story in Norway, a part which is at times put in the shade by the focus on its patently evil side. An unknown number of Jews were warned of the imminent arrests by patriotically minded policemen and many took heed of those warnings and were able to avoid being arrested. The majority of the Jews did after all escape and were assisted by resistance networks in order to reach and cross the border to Sweden. A moot question is whether escaping in itself can be considered an act of resistance as it certainly entailed an act of disobedience against the regime. It depends on whether an act of resistance presupposes not only disobedience on behalf of oneself to escape punishment but also disobedience on behalf of others, on behalf of a cause. At the time, the escape of the Jews was hardly seen as an act of resistance, but today we are, of course, free to take a different view.

Unlike the non-socialist parties which lapsed into passivity or the Labour Party which together with the trade union movement maintained an underground network but developed no resistance policy of its own, the communists continued to act as a party and to draw up their own particular resistance policy. Although the party became part of a national movement, its platform was never national but international, determined as it was by the policy and position of the Soviet Union. The communists started from almost nil at the beginning of the occupation but developed into an important element of the resistance movement in later years. Their full story could not be told and their impact properly weighed during the Cold War. In the first three-volume history of the war years, published in the late 1940s, they were hardly mentioned at all. Later, their existence was acknowledged and part of their story told but only in recent years have they been given their proper due. The time has come to assess their historical contribution more objectively.

The Communist Party, which had dwindled into insignificance in the 1930s and become even more negligible and stigmatized when it supported the Soviet Union in the Winter War, has traditionally been seen as being against all resistance as long as the non-aggression pact of 23 August 1939 between the Soviet Union and Germany was in force. This view is not wholly correct. After the party was prohibited on 16 August 1940, it strove to maintain its existence clandestinely, which may in itself be seen as an act of resistance. It also gave its support to civilian resistance against Nazification. What is true, however, is that the party could not follow the mainstream of early resistance. It saw the war between Great Britain and Germany as a war between imperialist powers which was of no concern to Norway, and, being mindful of the alliance between the Soviet Union and Germany, the communists could not orient themselves towards extra-territorial Norway, the war policy of its King and government, and their alliance with the British. The communists did not approve of any kind of military resistance prior to 22 June 1941. This stand was later used against them by their enemies in the mainstream resistance.

It took the party half a year after Germany's attack on the Soviet Union to adopt a radical resistance policy advocating sabotage and guerrilla warfare against the occupying power. This ran counter to the slowly evolving and more cautious policy of the mainstream resistance, which envisaged building an underground military organization that would not spring into action before the final liberation of the country. Sabotage not directly connected with the liberation was to be carried out only by special parties, organized jointly by the British Special Operations Executive (SOE) and the Norwegian High Command and sent in from Britain, returning there after the operation, like the famous sabotage against the heavy water plant at Rjukan in Telemark in February 1943. The Communist Party gradually built its own apparatus consisting of party cells, study circles, an underground press, an escape organization and military and sabotage units. For a period of time it left the task of carrying out sabotage to a person who had been part of a Moscow-led international sabotage organization before the war and whose loyalty in the final analysis was to Moscow, not to the Party. Later, the Party established a sabotage organization which was more properly its own. It was never able to organize any guerrilla warfare, nor was such warfare ever part of military resistance's operations except for some incidents at the very end of the war.

The communists worked from the outset against heavy odds as their radical policy meant an increased danger of exposure and of heavy reprisals against the population which was more than reticent in its attitude to such a policy. However, in the course of autumn 1943 to spring 1944 the mood of the country changed to a certain extent in favour of the communists and violence in the struggle against the regime. This had an impact on the mainstream resistance which also became radicalized. From spring 1944, the underground military organization changed its policy, starting to carry out sabotage aimed at targets not directly connected to the liberation although its main objective remained to prepare for the final liberation. The many sabotage operations which the underground military organization now carried out deprived the communists of an advantage they had had, and from the middle of 1944 the resistance leaders viewed the communists with less apprehension than before. Nevertheless, demands by the communists to be represented in the leading organs of resistance were invariably turned down.

The most celebrated sabotage heroes in Norway have been and still are the men who received their training in Britain and were secretly sent into the occupied country from abroad to carry out sabotage. It is still not generally recognized how much more widespread the purely homespun communist sabotage was in the years from 1941 to mid-1944. Between early 1941 and September 1944, approximately thirty sabotage operations were planned, attempted or completed from Britain, whereas in about the same period the communist sabotage apparatus executed some seventy operations. However, quantity is one thing, quality something else. To determine and compare the damage done by the various operations is a complex task.

The new emphasis on the communists in recent years has signified more prominence for sabotage and military forms of resistance. This underlines a tendency that has been prevalent in all the post-war years to see military resistance as the most typical kind of resistance, its very essence, so to speak. This, however, does not do justice to the overall character of the Norwegian resistance movement and poses two questions of balance in the portrayal of it.

The first concerns the balance between the civilian and military parts of the movement. In comparison with other countries, the civilian, basically non-violent, anti-Nazi mass protests of the Norwegian resistance movement appear as a more characteristic feature than its military underground, which is more comparable with other countries. Civilian resistance scored great successes in 1942 and 1944 and was surpassed by the military resistance only during the last year of occupation. The salience of the civilian movement was a reflection of the structure of the occupation regime in which a domestic Nazi party with the resources of the state at hand conducted a Nazification campaign against society. It was this campaign that triggered off civilian resistance, which incidentally created a stir in the Allied world in 1942 because it unfolded at a time when the Allies were still on the defensive. An analysis of the Norwegian resistance movement should assess more carefully than has been done so far the relative weight of its civilian and military components.

Secondly, to the extent that emphasis is placed on the military part of resistance, more attention should be paid to the relationship between resistance and its extra-territorial counterparts, the British authorities and the Norwegian authorities in exile. Military resistance ought to be viewed not primarily as a territorial movement in Norway but as part of a Norwegian/British whole in which the resistance received legitimacy, guidelines, instructors and equipment from Britain. This subordination to the Allied and Norwegian authorities abroad was, in fact, one of the mainstream resistance's weapons against the communists. The communists envisaged a resistance movement that was more independent of the authorities abroad, but its vision was met with the argument that the military underground received its orders from the Norwegian high command in exile and could not take into account the demands from a domestic political party.

Bibliography

The bibliography focuses on post-war debates and does not include general surveys or literature on specific topics.

Corell, Synne (2010), *Krigens ettertid. Okkupasjonshistorien i norske historiebøker*. Oslo: Scandinavian Academic Press.

Eriksen, Anne (1995), *Det var noe annet under krigen. 2. verdenskrig i norsk kollektivtradisjon*. Oslo: Pax.

— (2000), 'Krigsfortellinger. Episke strukturer i norsk erindringslitteratur om den 2. verdenskrig.' *Prosa - tidsskrift for skribenter*. 1/2000, pp. 32–41

Fure, Odd-Bjørn (1999), 'Norsk okkupasjonshistorie. Konsensus, berøringsangst og tabuisering'. In Stein Ugelvik Larsen (ed.), *I krigens kjølvann. Nye sider ved norsk krigshistorie og etterkrigstid*. Oslo: Universitetsforl.

Grimnes, Ole Kristian (2009), 'Hvor står okkupasjonshistorien nå?', *Nytt Norsk Tidsskrift* 3–4/2009.

— (1999), 'Kollaborasjon og oppgjør'. In Stein Ugelvik Larsen (ed.), *I krigens kjølvann. Nye sider ved norsk krigshistorie og etterkrigstid*. Oslo: Universitetsforl.

— (1997), 'Occupation and Collective Memory in Norway'. Ekman, Stig, and Edling, Nils (eds), *War, Experience, Self Image and National Identity: The Second World War as Myth and History*. Stockholm: The Bank of Sweden Tercentenary Foundation & Gidlunds Förlag.

— (2010), 'Okkupasjon og politikk i Norge' and 'Fra krig til fred i Norge.' In Dahl, Hans Fredrik (ed.), *Danske tilstander. Norske tilstander. Forskjeller og liheter under tysk okkupasjon 1940–45*. Oslo, Forlaget Press.

Maerz, Susanne (2008), *Die langen Schatten der Besatzungszeit. 'Vergangenheitsbewältigung' in Norwegen als Identitätsdiskurs*. Berlin. In Norwegian translation, (2010) *Okkupasjonstidens lange skygger. Fortidsbearbeidelse i Norge som identitetsdiskurs*. Oslo, HL-senteret, Unipub.

Figure 6 Sweden's *Aftonbladet* in 2000 gives front page coverage of an important milestone in Sweden's post-war response to the country's actions between 1939–45: The Stockholm International Forum on the Holocaust. [With kind permission of *Aftonbladet*.]

10

Realism and Idealism: Swedish Narratives of the Second World War

Historiography and Interpretation in the Post-War Era

Johan Östling

In the eyes of its own inhabitants, post-war Sweden was by all accounts a unique country. With its peaceful, evolutionary character, the course of modern Swedish history was certainly very different from the brutal developments on the European continent. Much of this was thanks to the simple fact that Sweden, like a few other major European countries, had been spared the horrors of World War II. At the same time, however, Swedish interpretations of the war underwent a transformation that closely paralleled wider European developments after 1945, not least from the late 1980s onwards. In an international historiographical perspective, therefore, this neutral northern democracy is of particular interest.

In this chapter, I will outline the major trends in the historiography of Sweden and World War II. Academic historiography falls into three main phases: 1945–70, 1970–90 and 1990 onwards. Although the characteristics of all three phases will be discussed, my emphasis is on the fundamental change in scholarly and public debate in the two most recent decades. Throughout, the historiographical shifts are related to the wider political, cultural and intellectual context of the post-war era, while the Swedish case is summed up in a broader geographical and historical perspective.[1]

The emergence of small-state realism: 1945–70

The first phase comprises the first 25 years of the post-war period, from 1945 to 1970. The period immediately after the war saw the publication in Sweden of a number of books on Nazism and the war years. In the 1950s and 1960s, however, this declined dramatically and, with a few exceptions, those that were published were not written by professional historians. The period can, thus, be further divided into two phases, 1945–50 and 1950–70, of which the publications from the former period have proved to be of more enduring historiographical significance. In truth, the aftermath of the war was by no means as turbulent for Sweden as it was for many other countries. With the exception of a few minor trials, no legal action was taken against former Nazis. Given that there was no resistance movement set on monopolizing the interpretation of the war and no occupying power to dictate post-war conditions, it becomes clearer why World War II did not really become part of the official national memory.

Despite this, in the late 1940s a powerful narrative of Sweden and World War II did emerge, a hegemonic interpretation that was to dominate the entire post-war era. It may best be characterized as the *small-state realistic narrative*. The argument went that, being a small state, Sweden had no choice but to tailor her responses to aggressive German power. This much was undisputed in the dominant Swedish interpretation. However, it was also held that Sweden's concessions had been limited, and the price paid – having to acquiesce in the face of Nazi aggression – was seen as stemming directly from the threat of occupation in the event of non-compliance. Sweden's policy of neutrality had, thus, been to the lasting benefit of the nation, its neighbours and peace itself. 'The role of a small state gave Sweden moral absolution', as the historian Alf W. Johansson wrote in a paradigmatic article on small-state realism and Swedish self-image: 'All the difficult questions which the policy of concessions posed about the Swedish social ethos during the war years, about the will to resist and submission, about fidelity to one's own ideals and ideological principles, were swept under the carpet by the triumph of small-state realism.'[2]

This small-state realistic narrative fits into a larger European pattern. The historian Étienne François has characterized the national narratives of World War II that emerged in the first decades after 1945 as 'patriotic'. This is somewhat misleading, since the narratives are not notable for their chauvinistic rhetoric or even for their love of country. 'Patriotic', however, refers to the simple fact that in this period the narratives defended the cause, the people and the actions of a nation during the war. According to the patriotic interpretation, victory over Nazism could be ascribed to national achievements, in the shape of the resistance movement, superior fighting skills or a more advanced social system. This view was a national article of faith, and the arguments drew their force from a self-righteous ethos: the war years had brought hardship and suffering, but thanks to the ideals and virtues we held dear, we gained strength and managed to mitigate the evil of the aggressive invading power. In countries that had had strong Nazi or fascist organizations, such as Germany, Austria and Italy, these political currents were often regarded as foreign elements, as alien powers that had taken control over their own people.[3]

Despite the lack of heroic acts, the dominant Swedish narrative incorporated elements similar to those of other European countries and can reasonably be regarded as a patriotic narrative. Moreover, small-state realism was a 'progressive narrative', in which the evil of National Socialism was located in a historical epoch that belonged firmly in the past.[4] It was by these means that Sweden's coalition government appeared as a stable guarantor of peace and sovereignty, with a policy of neutrality that had spared Sweden war and occupation. Sweden's humanitarian efforts in war-torn Europe were also emphasized, a proud and important tradition that continued in the reconstruction after 1945, and in an ever-increasing international commitment in the 1950s and 1960s.

The structure of the patriotic narrative also required a set of scapegoats. The most obvious ones were quislings and fifth columnists, in other words, the Swedish Nazis and communists of dubious loyalty who were all actual or potential traitors. The ranks of whipping boys were swelled with the open opponents of National Socialism from the fields of publishing, culture and intellectual debate, including Torgny Segerstedt, Ture Nerman and Karl Gerhard. With their treacherous, disruptive opposition to the government policy of neutrality and censorship, they were viewed as self-conceited idealists who threatened to bring Sweden into the war.

The origins of the small-state realistic narrative can be traced back to the war years. In a speech given in May 1945, on the very last day of the war, the Swedish Prime Minister Per Albin Hansson declared, 'We have made our contribution, we have struggled in our own way', thus asserting that his wartime coalition government had not only acted successfully, but also that the whole Swedish social order and way of life was superior. Admittedly, Sweden had in some ways deviated from strict neutrality, but on the whole, the Swedish approach had combined resistance with a major effort for peace. Self-righteousness was a salient feature, and small-state realism was at the heart of national identity in the post-war period.[5]

In the years immediately following the end of war, however, small-state realism had not yet obtained its standing as the hegemonic Swedish interpretation of World War II. Until the late 1940s, competing narratives thrived in the public debate in a way that would be unthinkable a few years later. For example, a moral counter-narrative was much in evidence in a number of critical accounts of Swedish wartime policies. The leitmotif of these interpretations was that the coalition government, with its concessions to Nazi Germany, had pursued a morally irresponsible line, whose sole purpose had been to keep Sweden completely out of the great power conflict. The guiding star had been unscrupulous pragmatism. The wartime government was accused of being incapable of seeing World War II for what it really was – a moral struggle between democracy and dictatorship, liberty and oppression, good and evil – and leading Swedish politicians, who had sunk to using the fundamental democratic values as bargaining chips, were castigated for their cowardice and nationalistic narrow-mindedness. According to this moral narrative, the policy of concession served only to prolong the war and prevented the world from recognizing earlier the full scope of the Nazis' crimes.[6] From the late 1940s' onwards, however, the small-state realistic narrative prevailed, and the counter-narratives were gradually marginalized. The same tendency was matched in many other parts of Europe, where the war had demolished social cohesion and diluted human trust. The Manichaean heroism of the patriotic narratives offered a remedy.[7] The historian Tony Judt has argued that in this respect Europeans were faced with a tricky balancing act: they had to revitalize the continent economically and politically by ignoring the recent past, while at the same time cultural and moral invigoration demanded that they learn from the very events they were trying to put behind them.[8]

Of course, the need for a unifying memory of the war was not as urgent in Sweden as it was in many European countries. Nevertheless, the small-state realistic narrative served to underpin and strengthen national traditions in post-war Sweden. For example, criticism of wartime small-state realism was regarded as amounting to criticism of Cold War small-state realism. This is not contradicted by the idea – suggested, for example, by the historian Bo Stråth – that neutrality was in part a construction after the event and that the doctrine itself did not take shape until the beginning of the 1950s. At the heart of the small-state realistic narrative was a plea for the maintenance of fundamental principles in post-war Swedish society: peace and security, sovereignty and neutrality, welfare, modernity and progress.[9]

In the 1950s and 1960s, only a few substantial contributions were made to the history of Sweden during World War II, the majority of them written in the spirit of small-state realism. In 1958, for instance, the senior diplomat Gunnar Hägglöf published a book on Swedish trade policy towards both Germany and the Allies. Hägglöf, who himself had been one of the key wartime negotiators, described it as a balancing act, without discussing the moral dilemma of Sweden's exports of iron ore to Nazi Germany. Four years later, the historian Åke Thulstrup wrote a book on German attempts to influence Swedish public opinion in 1933 to 1945. Although Thulstrup had been actively engaged in anti-Nazi circles during the war, his overall assessment of Sweden's actions was not particularly harsh. As with the school textbooks and general histories of the period, the paradigm of Thulstrup's account was *Realpolitik*.[10] In retrospect, the years 1945–70 must be regarded as a phase when the foundations of the small-state realistic narrative were laid. After a short period of intense debate in the immediate post-war period, memories of World War II faded fast. Only a handful of significant books was published, and academic interest was almost non-existent. Things were to change, however.

Small-state realism – the historiographical paradigm: 1970–90

The second phase in Swedish historiography is marked by the beginnings of scholarly interest. The period encompasses the 1970s and 1980s, and marks the historiographical consolidation of small-state realism. It is very much associated with a large research project at the Department of History at the University of Stockholm, 'Sweden during the Second World War' (*Sverige under andra världskriget, SUAV*). Within this project, some twenty doctoral theses were published in the 1970s. A whole range of new empirical fields was analysed, with an emphasis on political, economic and social history. Many of the studies drew on official sources and were discussed in historical journals such as *Historisk tidskrift* and *Scandia*. By contrast with many other western European countries, however, no institutes or chairs exclusively dedicated to World War II were inaugurated.[11]

Back in the late 1960s, the historian Wilhelm M. Carlgren, the head of the Foreign Office's archive in Stockholm, had been commissioned by the government to write a history of Swedish foreign policy during World War II. His 600-page book, *Svensk utrikespolitik 1939–1945*, was published in 1973 and is still an important work of reference. Carlgren's thorough if somewhat deferential study benefited from his outstanding command of the diplomatic and political sources. Although he touched on the moral issues in different ways, his fundamental assumption was that the military threat from Germany was a real one and must be considered when judging Sweden's concessions. On the whole, Carlgren showed a far-reaching understanding of Swedish foreign policy during the war, and many of the politicians responsible, for example, the Minister of Foreign Affairs Christian Günther and the Minister of Justice Karl Gustaf Westman, were depicted with sympathy. His *magnum opus* is an impressive monument to the historiographical paradigm of his day, small-state realism.[12]

Young researchers within the SUAV project did not have the same free access to the archives that Carlgren had enjoyed, but they shared many of his basic assumptions and perspectives. With hindsight, many have regretted that their licentiate and doctoral dissertations were not brought together in a proper synthesis, for the unfortunate consequence was that broad questions concerning Sweden's policy were not addressed in depth, and the framework of small-state realism hampered an ethical or ideological discussion. Refugee policy, for example, was a field of research in the SUAV project, but the moral implications of Sweden's part in the destruction of European Jewry were never discussed, albeit that this was in accordance with the avowedly objectivistic ideals of the day. Thus, the Holocaust was not considered a part of Sweden's wartime history.[13]

There were some works, however, that tried to summarize the research and present a comprehensive picture. The historian Alf W. Johansson had written a SUAV dissertation, and in 1985 he published an important study on the coalition government and foreign policy during World War II, centred on the wartime prime minister, Per Albin Hansson. Johansson described Swedish policy as one of negotiation rather than of concession. When at the end of the book he formulated his overall assessment, his conclusions tended to confirm the small-state realism narrative. He characterized the foreign policy of the coalition government – in a much-quoted phrase – as 'good management of fortunate circumstances'.[14] A limited number of studies in the 1970s and 1980s took an alternative stance. Often they were written not by historians but by specialists in literature, film and theatre. Yet despite their focus on the intellectual and spiritual resistance to Nazism among writers and artists, they helped to reinforce an impression that was fully in line with small-state realism: the Swedes had done what they could to keep the Nazis in check.[15] Openly critical studies of the political and cultural trends of the 1930s and 1940s were rare, and thanks to their rarity they tended to be regarded as exceptions to a general rule.[16] On balance, research on Sweden and World War II gained momentum in the 1970s and continued to expand in the 1980s. Historiography continued to be pervaded by small-state realism, an interpretation that buttressed the majority of the studies and shaped the overall scholarly debate.

The moral narrative: 1990 onwards

The third phase in Swedish historiography began in the late 1980s and early 1990s. Against the background of deep-seated changes in world affairs, the strong small-state realistic narrative started to moulder. A new moral interpretation of the war emerged in the course of the 1990s, which saw the publication of a large number of scholarly studies of Swedish antisemitism and racial biology, as well as Sweden's relationship with Nazi Germany and attitudes to the Holocaust. Explicitly or not, they were united in a moral stance that earlier academic studies had lacked.[17]

The changes in Swedish historiography must be seen in connection with the fundamental transformation of European memory towards the end of the twentieth century. In the Federal Republic of Germany, in many ways an exception because of its history as a successor to Nazi Germany, a new attitude towards its own dark past emerged in the early 1960s, but German lessons remained exclusively German, and strengthened rather than softened the self-righteous tone in other parts of Europe. German *Vergangenheitsbewältigung* (the process of coming to terms with the past) probably had the effect that the Nazis continued to be seen primarily as a German problem, and other European countries could remain onlookers. More deep-seated national confrontations were delayed.[18] However, as a general rule, the *leitmotifs* of the national narratives of World War II have undergone a fundamental change in recent decades, from *patriotism* to *universalism*. If heroic deeds and brave resistance were to the fore until the 1980s, the new universalistic narratives take grievous, traumatic experience as their starting point. The Holocaust was the *sine qua non* in this universalistic tendency. The extermination of European Jewry had been known about during the war, but it was not until the 1980s and 1990s that the Holocaust became the focus of attention and the predominant moral lesson of World War II. In a world that had experienced Stalinism, fascism and imperialism, the Holocaust marked a dark century's deepest abyss.[19]

As a result, patriotic narratives came in for tremendous criticism in the 1980s and 1990s. Across Europe, heated public controversies broke out over issues related to World War II, from the *Historikerstreit* in West Germany to the arguments over the Vichy regime in France, *la Resistenza* in Italy and the Kurt Waldheim scandal in Austria. Suddenly, the legacy of the war years was found to be a rich source for political and moral discussion, a challenging question for politicians, intellectuals and historians alike. At the same time, victims were drawn into the public sphere as never before, and many of the villains were finally brought to justice decades after the end of the war. The Eichmann trial in Jerusalem in 1961 and the Auschwitz trial in Frankfurt in 1963–65 anticipated the legal proceedings of the 1980s and 1990s. Moreover, companies, banks and states were forced to repay profits illegally earned in the 1930s and 1940s. An additional component in the new attitude towards World War II was the emergence of an official culture of grief and commemoration, above all, in the tributes paid to the memory of the murdered Jews. With monuments, exhibitions and memorial days, World War II in general and the Holocaust in particular were brought to the centre of public attention. States, organizations and individuals took upon themselves the blame for crimes committed during the war. The Stockholm International Forum on the Holocaust in 2000 was a decisive moment for this new universalistic narrative.[20]

In Sweden, the small-state realistic narrative was replaced by a moral narrative in the 1990s. In the preface to *Heder och samvete* (1991), a hugely influential book that heralded a new attitude towards Sweden's history during World War II, the author and journalist Maria-Pia Boëthius declared:

> This is a history book for those who were born after the war; an indictment, a list of sins and a polemic. The post-war generation in Sweden knows extraordinarily little about Sweden and the Second World War. This may be a part of our general lack of a sense of history, this may be a conspiracy of silence. Sweden's role during the Second World War was not an honourable one.[21]

Boëthius' polemic marked the starting point of the latest controversy over small-state realism. Older reviewers tended to dismiss her book as superficial, but younger ones, many of whom were born after the war, were more receptive. In that respect, *Heder och samvete* paved the way for a whole range of critical books and articles in the 1990s on everything from Nazi gold to Swedes who had fought for Hitler.[22] In an official confirmation of the widespread acceptance of the new moral narrative, in 1997 the prime minister Göran

Persson launched the project 'Living History' (*Levande historia*) to promote efforts to advance democracy, tolerance and human rights, prompted by the memory of the Holocaust.[23]

Simultaneously, Swedish historiography on World War II shifted focus. An event of symbolic significance occurred in 1995, when Alf W. Johansson, one of the leading experts in the field, delivered a personal speech at a major conference to mark the 50th anniversary of the end of the war that was to have far-reaching implications. In his soul-searching account, Johansson described the view that had permeated the post-war interpretation of Sweden's behaviour during the war, including the SUAV project: 'Sweden had been confronted with a ruthless and aggressive great power and had no choice but to give way. This had been a wise policy, because it had saved the peace. However, the ideological perspective on the war had to be pushed aside if this line was to be consistently argued, and this created a strange duality in the Swedish consciousness'.[24] It was precisely this perspective that was the target of the moral criticism of the 1990s. Small-state realism had had the effect of excluding important aspects of World War II from the analysis. Historians had unquestioningly adopted the coalition government's perspective as their own and had neglected to raise moral questions. In his self-critical speech, Alf W. Johansson discussed Wilhelm M. Carlgren's comprehensive account from 1973 and his own book from the mid-1980s. Both, in his opinion, were firmly within 'the framework of the same paradigm, namely small-state realism, and in that sense were a defence of wartime policy'.[25]

Alf W. Johansson's reconsideration was not an isolated phenomenon. On the contrary, in the late 1990s and early 2000s a whole range of new studies on antisemitism, racial biology, the Holocaust and Swedish relations with Nazi Germany were published. The majority of them were written by a younger generation of researchers, often born in the 1960s, including Lars M. Andersson, Lena Berggren, Heléne Lööw and Mattias Tydén. With their critical and moral approach, they differed from the older historians in the SUAV project, who had been born in the 1930s or 1940s.[26] Two books exemplify the historiographical shift. In 1996, the historian Gunnar Richardson published a new book on an old theme: Swedish links and concessions to Nazi Germany. In contrast to older studies, for example, Åke Thulstrup's from 1962, he also included Sweden's close military, clerical and sporting contacts with its southern neighbour. Richardson regarded them as a part of a Swedish adaptation to the Third Reich. By comparing Richardson and Thulstrup, the intellectual historian

Jonas Hansson uncovered significant historiographical differences between the 1960s and 1990s:

> For Richardson, it is Swedish actions that are visible, while for Thulstrup it was more interesting to know what the German side were up to. Richardson talks about admiration and fear in Sweden, while Thulstrup, mostly with Swedish press opinion in mind, describes a pendulum movement from 'sharp rejection' to 'cautious objectivity' and back again. The difference in the assessment of the Swedish attitude cannot be reduced just to a difference in material but must be viewed in the context of a change in the spirit of the age.[27]

In 2000, the Swedish Research Council launched a new major research project, 'Sweden's Relations with Nazism, Nazi Germany and the Holocaust' (*Sveriges förhållande till nazismen, Nazityskland och Förintelsen, SweNaz*). It drew scholars from across the humanities and social sciences. In contrast to the SUAV project of the 1970s, SweNaz specifically took the Holocaust as its departure point.[28] Sweden and the Holocaust had first been treated in a historical analysis in 1987, notably by an American historian, Steven Koblik, and another American historian living in Sweden, Paul Levine, wrote the second monograph on the theme.[29] In the early 2000s, however, Swedish historians not only began to publish on the subject, but also scholars from many other disciplines made important contributions to the history of Sweden and the Holocaust.[30]

Swedish historiography in perspective

To grasp fully the recent fundamental changes in conceptions and interpretations of Sweden's war years, they must be related to a series of broader issues. A look at two of Sweden's Scandinavian neighbours reveals some interesting trends.

In contrast to Sweden, both Denmark and Norway were occupied by Nazi Germany between April 1940 and May 1945. In Denmark, the historians Claus Bryld and Anette Warring have examined how a hegemonic narrative of the German occupation emerged straight after the war. In its character, this 'basic narrative of the occupation' (*grundfortælling om besættelsestiden*) was markedly nationalistic. One entrenched belief was that the Danes to a man had supported the Danish Resistance; of course, a distinction was drawn between active and passive opposition, but with the exception of a few traitors, the whole Danish people had joined in the struggle against the foreign invaders.

Under the influence of the unfolding Cold War, the narrative gradually took on more mythical proportions: good versus evil, democracy versus dictatorship, universalism versus racism. This national interpretation dominated textbooks, television programmes and historical jubilees throughout the entire post-war period and strongly underpinned Danish national identity.[31] However, a critical counter-narrative had been formulated by members of the Danish Resistance at the very end of the war. In their version, the Danish establishment was a nest of collaborators and traitors. In the public sphere, the counter-narrative was marginalized in the late 1940s, but it survived to be reinterpreted by various groups and for various purposes in the last decades of the twentieth century. For example, this nationalistic narrative was taken as an argument against Danish membership of the European Community, and again as a right-wing argument in the 1980s when criticizing asylum legislation.[32]

According to the ethnologist Anne Eriksen, a similar patriotic narrative emerged in Norway after the war. As in Denmark, it had a strong national appeal and a mythic character. Eriksen viewed the narrative as amounting to modern Norway's creation story, a master narrative in which the brave resistance of the common people against their foreign oppressors emphasized the spirit of national liberty that had been so important to the Norwegian tradition since at least the nineteenth century. From the 1980s, somewhat earlier than in Denmark and Sweden, a new generation of historians began to challenge this patriotic interpretation. They raised new and controversial questions regarding the fate of the Norwegian Jews, the volunteers in the *Waffen-SS* and the fate of the quislings and their children after 1945. Although an important shift took place in Norwegian historiography, the exact impact new research has had on the public opinion remains an open question.[33] The narrative of World War II seems to have played a very similar role in Norway and Denmark after 1945. In general, interpretations of the war underpinned national identity and were interwoven with strong currents in political and cultural life in the post-war period. To uncover the nature of the transformation of Swedish narratives in the 1990s, the perspective must, thus, be widened beyond the realm of academic historiography.

In spite of the symbolic importance of Maria-Pia Boëthius' indictment, there was a prelude to the collective self-examination of the 1990s back in the late 1980s. The example of the 1988 debate over Zarah Leander's career in the Third Reich is illustrative. After the war, the Swedish star had not at first been regarded as a political animal, but rather as a diva, a naïve but successful prima donna who had charmed audiences in Nazi Germany and elsewhere. By the end of the 1980s, however, a much more critical narrative won through, in which Leander was portrayed as a woman of doubtful reputation who had enjoyed the company of senior Nazis without demur. At the same time, Ingmar Bergman's memoir *Laterna Magica* caused a stir on account of his admission of his fascination with National Socialism in his youth. A few years later, a book on the Wallenbergs, an important financial dynasty, and their relationship to Nazi Germany also sparked a public debate.[34]

This change in mood must be seen against the backdrop of international events in the late 1980s. For instance, the *Historikerstreit* in West Germany in 1986–88 was debated in Sweden and may well have spurred Swedish self-examination. Other national controversies, such as those surrounding the Austrian president Kurt Waldheim, the philosopher Martin Heidegger and members of the French Vichy regime, were all commented on in the Swedish media. Generally speaking, European public disputes in the late 1980s can be seen as harbingers of the intense struggle with the legacy of the war that would take place in the 1990s.[35] Although it is impossible to establish a specific date when the change occurred, the years around 1990 marked the beginning of the gradual transition from a patriotic to a universalistic narrative of World War II in Sweden. In essence, the dominant national interpretation underwent a simultaneous transformation in Sweden and the rest of Europe. Self-righteousness gave way to self-criticism, national sovereignty to international commitment and security to human dignity. The narrative became eminently moral when the Holocaust became its origin and object.

In a broader international perspective, certain peculiarities in the Swedish confrontation with its patriotic narrative stand out. The criticism of small-state realism coincided, and partly overlapped, with a more general criticism of the configuration of post-war society. In a series of conflicts over instrumental rationality, eugenic sterilization and respect for individual freedom, the Swedish welfare state was brought under the microscope. The policy of neutrality and non-alignment, the cornerstones of Swedish foreign policy during the Cold War, was portrayed as an exercise in hypocrisy. In general, the 1990s can be regarded as 'the decade of debates', a time when the whole post-war construction was challenged and discussed.[36]

It was no coincidence that Sweden's confrontation with small-state realism ran parallel to a more general examination of post-war society. For Sweden after 1945, as in other parts of Europe, the patriotic interpretation of World War II had lived in symbiosis with broader post-war narratives. The strength of the Swedish interpretation can be explained by the fact that it formed a solid argument for the welfare state in the Cold War era. It efficiently underpinned the idea of Sweden as a neutral, democratic and flourishing country, where everyone worked for the common good and where peaceful solutions were preferred. Furthermore, small-state realism merged smoothly with the hegemonic master narrative of modern Sweden to which the Social Democrats and the majority of the centre-right opposition adhered in the post-war period. Although this narrative of democracy, welfare and rationalism was challenged from the 1960s onwards (by, in turn, the New Left, the women's movement, the Green movement and new liberal currents), Sweden's role in World War II was never a prime target for their attacks. Small-state realism would remain an important part in Swedish self-understanding even when the master narrative was called into question.[37] All the same, it is misleading to interpret small-state realism as 'a conspiracy of silence,' as a cunning form of manipulation by a malevolent government. Both as an identity and as a historical understanding, the patriotic narrative originated in conclusions drawn in the late 1940s and early 1950s from direct experience of World War II. Equally, the transformation of the patriotic narrative into a universalistic narrative in the 1990s was facilitated by the fact that the patriotic Swedish interpretation was so universalistic in substance. With its progressive character that underscored universal values such as international solidarity, civil rights and social welfare, much of the content could remain intact even when the structure had changed. In other words, the moral focus of small-state realism remained even when small-state realism itself was discredited.

The crisis of consensus paved the way for a new kind of consensus. The moral narrative that emerged in the early 1990s became increasingly hegemonic.[38] Indeed, while these changes reflect a general European development, it is nevertheless important to take specifically Swedish characteristics into account. The new universalistic narrative was not just a historical interpretation; as always, historical narratives have at least as much to do with the present and the future as with the past. Some commentators, including the historian Klas-Göran Karlsson, view recent developments in the light of various Europeanization processes in Sweden in the 1990s. In order to take a full part in the wider European project, as signalled by Sweden's membership of the European Union in 1995, the country 'also had to come to terms – albeit belatedly – with the unifying experience of war and its symbolism'. A new approach to the history of Sweden and World War II was called for, and the answer was found in a moral narrative.[39]

Notes

1. This article enlarges on earlier work, primarily Östling, Johan (2008a), 'Swedish Narratives of the Second World War: A European Perspective', *Contemporary European History*, Vol. 17, No. 2; Östling, Johan (2008b), *Nazismens sensmoral: Svenska erfarenheter i andra världskrigets efterdyning*. Stockholm: Bokförlaget Atlantis; and Östling, Johan (2011), 'The Rise and Fall of Small-State Realism: Sweden and the Second World War', in Stenius, Henrik, Österberg, Mirja and Östling, Johan (eds), *Nordic Narratives of the Second World War: National Historiographies Revisited*. Lund: Nordic Academic Press. Excellent bibliographical works on Sweden and World War II include Ekman, Stig and Åmark, Klas (eds) (2003), *Sweden's Relations with Nazism, Nazi Germany and the Holocaust: A Survey of Research*. Stockholm: Almqvist and Wicksell International; and Vonderau, Patrick (ed.) (2003), *Schweden und das nationalsozialistische Deutschland: Eine annotierte Bibliographie der deutschsprachigen Forschungsliteratur: 825 Einträge – 439 Annotationen*. Stockholm: Almqvist and Wicksell International.
2. Johansson, Alf W. (1997), 'Neutrality and Modernity: The Second World War and Sweden's National Identity', in Ekman, Stig and Edling, Nils (eds) *War Experience, Self Image and National Identity: The Second World War as Myth and History*. Stockholm: Bank of Sweden Tercentenary Foundation [Riksbankens jubileumsfond], p. 176. See also Liljefors, Max and Zander, Ulf (2003), 'Det neutrala landet Ingenstans: Bilder av andra världskriget och den svenska utopin', *Scandia*, Vol. 69, No. 2, and Bryld, Claus (2007), 'The Five Accursed Years: Danish Perception and Usage of the Period of the German Occupation, With a Wider View to Norway and Sweden', Scandinavian Journal of History, Vol. 32, No. 1.
3. François, Etienne (2004), 'Meistererzählungen und Dammbrüche: Die Erinnerung an den Zweiten Weltkrieg zwischen Nationalisierung und Universalisierung', in Monika Flacke (ed.) (2004), *Mythen der Nationen: 1945 – Arena der Erinnerungen*, Vol. 2. Berlin: Verlag Philipp von Zabern GmbH, pp. 16–20.
4. Alexander, Jeffrey C. (2004), 'On the Social Construction of Moral Universals: The "Holocaust" from War Crime to Trauma Drama', in Alexander, Jeffrey C. et al. (eds) (2004), *Cultural Trauma and Collective Identity*. Berkeley: University of California Press, p. 209.
5. Johansson, Alf W. (2006), *Den nazistiska utmaningen: Aspekter på andra världskriget*. Stockholm: Rabén Prisma, p. 277.
6. Östling (2008a), pp. 202–3; Östling (2008b), pp. 105–12. Critical counter-narratives appeared in, for example, Nerman, Ture (1942), *Sverige i beredskap*. Stockholm: Trots allt; Moberg, Vilhelm (1945), *Segerstedtstriden*. Stockholm: Bonnier; Boldt-Christmas, Emil (1946), *Voro vi neutrala*. Stockholm: Bonnier; and Sastamoinen, Armas (1947), *Hitlers svenska förtrupper*. Stockholm: Federativs förl.

7   François (2004), p. 17. See also Conway, Martin and Romijn, Peter (2004), 'Introduction', *Contemporary European History*, Vol. 13, No. 4, pp. 377-88.
8   Judt, Tony (2005), *Postwar: A History of Europe Since 1945*. London: Heinemann, pp. 61-2 and pp. 803-31.
9   Johansson (2006), pp. 280-7; Stråth, Bo (1993), *Folkhemmet mot Europa: Ett historiskt perspektiv på 90-talet*. Stockholm: Tiden. See also Johansson, Alf W. (2001), 'Inledning: Svensk nationalism och identitet efter andra världskriget', in Johansson, Alf W. (ed.) (2001), *Vad är Sverige? Röster om svensk nationell identitet*. Stockholm: Prisma.
10 Hägglöf, Gunnar (1958), *Svensk krigshandelspolitik under andra världskriget*. Stockholm: Norstedt; Thulstrup, Åke (1962), *Med lock och pock: Tyska försök att påverka svensk opinion 1933-45*. Stockholm: Bonnier. See also Ekman, Stig (2003), 'Introduction', in Ekman (2003), pp. 16-22.
11 Ekman (2003), pp. 20-7; Johansson (2006), pp. 284-5.
12 Carlgren, Wilhelm M. (1973), *Svensk utrikespolitik 1939-1945*. Stockholm: Allmänna förl. An abridged English edition was published a few years later, Carlgren, Wilhelm M. (1977), *Swedish Foreign Policy During the Second World War*. London: E. Benn.
13 Ekman (2003), pp. 22-30; Johansson (2006), pp. 284-5.
14 Johansson, Alf W. (1985), *Per Albin och kriget: Samlingsregeringen och utrikespolitiken under andra världskriget*. Stockholm: Tiden, p. 416. See also Ekman (1986), *Stormaktstryck och småstatspolitik: Aspekter på svensk politik under andra världskriget*. Stockholm: LiberFörlag.
15 Landgren, Bengt (1975), *Hjalmar Gullberg och beredskapslitteraturen: Studier i svensk dikt och politisk debatt 1933-1942*. Uppsala: Univ.; Lind, Martin (1975), *Kristendom och nazism: Frågan om kristendom och nazism belyst av olika ställningstaganden i Tyskland och Sverige 1933-1945*. Lund: H. Ohlsson; Drangel, Louise (1976), *Den kämpande demokratin: En studie i antinazistisk opinionsrörelse 1935-1945*. Stockholm: LiberFörlag; Sauter, Willmar (1979), *Theater als Widerstand: Wirkung und Wirkungsweise eines politischen Theaters: Faschismus und Judendarstellung auf der schwedischen Bühne 1936-1941*. Stockholm: Akademilitt.
16 Forser, Tomas (1976), *Bööks 30-tal: En studie i ideologi*. Stockholm: PAN/ Norstedt; Olsson, Jan (1979), *Svensk spelfilm under andra världskriget*. Lund: LiberLäromedel.
17 Levine, Paul A. (1996), *From Indifference to Activism: Swedish Diplomacy and the Holocaust, 1938-1944*. Uppsala: Univ.; Richardson, Gunnar (1996), *Beundran och fruktan: Sverige inför Tyskland 1940-1942*. Stockholm: Carlsson; Oredsson, Sverker (1996), *Lunds universitet under andra världskriget: Motsättningar, debatter och hjälpinsatser*. Lund: Lunds universitetshistoriska sällsk.; Berggren, Lena (1999), *Nationell upplysning: Drag i den svenska antisemitismens idéhistoria*.

Stockholm: Carlsson; Bachner, Henrik (1999), *Återkomsten: Antisemitism i Sverige efter 1945*. Stockholm: Natur och kultur; Andersson, Lars M. (2000), *En jude är en jude är en jude. . .: Representationer av 'juden' i svensk skämtpress omkring 1900-1930*. Lund: Nordic Academic Press; Götz, Norbert (2001), *Ungleiche Geschwister: Die Konstruktion von nationalsozialistischer Volksgemeinschaft und schwedischem Volksheim*. Baden-Baden: Nomos; Tydén, Mattias (2002), *Från politik till praktik: De svenska steriliseringslagarna 1935-1975*. Stockholm: Fritzes offentliga publikationer; Carlsson, Henrik (2004) *Medborgarskap och diskriminering: Östjudar och andra invandrare i Sverige 1860-1920*. Uppsala: Acta Universitatis Upsaliensis; Blomqvist, Håkan (2006), *Nation, ras och civilisation i svensk arbetarrörelse före nazismen*. Stockholm: Carlsson; Rosengren, Henrik (2007), *'Judarnas Wagner': Moses Pergament och den kulturella identifikationens dilemma omkring 1920-1950*. Lund: Sekel; Petra, Garberding (2007), *Musik och politik i skuggan av nazismen: Kurt Atterberg och de svensk-tyska musikrelationerna*. (Lund: Sekel. See also Svanberg, Ingvar and Tydén, Mattias (eds) (1997), *Sverige och Förintelsen: Debatt och dokument om Europas judar 1933-1945*. Stockholm: Arena; Blomqvist, Håkan (1999), *Gåtan Nils Flyg och nazismen*. Stockholm: Carlsson; Blomqvist, Håkan (2001), *Socialdemokrat och antisemit? Den dolda historien om Arthur Engberg*. Stockholm: Carlsson; Blomberg, Göran (2003), *Mota Moses i grind: Ariseringsiver och antisemitism i Sverige 1933-1943*. Stockholm: Hillelförl.; Karlsson, Henrik (2005), *Det fruktade märket: Wilhelm Peterson-Berger, antisemitismen och antinazismen*. Malmö: Sekel; Byström, Mikael (2006), *En broder, gäst och parasit: Uppfattningar och föreställningar om utlänningar, flyktingar och flyktingpolitik i svensk offentlig debatt 1942-1947*. Stockholm: Acta Universitatis Stockholmiensis; and Geverts, Karin Kvist (2008), *Ett främmande element i nationen: Svensk flyktingpolitik och de judiska flyktingarna 1938-1944*. Uppsala: Acta Universitatis Upsaliensis. For a summary of the new research of the 1990s and 2000s, see Brylla, Charlotta, Almgren, Birgitta, and Kirsch, Frank-Michael (eds) (2005), *Bilder i kontrast: Interkulturella processer Sverige/Tyskland i skuggan av nazismen 1933-1945*. Aalborg: Institut für Sprache und internationale Kulturstudien, Univ. Aalborg; and Andersson, Lars M. and Tydén, Mattias (eds) (2007), *Sverige och Nazityskland: Skuldfrågor och moraldebatt*. Stockholm: Dialogos.

18 See, for example, Frei, Norbert (2005), *1945 und wir: Das Dritte Reich im Bewußtsein der Deutschen*. Munich: C. H. Beck.

19 François (2004), pp. 19-25. The Holocaust in contemporary European history culture is analysed in Karlsson, Klas-Göran (2003), 'The Holocaust as a Problem of Historical Culture', in Karlsson, Klas-Göran and Zander, Ulf (eds), *Echoes of the Holocaust: Historical Cultures in Contemporary Europe*. Lund: Nordic Academic Press.

20 François (2004), pp. 21-2.
21 Boëthius, Maria-Pia (1991), *Heder och samvete: Sverige och andra världskriget*. Stockholm: Ordfront, p. 9. The original reads: 'Detta är en historiebok för efterkrigsfödda; en anklagelseakt, ett syndaregister och en debattbok. Efterkrigsgenerationerna i Sverige vet synnerligen lite om Sverige och andra världskriget. Det kan vara en del av vår allmänna historielöshet, det kan vara en tystnadens konspiration. Sveriges roll under andra världskriget var inte ärofull.'
22 Zander, Ulf (2001), *Fornstora dagar, moderna tider: Bruk av och debatter om svensk historia från sekelskifte till sekelskifte*. Lund: Nordic Academic Press, pp. 445-55.
23 Ludvigsson, David, 'Levande historia' - inte bara levande historia', in Nielsen, Carsten Tage, Simonsen, Dorthe Gert, and Wul, Lene (eds) (2001), *Rapporter til Det 24. Nordiske Historikermøde, Århus 9.-13. august 2001: Mod nye historier*. Århus: Jysk Selskab for Historie; Karlsson, Klas-Göran (2004) 'The Holocaust as Politics and Use of History – the Example of Living History', in Almqvist, Kurt and Glans, Kay (eds), *The Swedish Success Story?* (Stockholm: Axel and Margaret Ax:son Johnson Foundation.
24 Johansson (1997), p. 176.
25 Johansson (1997), p. 181.
26 Of course, there were exceptions: Gunnar Richardson was born in 1924 and Sverker Oredsson in 1937.
27 Hansson, Jonas (2003), 'Sweden and Nazism', in Ekman, Stig and Åmark, Klas (eds), *Sweden's Relations with Nazism, Nazi Germany and the Holocaust: A Survey of Research*. Stockholm: Almqvist and Wicksell International, p. 182.
28 Forskningsprogrammet 'Sveriges förhållande till nazismen, Nazi-Tyskland och Förintelsen' http://www.vr.se/download/18.bfcea3310ab2bd97898000214/Nazismen.pdf. accessed 3 May, 2012. Klas Åmark's (2011) massive *Att bo granne med ondskan: Sveriges förhållande till nazismen, Nazityskland och Förintelsen*. Stockholm: Bonnier, synthesizes much of the new research on Sweden's relations with Nazi Germany. John Gilmour's (2010) *Sweden, the Swastika and Stalin: The Swedish Experience in the Second World War*. Edinburgh: Edinburgh University Press, the first comprehensive introduction for English-speaking readers to the topic, also benefits from many of the new studies.
29 Koblik, Steven (1987), *'Om vi teg, skulle stenarna ropa': Sverige och judeproblemet 1933-1945*. Stockholm: Norstedt; Levine (1996).
30 Ohlsson, Anders (2002), *'Men ändå måste jag berätta': Studier i skandinavisk förintelselitteratur*. Nora: Nya Doxa; Andersson, Greger and Geisler, Ursula (eds) (2006), *Fruktan, fascination och frändskap: Det svenska musiklivet och nazismen*. Malmö: Sekel; Jarlert, Anders (2006), *Judisk 'ras' som äktenskapshinder i Sverige: Effekten av Nürnberglagarna i Svenska kyrkans statliga funktion som lysningsförrättare 1935-1945*. Malmö: Sekel; Richardson (1996); Almgren,

Birgitta (2001) *Illusion und Wirklichkeit: Individuelle und kollektive Denkmuster in nationalsozialistischer Kulturpolitik und Germanistik in Schweden 1928–1945*. Huddinge: Södertörns högsk.; Liljefors, Max (2002), *Bilder av Förintelsen: Mening, minne, komprometttering*. Lund: Palmkron; Almgren, Birgitta (2005), *Drömmen om Norden: Nazistisk infiltration i Sverige 1933–1945*. Stockholm: Carlsson; Lomfors, Ingrid (2005), *Blind fläck: Minne och glömska kring svenska Röda korsets hjälpinsats i Nazityskland 1945*. Stockholm: Atlantis; Karlsson, Birgit (2007), *Egenintresse eller samhällsintresse: Nazityskland och svensk skogsindustri 1933–1945*. Lund: Sekel; Fritz, Martin (2007), *Sveriges tyskgruvor: Tyskägda gruvor i Sverige under andra världskriget*. Lund: Sekel.

31 Bryld, Claus and Warring, Anette (1998), *Besættelsestiden som kollektiv erindring*. Gylling: Roskilde Universitets Forlag.

32 Sørensen, Nils Arne (2005), 'Narrating the Second World War in Denmark since 1945', *Contemporary European History*, Vol. 14, No. 3.

33 Eriksen, Anne (1995), *Det var noe annet under krigen: 2. verdenskrig i norsk kollektivtradisjon*. Oslo: Pax; Bryld (2007).

34 Östling (2008b), pp. 284–6.

35 Ibid., p. 284.

36 Zander (2001), pp. 402–59; Linderborg, Åsa (2001), *Socialdemokraterna skriver historia: Historieskrivning som ideologisk maktresurs 1892–2000*. Stockholm: Atlas, pp. 419–23; Rosenberg, Göran (2002), 'The Crisis of Consensus in Postwar Sweden', in Witoszek, Nina and Trägårdh, Lars (eds) (2002), *Culture and Crisis: The Case of Germany and Sweden*. New York: Berghahn.

37 Wiklund, Martin (2006), *I det modernas landskap: Historisk orientering och kritiska berättelser om det moderna Sverige mellan 1960 och 1990*. Eslöv: Östlings bokförlag Symposion.

38 See, however, Zetterberg, Kent (2000), 'Det neutrala Sveriges skuld och ansvar: Till frågan om den svenska politiken under det andra världskriget och den svenska debatten efter kriget', in Zetterberg, Kent and Åselius, Gunnar (eds) (2000), *Historia, krig och statskonst: En vänbok till Klaus-Richard Böhme*. Stockholm: Probus, for a critical view.

39 Karlsson (2004), p. 245.

Figure 7 Finland's *Iltalehti* newspaper in this 2011 special supplement commemorates the wartime service by soldiers and civilians alike in the controversial 'Continuation War' ('*Jatkosota*') when Finnish forces fought alongside the German *Wehrmacht* against the Soviet Union. [With kind permission of Iltalehti/Alma Media.]

11

Two Shadows over Finland

Hitler, Stalin and the Finns Facing the Second World War as History 1944–2010

Juhana Aunesluoma

Remembering the Second World War

The Second World War is the most celebrated and debated moment in Finnish history. No other event, period or historical process matches the extent to which the war – or wars in Finnish vocabulary – is and has been represented in different forms of Finnish historical culture.[1] The significance of the war is in part explained by its human dimension and the direct influence it had over the lives of many Finns. The war left Finland with more than 90,000 people dead, most of them troops killed in combat. Territorial changes forced 400,000 Finns to leave their homes and to find new habitation in the remaining parts of the country. Out of a population of four million, these are high figures by general European and Scandinavian standards, although they pale in comparison with the worst experiences of the eastern European 'bloodlands' located in the contested regions between Germany and the Soviet Union.[2]

The war shadowed the life of ordinary Finns for years to come. In 2004, there were still some 100,000 people alive who had fought in the war, and more than one million people who had personally experienced it on the home front.[3] Despite the fact that the younger generations do not share the memories of the older population, they still express a keen interest in the war. This can be seen in the popularity of the war and related topics in film and plays, fiction novels, personal memoirs and in other representations of history.[4] As the historian Tony

Judt has said, for most Europeans, forgetting was an important way of coping with the past as soon as the war had ended in Europe.[5] For Finns, however, forgetting about the war was not and has never been an option. On the contrary, actively, even obsessively, remembering and commemorating the war has been a central component of Finnish national identity.[6] An idea of a 'nation forged in the crucible of war' has for long formed the keystone of a national narrative which is still rehearsed in a remarkably coherent form in schools, popular historical literature, days of commemorating the nation's sacrifices and so on.[7]

According to the 'nation-building view' of the significance of World War II, the following narrative has usually been adopted: first in the mid-nineteenth century the Finnish cultural nation was born within the Russian empire, inhabiting a semi-state, an autonomous Grand Duchy. In 1917, an independent state was created during the chaos of the Russian revolution, but the nation-building process was disturbed by a fierce civil war in 1918. Despite a clear victory for the non-socialist right, the country remained politically and socially divided in the interwar period. Hence, it was only in the Winter War of 1939–40, a 'holy war' for many Finns, and in the far more controversial Continuation War of 1941–44, that a unified society and a nation grew in and out of it, and took its place in the European community of peoples. In this narrative, it was in World War II that Finns had passed the test of history and finally earned their own state and full nationhood – with their blood. This is the traditional grand narrative which provides the framework within which World War II is commemorated in Finland every 6 December, the national day of independence.[8] A remarkable feature in Finnish historical culture is how wartime sacrifices and events are paraded in independence-day celebrations and how World War II has over time eclipsed the events of 1917 as the critical moment for Finnish independence.[9] In Europe, it may be argued, only the Soviet Union, and more recently Russia, has made more of its efforts in the Great Patriotic War than Finns have made of theirs.

The war lives on in contemporary political parlance. It is not at all unusual that issues dealing with the 'common interest' or the 'national interest', and how these are produced and constructed in politics, are often framed in wartime rhetoric. In Finland, one can still periodically hear contemporary politicians appeal to the wartime national consensus while trying to create one now, or to the 'spirit of the Winter War' when seeking, for example, parliamentary approval for emergency measures to counter international financial and economic turmoil. Not all connexions of the war with today's politics and attitudes are merely rhetorical. Lessons drawn from World War II loom large in Finnish attitudes towards military defence, especially in the widespread support to maintain a nineteenth century-style conscript army tasked with a twentieth century-style commitment to territorial defence. It worked then, so it still might. Seventy years on, the war is still with us.

Makers of historical culture

The continuing presence of World War II in contemporary Finnish society and culture, and the interest in the various phases and events of it, does not mean that the war's historical image is without tensions or inherent contradictions. One of the reasons why the war is so keenly commemorated and discussed arises from the very fact that many of the memories associated with it and key elements of the historical narratives are still controversial and subject to often heated debate. A notable feature in Finnish Second World War historical culture has been how intensively the wider public, professional historians and political actors have interacted in it. The triangular relationship involving these producers and consumers of historical knowledge has not been an easy one. Despite certain pluralism and fragmentation of popular notions of history and also the more polyphonic nature of professional historical scholarship, views concerning the war have had a strong tendency to polarize around traditionalist and revisionist views.[10] The often rather conflicting interaction of different producers and interpreters of historical knowledge has also slowed down the coagulation of consensual views on certain key themes of Finland's experience of the war and the writing of a broad-ranged and balanced historical synthesis of it.

Finnish Second World War historical culture has not merely reflected or augmented particular or pre-existing notions of history, but it rather has created views and understanding of history through its own dynamics. It may well be that it is the very nature of this interaction and its intensity that explain the persistence of polarized views of the war and how difficult it is to carve out room for more nuanced and less clear-cut interpretations of the war. In the making of this historical culture different actors have had their own roles, interests and voice.

For post-war political actors who sought a political accommodation with the Soviet Union, World War II and the decisions made by political leaders during it were nothing but politically irrelevant. But no one, not even the communists who re-entered Finnish political life as an organized political force in 1944, could start with a clean slate. The continuity of Finland's political elite from the war to the Cold War ensured that the wartime record remained on the agenda long into the future. As participants of historical debates, their views of wartime events were also politically significant.

Given the extent to which Finnish society and people were directly influenced by the war and the reconstruction period that followed it, it is no surprise that such a vibrant field of popular histories, commemoration and diverse forms of historical representations emerged in post-war decades, and that it continues even today. Between different voices and views, professional historians have been not only a moderating force. By providing new archive-based knowledge and novel interpretations for a field that is already crowded with historical representations, academic historians have in fact played a key role in fomenting controversy. As participants in history debates with the wider public, many Finnish historians have also become well-known public personalities, with a distinct role as intermediaries and interpreters of the past in the present.[11]

Notwithstanding the opportunities this has provided for professional historians to practise their craft, the intensity of Finnish Second World War historical culture has also been a challenge. To the apparent frustration of some historians, it has been quite difficult to change the parameters of the existing debate, let alone to cause fundamental shifts in the wider historical understanding of the war in Finland. The prime example of the persistence of popular views of history that run against the main current of academic history writing is the thesis that Finland's war against the Soviet Union in 1941–44 should be considered a 'separate war' from the war waged between Hitler and Stalin. This view of Finland's war in relative isolation from the wider Second World War still has a keen following especially outside the realm of professional historians. The separate war thesis follows closely the wartime efforts of the Finnish government, and President Risto Ryti in particular, to convince a sceptical public in the west that Finland had not irreversibly allied itself with Germany, although they shared a common enemy in the east.[12] Pre-eminent historians, such as Eino Jutikkala and Mauno Jokipii, both of whom served in different functions during the war and could hardly be suspected of harbouring 'unpatriotic' views of history, also faced a sceptical public when in the 1970s and

1980s they took issue with widely held views that Finnish wartime leaders had merely drifted into war against their will in 1941 and had not made conscious or deliberate decisions to this effect.[13]

Points of interest, points of controversy

The points of controversy have shifted somewhat over time from one issue or theme to another. As can be seen from Oula Silvennoinen's chapter in this book, perhaps the most impassioned controversy now arises from the relationship of Adolf Hitler and the Nazi regime with Finland – or perhaps rather the other way around: the Finns' relationship with the Nazis. As time and decades have passed, we can see that the continuing Finnish interest in the war has been increasingly concerned with a Finnish version of *Vergangenheitsbewältigung*, that is, how to cope with the legacy of fighting alongside Hitler and the Nazis in 1941–44.

For a long time, the historical comprehension of Finns in World War II revolved around the twin concepts of victimhood and being alone. The starting point was simple enough: unprovoked Soviet aggression in November 1939. Finns faced evil on their own. Furthermore, as Germany had aligned itself with the Soviet Union in the August 1939 Molotov-Ribbentrop Pact, all the evil in World War II was on the other side. Everything else that subsequently happened followed from that basic premise. The course of the Winter War of 1939–40 was a relatively straightforward story, but how then should we consider and describe the relationship between Finland and Germany during the years 1941–44? An alliance, coalition, co-belligerency, comradeship in arms, an alliance of kind, or what? How did Finland go to war again in 1941?

A related issue that has attracted considerable interest concerns Finnish behaviour regarding the atrocities committed by the Nazi regime and its supporters on the eastern front and in various parts of Europe – the Holocaust and other crimes against humanity.[14] A thorough investigation was conducted in 2004–08 on the conditions and fatalities of Soviet prisoners of war in Finland, and how many Jews and other people were eventually shipped to their deaths in territory under German control from Finland.[15] However, despite the paramount importance of the integration of Finland into the history of the Holocaust, Finnish *Vergangenheitsbewältigung* has not been the whole story. The more salient political and politicized aspects of analysing or narrating Finland's war have coexisted with a different, wider, lower and more diffuse level of historical culture, the experiential, the personal and the communal. In the discussion of

Finland's relationship with Hitler and the Holocaust, but also in the ways in which ordinary Finns coped with wartime conditions and experiences, we can see a discernible trend over the last decades. The human dimension, the personal and the experiential, has gradually overtaken the level of high politics, grand strategy and questions of state. As the big political and strategic decisions of wartime leaders have somewhat receded into the background, the human and humanitarian aspects have taken the foreground. Against this background, a discussion of Finland's place in the wider history of the Holocaust has been unavoidable.

The reasons behind this development can be traced to international trends in how the war has been viewed as a personal experience, the centrality of the Holocaust perspective, but also in the ways in which wartime political and military decisions eventually became irrelevant politically in Finland after the dissolution of the Soviet Union. The breaking of the linkage between current Finnish foreign and domestic politics with the 'lessons' and in particular the end result of the war created more room for other themes and viewpoints to emerge in the 1990s and 2000s.

In addition to the relationship and role of Finland in the Holocaust, the personal and humanitarian aspects can be seen in how the lives of ordinary Finns have been expressed in history writing and historical culture. The fate of the 80,000 or so children shipped over to safety in Sweden, and the long-term personal consequences of these children's lonely exile, is clearly a sore point for those involved. The Soviet strategic air force's heavy bombing of Helsinki and other cities in 1944, and civilians slaughtered by Soviet partisans in remote villages, have proved to be difficult topics to handle in history writing, not to mention commemoration, and are also sensitive issues in today's Russia. The Finnish authorities' rounding up of Soviet citizens into concentration camps, and by and large their responsibility for wartime conditions in the occupied territories in Eastern Karelia, has been a point of dispute between more critical voices and those who stress the absence of genocidal motives or behaviour on the part of Finns.[16]

Previous decades have seen many other controversies as well, and some issues return from time to time. If the humanitarian and also the moral aspects of the war seem so important today, the crucial political and military-strategic decisions made by the nation's highest leadership during the war were where most of the controversy previously lay. Decades rolled by in the debate between the supporters and opponents of the so-called 'driftwood theory' of Finland's entry into the war alongside Germany in 1941. Did Finland choose war in 1941, or was it forced into it against its own will? What was the precise range of choice its leaders had at the time? It is worth noting that, as the range of choices available for Finnish wartime leaders was assessed by historians and a keenly interested general public in the 1960s and 1970s, the question as to whether the Soviet attack on Finland could have been avoided altogether in 1939 by a more efficient diplomacy and willingness to negotiate from the Finnish side divided opinions in Finland. In the creation of historical knowledge and understanding, this debate was probably a more useful exercise than the disputes between Finnish and Soviet historians over who actually had started the war in 1939. Before the *perestroika* of the late 1980s influenced Soviet historical interpretations, the official view was that an aggressive and adventurous Finland had started it, a claim against material evidence and which Finnish historians could not but regard as plainly outrageous. Another volley of the Soviet historians' shots was fired on the original Finnish version of the outbreak of hostilities in 1941, when the wartime government claimed that the Soviet Union started them. As the Soviet airforce indeed had struck targets in Finland just before the latter's ground forces moved to the east in July 1941, there was a technical truth in the Finnish version, but in all other aspects the claims of a Soviet offensive against Finland in the summer of 1941 were pure nonsense.

The debates on who started the war, not to mention why, were conjoined with a debate on whether Finland might have averted its worst losses in the war by suing for peace in the first half of 1944 and accepted the peace terms that the Allied powers offered it then. Thus, it might have avoided the great battles, and fatalities, of the eastern front in the summer of 1944. Nevertheless, as the leaders at the time and subsequent historians have reasoned, such a move would have risked a German counteroffensive and an intervention in Finland along the lines of action taken in Italy and in Hungary in 1943–44. According to this scenario, Finland almost certainly would have shared the experiences of our neighbours in the 'bloodlands' south of the Gulf of Finland.

On a quite different note, there has also been a lively debate in Finland about whether we should in fact regard ourselves as one of the victor nations of the war – instead of having ended up on the losing side in 1944. The justification for that view lies in the events of the summer of 1944 in particular, when Finland, by achieving a 'defensive victory', narrowly avoided military occupation by the Red Army.[17] The fact that no Soviet troops 'liberated' mainland Finland is directly relevant to what happened in 1944–48, when Finland also avoided the fate of becoming a people's democracy under Communist Party rule. Perhaps against the odds – at least that was the view in the west at the time – Finland preserved not only its independence but also its traditional societal and political Nordic institutions, its democracy and a western-style export-driven market economy.

There is no shortage of controversial issues on a more detailed level either. In the early 2000s, a debate raged on the peacemaking which ended the Winter War in March 1940. The historian Heikki Ylikangas claimed that the Finnish government had already during early 1940 received assurances from Germany, and from Hermann Göring in particular, that it could accept peace there and then. As Germany's geopolitical destiny would soon have outlived its partnership with the Soviet Union, it would turn to the east and bring Bolshevism down together with the Soviet state.[18] Finland could expect a handsome compensation for its losses. Recently, the domestic situation in 1940 has also been under scrutiny, in particular, what the local communists were up to in Finland as the Baltic states were sovietizised and whether Finland was moving, or was being moved, in the same direction. We should also not forget military historians, who debate the course of campaigns and individual battles, or economic historians who have yet to reach an agreement on what precisely happened to Finland's gross national product during the war. After decades of historical research and debates, views differ and the war arouses emotions. However, irrespective of what one thinks about World War II as a whole or its specific features, its centrality as a national experience is widely acknowledged. Remembering and commemorating Finland's war, in agreement or in disagreement, is still a part of being a Finn in today's world.

Guilty as charged?

Finnish Second World War historical culture has taken shape and evolved through the interplay of different articulations and uses of history. In order to understand how all this has happened, it is important to acknowledge and analyse the role, the function and the motivations of the different actors. However, the interplay has also been time-specific, meaning that is has taken place in a particular social, cultural and political setting, in a given time and a place.

The evolution of balanced views of Finland's experience of the war did not have an auspicious start. The first act was played out in a politically supercharged atmosphere, in the so-called war-guilt trial of 1945–46, which set the parameters for debate on the war for decades to come. The trial was instigated by the Allies, who demanded that not only those who had committed war crimes or crimes against humanity, but also politicians who had cooperated with the Nazis, should be put on trial. Finland's wartime President Risto Ryti received the longest sentence, 10 years, others shorter ones, with the notable exception of the wartime military Supreme Commander Gustav Mannerheim, President of the republic 1944–46, who was not prosecuted at all, as he was needed to steer Finland onto a new path in the immediate post-war confusion.

Although the sentences were lenient by European standards, anyone in Finland who felt that their nation as a whole had been treated unjustly in the war could regard the imprisoned leaders as their martyrs. The trial's legitimacy was widely disputed at the outset, with the far left an exception to this.[19] It was based on retroactive law, and besides most Finns did not believe that their leaders had done much wrong in the first place. The whole nation had met a misfortune on a massive scale, squeezed between the ambitions of two dictators, and it seemed futile to blame a handful of Finnish leaders for what had happened in 1940–41, with the decision to go to war, nor in 1943–44, with the decision to continue it against mounting Allied military and diplomatic pressure.

The war guilt trial, however, had important long-term consequences that were felt long after the men had served their sentences. The Allied and Soviet Union's interests were fulfilled in the short term, as their demands to purge wartime leaders from post-war politics were met in Finland, with the exception of Mannerheim. In the longer term, the trial proved to be Pyrrhic victory. From the Allied perspective, the war guilt trial led to unintended consequences. As the wartime leaders were prosecuted, they were able to develop, articulate and argue a case in their defence and make it public.[20] The trial gave them a voice. In this they were helped by other wartime insiders, professional historians, and by and large a public that was sympathetic to their case.

It is very likely that an apologetic version of wartime events would have emerged in any case soon after the war, but an illegitimate trial, in a curious fashion, legitimated the defence's case beyond what it probably would have been in other circumstances. As they mounted their case, a legitimate exercise for anyone facing the prospect of imprisonment, the defendants composed a rather extreme version of wartime events and decisions that stretched and omitted evidence as suited them best, and was anything but a thorough and objective account of what had happened. At the core of the defence's case was an interpretation of Finland as having being forced against its will into the war in 1941. Events in the main theatres of the war and actions of powers beyond Finland's control had dragged Finland into war against the Soviet Union. Furthermore, the country was an object of aggression and not really a willing partner in Hitler's coalition, as the prosecutors suggested.

Soon after the trial, the defence's argumentation became the staple of historical accounts and memoir literature.[21] It was rehearsed in the memoirs of a German diplomat, Wipert von Blücher in 1950, who compared Finland's destiny to driftwood that was pulled into the torrent of great power politics, and thus it provided the key metaphor for Finns to describe their relationship with Hitler, Operation Barbarossa and all that went into and followed from that.[22] Thanks to the activities of the defence's historical advisors, the western public was also soon able to familiarize itself with their case in John H. Wuorinen's edited volume *Finland and World War II, 1939–1944*, published in 1948 in the United States. It was in fact the work of the eminent Finnish historian Arvi Korhonen, Risto Ryti, Väinö Tanner, the wartime Social Democratic Minister and others, translated into English and published in the United States in Wuorinen's name.[23] After resigning from the presidency in 1946 and after moving to Switzerland to spend his remaining years in a less arduous climate than that of Cold War Finland, Marshal Gustav Mannerheim also wrote his memoirs, where the same line of argument was elaborated and defended forcibly, and was well received by the reading public in Finland.[24]

Between the two dictators

The trial of 1946 entrenched and legitimated the apologetic version of the wartime leaders. To defend the 'driftwood' theory of Finland's entry into the war in 1941, and by and large the case in defence of the prosecuted politicians, became a patriotic duty for Finns. Finland had not been an active agent but a passive victim in the war. If one held different views, one sided either with the communists or with the proponents of the 1946 sentences – in Finland or in the Soviet Union, it did not matter which. The new political leadership of Cold War Finland found this discourse most uncomfortable, but such was the strength of the argument that even Urho Kekkonen, who as Minister of Justice had been responsible for orchestrating the trial, avoided taking issue with the defence's case when he later became President of the republic and served almost twenty-five years in office.[25]

A hegemonic discourse was established, but not of a type that the victors of the war would have preferred to see taking root in post-war Finland. In this exercise of politicizing history and coping with a difficult past, Finns started to play the wartime dictators against each other. According to this view, the one shadow provided by Hitler was eclipsed by an even stronger and darker shadow, the shadow of Stalin. Compared with the existential threat of Stalin to Finns, Hitler's legacy was seen as relative. As one wartime veteran later put it: 'Of course no one of us really knew, what man this Adolf Hitler was and what he might bring about. It was quite natural that we here in Finland were more afraid of Stalin than we were of Hitler, and that we knew, that if the situation grew worse again, we would have to devise our own solutions so that the independence of our country would be secured.'[26] From instrumentalizing and relativizing Hitler it was not a large step to remove the Nazi experience from Finland's own, separate the wars altogether and see Hitler as not much more than an external, if somewhat distant, evil force compared with Stalin. With Stalin and the Soviet Union as the main players in the story of Finland's national survival, Hitler was encapsulated and isolated from this narrative, and for the first one and a half decades after the war or so remained largely absent from Finnish popular or professional historical accounts.

A key concept in the making of this version of wartime history was agency – or rather, the lack of it. As Finland had faced not only one dictator but two of them, their leaders had to make whatever decisions they made within very narrow margins. From April 1940 onwards, with Hitler in command of Scandinavia, the course of war had left very little room for agency for Finns, who had become the victims of nearly deterministic historical forces that they were in no position to control. Given the forces at play around the country, this view of the two dictators signified only limited room for individual agency on all levels – not only at the top, but also in the rank and file and in society at large. In a sense, it let not only the top leaders but also the whole nation off the hook.

It is difficult to say what would have happened in this strategy of throwing the shadow of one dictator, Stalin, over the shadow of another one, Hitler, had there been no Cold War and the ensuing vilification of 'Uncle Joe' in the west. It certainly helped, since there were many others in Europe who wanted to forget about Hitler as well. In any case by turning the attention away from Hitler and emphasizing the shadow of Stalin, Finns were able to underline the existential nature of their wartime struggle in a manner that is reminiscent of the 'bloodlands' historiographies rather than of the Scandinavian experience.

Obligation to overcome animosity

It took many years before the apologetic account of the events of 1941–44 could be challenged. What is particularly interesting was its persistence. After all, views such as these on the recent war fitted most uneasily with the realities of post-war Finland and its position as a defeated country within the Soviet sphere of influence. President Juho Kusti Paasikivi (1946–56), who succeeded Mannerheim in 1946, described the wartime leaders as irresponsible 'adventurers' and called for a new *modus vivendi* with the eastern superpower. Paasikivi's successor, Urho Kekkonen (1956–82), was in turn well known for his critical views of wartime politicians and their politics, and he did not shy away from expressing his criticism in public debates. Kekkonen had himself shifted his warmongering views and joined the opposition against continuing the war in 1943 and was not sympathetic at all to the apologetic driftwood thesis. To accept it openly would be to side with the men in jail and also to take a stand against the Soviet Union. On the other hand, and as has been pointed out by the Finnish historian Henrik Meinander, to embark upon a domestic debate over the topic would risk going too far against the grain of popular opinion and challenging widely shared and cherished views of the war. So, Kekkonen dodged the issue.[27] But neither was the Soviet Union happy with the situation. It nonetheless became, for a while, one of the post-war compromises between Soviet Union and mainstream Finnish society. The whole issue was brushed under the carpet. Meanwhile, and as a part of this compromise, the Finnish people were faced with the challenge of overcoming their wartime and pre-war animosity towards the Soviet Union, as post-war foreign policy rested on the foundations of the Friendship, Cooperation and Mutual Assistance (FCMA) Treaty of 1948. An obligation to overcome animosity between the two nations and become 'friends', as the treaty stated, was neither easy nor achieved overnight.

As the hegemonic discourse of the war could hardly be challenged outright, the tension arising from Finland's new geopolitical position, its new foreign policy and relationship with the Soviet Union found outlets in the 1950s in the third pillar of historical culture mentioned above: in public history and, in particular, remembering the war and its cultural representations.

While the FCMA-treaty and its application obliged Finns to forget the mutual animosity between the Soviet Union and Finland and to build a different kind of future horizon for themselves, when looking at and thinking about the recent past their gaze turned elsewhere: to the experience of the war at the front and the experience of the human being in it. The uneasy compromise on the Finnish agency question and the silence or complicity of professional historians with the established views impelled artists and ordinary people to create their own histories of the war. From the mid-1950s' onwards and all the way to the present in the 2010s, this level of writing, experiencing and displaying World War II history has made up the most voluminous, and – when it comes to the wider public – probably the most accessible and influential part of all historical representations of it.[28]

The decisive turning point in the artistic expressions and representations of the war was Väinö Linna's novel *Unknown Soldier*, published in 1954, which was the first realistic fiction account of the war at the front. It achieved immense popularity as soon as it was published.[29] A subsequent film version became the biggest box office success in the history of the Finnish film industry. Characteristic of Linna's, but also of other popular or artistic representations of the war, was, however, that it took no explicit stand on the big debate about Finland and Germany. By looking at the individual soldier's experience, it avoided the thorny issue of who fought with whom and for what purpose, and removed politics almost completely from the picture.

Introducing Finnish agency

The professional historians' loyal silence could not last forever. Neither would the war guilt trial's defendants' case survive the test of a hard look into the archives. The relative calm around the driftwood-explanation started to show its first cracks in the late 1950s. Within the Cold War international system, Finland followed a 'realist' foreign policy of accommodation with the Soviet Union, accepted the geopolitical realities and by emphasizing neutrality tried to avoid being entangled further in the Cold War between the superpowers than the country's geographical location dictated. While relations with the Soviet Union had in the mid-1950s settled on a course of 'peaceful coexistence', it also seemed that the new foreign policy was working as well. As exercised by Presidents Paasikivi and Kekkonen, Finnish agency appeared not as wrong-headed as during the war.

In historical revisionism, however, Finnish historians were not the agents of change, at least not in the first wave. Utilizing German and western archival materials, American and British historians C. Leonard Lundin, Anthony Upton and Hans Peter Krosby punctured the driftwood thesis and sank it in the course of the late 1950s and 1960s.[30] According to them, it had been clear that the Finnish leadership had deliberately chosen war in 1941, planned their offensive operations in cooperation with the Germans and taken a calculated risk to correct the wrongs of the Moscow Peace of 1940. Finnish historians, spearheaded by Arvi Korhonen, put up yet again a heroic defence, eventually to be overwhelmed by documentary evidence and the compelling logic of the revisionist historians' works.[31] As agency had become the keyword of Finnish foreign policy in the late 1950s and 1960s, so it became the *leitmotif* of the new histories of Finland's war as well. Introducing agency in Finnish decision-making in 1940–41, however, opened up controversial questions over particular actions and personalities that had been avoided previously. The key question was simple and big. If the choices made either on the individual level or among the collective political and military decision-making machinery were not dictated by necessity, but were rather the result of rational deliberation and choice, then the nature and consequences of these choices had to be considered. Were the decisions right?

Agency opened up a whole new range of themes that had to be addressed and a whole new registry of attributes that could be used in portraying the decisions, choices and the personalities behind them. A debate on, and representations of, wartime events, in particular, the forging of the alliance of a kind with Germany in 1941 and the events of summer 1944 thereafter, began to revolve around concepts such as heroism, betrayal, opportunism, statecraft, risk-taking, irresponsibility and ideology – all depending on the viewpoint and the nature of those conducting the argument. That debate, which has continued until this day, is not without ideological or moral undertones and links the Finnish debate with debates elsewhere in Europe.

The questioning of the 1946 defence case was in many ways also connected to the environment and the cultural and intellectual atmosphere of the 1960s. The rising tide of left-wing movements and sentiments in national political life took one of its cues from criticism of the actions of the wartime generation, including its leaders. To accept the revisionist views of the wartime decisions, and in particular of Finland's partnership with Hitler, also indicated a discontinuity in Finnish political life. The contemporary societal conditions as well as the historical record suggested that Finns should now, finally, make a break with the war generation and with the one that had preceded it. This process, however, remained in many ways incomplete. Both on the political level, where continuities proved strong (as had happened after 1944), and on the level of historical culture, a sizeable tranche of opinion would still in the future show sympathy for the men on trial in 1946. At the very top, high up in President Kekkonen's chancellery, things, however, could not have looked better. Although it is difficult to show that there existed a direct link between revisionist historiography and Finnish political leadership and foreign policy, the new historical views that gained currency suited Kekkonen very well indeed.

Two birds were killed with one stone. First, the historical record showed that a country like Finland could, even in the most difficult of circumstances, make its own foreign policy and have a say in its destiny. Its leaders simply had to follow the right kind of policy and make the right decisions. For Kekkonen, there were at least three lessons learnt from the war – all controversial and disputed freshly by professional historians. As Kekkonen saw it, the outbreak of hostilities in 1939 could have been avoided had there been more effective diplomacy and trust between the two countries and their representatives. The entry into the war in 1941 had been a calculated decision, but it was also driven by heated domestic feelings of revanchism and ideological motivation. Hence, rational *Realpolitik,* which should have guided all decisions, had been cast aside. The third lesson was that the possibilities of neutrality, the cornerstone of Kekkonen's own Cold War foreign policy, were never exhausted during the war, including particularly in 1941. And finally, on a more personal note, the historical evidence culled from the archives proved to Kekkonen that he had been right in pursuing the wartime leaders in the trial of 1946. As it seemed to him, not only was he right about the present and the future, but he was right about history too.

From agency to distance

After agency was introduced into the Finnish comprehension of the nation's experience of the war, in the 1960s and 1970s, debates on particular decisions, events and personalities have come and gone. Confronted with masses of documentary evidence pulled from archives around Europe, even the most hard-boiled traditionalists had to accept the validity of the thesis that the wartime leaders 'had not been zeros', as Eino Jutikkala phrased it. They had made decisions – rational, calculated decisions – to re-enter the world war alongside Germany in 1941. What was debatable was how willingly they made the choices they made, and the extent to which some of them went, or wanted to go, in throwing in their lot with Hitler's Germany. Whether all the decisions made had been the right ones could also be questioned, as could the intricacies of Finland's political relations with Germany, but what could not be challenged any longer was that 1941 had been a year of decisions.

With Finnish agency accepted in principle, the debate took different directions. In the aftermath of the dissolution of the Soviet Union and the end of the Cold War in 1989–91, views on the Finnish leadership's agency in the war were turned on their head once again, at least when compared with Kekkonen's critical views. As a form of Finnish post-Cold War triumphalism, a view became commonplace in the 1990s that stressed the ultimate wisdom of the choices that had been made during the war. President Mauno Koivisto (1982–94), who himself had served at the front, was a high-profile defender of the decisions made by his predecessor Risto Ryti and other leaders. In his view, they had not been able to choose their course of action freely, but their decisions were the best that could be made with the information to hand, and in any case they saved the country and its people.[32] A corollary to the thesis that stressed the positive aspect of Finnish agency has been a popular view that has emphasized the final outcome of the great battles of the eastern front in the summer of 1944. There, Finnish forces had then, with strong support from the Germans, halted the Soviet offensive. This saved the country from occupation. The 'defensive victory' thesis has not quite put Finland on the winners' side in the 1945 endgame, but not on the losers' side either.

Looking at historical scholarship and other representations of history from the late 1980s until the present day, it is apparent that how to deal with Finnish agency in the war still remains a problematic issue. But the more we look at agency, and the more salient the universal humanitarian aspects of the war have become, the more problematic that consideration becomes. The ghost that rises on the horizon is the Holocaust. As the war slowly moves further back into history, and as the numbers of veterans and other people who experienced it directly are reduced and their voices less heard, what remains is what is unique in World War II in a much broader historical perspective: the scale and scope of genocide. How are we to cope with this, when the memories of wise statesmen making wise decisions and heroic soldiers fighting heroic battles are a lesser part of the broader historical panorama, and Auschwitz remains the lens through which everything else is seen? The strategy adopted is also familiar and, as it happens, is quite well in line with the basic Finnish foreign and security policy doctrine during the Cold War as well: isolation and distance.

Assuming and accepting a role for Finnish agency, the strategy adopted in a certain neo-traditionalist strand of Finnish *Vergangenheitsbewältigung* has been to make sure that Finland's war is as distinct a part of the Second World War as possible. Just as was the case in the 1940s, the passing of time has increased rather than decreased the need to distance and isolate Finland's war from the wider context of World War II – including how the war was experienced in the neighbouring Scandinavian countries. Although not shared by professional historians, in the culture of popular commemoration and popular representations of the war, this tendency has been discernible since the 1990s and does not show signs of weakening.

Just as during the war and immediately thereafter, it is as important as ever to make sure that Finland's Second World War is always dealt with and remembered as a continuity of two or three wars, with their own names and chronological frames from 1939–40 to 1941–44, culminating in the War in Lapland in 1944–45, where, most importantly, Finland fought against Germany. The main goal of this projection of Finland as a special category has undoubtedly been to do justice to the great number of Finns who served, fought and died in the war, but also to gain distance from the Holocaust and other Nazi atrocities. Nonetheless, it also has served a purpose in helping to construct the war as a tragic event in the short term with positive outcomes in the long term, with defeat becoming victory in time, risk-taking wise statecraft and traumatic individual experiences the building blocks of a coherent national culture with a shared past and a future. Stalin's shadow still eclipses that of Adolf Hitler.

Notes

1   On 'historical culture', I follow the definition of Jürn Rusen (1994), 'Was ist Geschichtskultur? Überlegungen zu einer neuen Art, über Geschichte nachzudenken', in Jörn Rüsen, Theo Grütter and Klaus Füssman (eds), *Historische Faszination: Geschichtskultur heute*. Köln u.a., pp. 3–26, and Pilvi Torsti (2008) 'Why do history politics matter? The Case of the Estonian Bronze Soldier', in Juhana Aunesluoma & Pauli Kettunen (eds) (2008), *The Cold War and the Politics of History*. Helsinki, Edita Publishing and University of Helsinki Department of Social Science History, 22. In this chapter, I use the derivative concept 'Second World War historical culture' to describe this particular aspect of (Finnish) historical culture.

2 What Finland narrowly escaped can be imagined from Timothy Snyder (2010), *Bloodlands. Europe Between Hitler and Stalin*. London, The Bodley Head. For recent figures of victims in the 'bloodlands' see Timothy Snyder (2011), 'Hitler vs. Stalin: Who Killed More?' *New York Review of Books*, 10–23 March 2011, Volume LVIII, No 4, 35–6.

3 Markku Jokisipilä (2004), *Aseveljiä vai liittolaisia? Suomi, Saksan liittosopimusvaatimukset ja Rytin-Ribbentropin-sopimus*. Helsinki, Suomalaisen Kirjallisuuden Seura, 23.

4 Good examples of the Finnish media's (commercial) interest in Second World War historical culture are the 66-page 'Continuation War' supplement of a national daily newspaper published in June 2011 as 'Jatkosota Extra. Kun Suomi Pelastui', *Iltalehti* 31/2011, and the extensive television and radio documentaries by the *Finnish National Broadcasting Company YLE* on the Winter War in 2009 and the Continuation War in 2011.

5 Tony Judt (2008), 'The Problem of Evil in Postwar Europe', *New York Review of Books*, 14 February 2008, Volume LV, No 2, 33–5; Tony Judt (2002), 'The past is another country: myth and memory in post-war Europe', in Jan-Werner Müller, *Memory & Power in Post-War Europe. Studies in the Presence of the Past*. Cambridge, Cambridge University Press, pp. 157–83.

6 A recent expression of the identity building thesis is Henrik Meinander (2009), *Suomi 1944. Sota, yhteiskunta, tunnemaisema*. Helsinki, Kustannusosakeyhtiö Siltala, pp. 392–8. Meinander also stresses the uniform nature in which the war has been remembered, although he anticipates that in the future more fragmented and pluralist views may appear, following what he sees as 'Western European' developments. Pilvi Torsti's research on Finnish historical consciousness indicate that this is happening, although it is yet to be ascertained how these more pluralist views may change the war's significance for Finnish national identity. Pilvi Torsti, History Consciousness in Finland – project at the University of Helsinki, www.historiatietoisuus.fi; Pilvi Torsti (2011), 'Sotasankaruuteen suhtaudutaan jo kriittisesti. Tuore tutkimus osoittaa, että kansalaisten enemmistö ei tue ahdasta näkemystä Suomen historiasta', *Helsingin Sanomat* 15 January 2011.

7 A thorough account of commemorating anniversaries is Heino Nyyssönen (2008), 'Commemorating two political anniversaries in cold war Finland: Independence and the Beginning of the Winter War', in Auesluoma & Kettunen (2008), *The Cold War and the Politics of History*. Helsinki, Edita Publishing and University of Helsinki Department of Social Science History, pp. 207–25. How the Winter War was viewed during the Cold War in Finland is outlined in Markku Jokisipilä (2010), 'Myyttinen tabu – talvisota suomalaisessa historiankirjoituksessa kylmän sodan kaudella', in Tiina Lintunen & Louis

Clerc (toim.), *Kenen sota? Uusia näkökulmia talvisotaan*. Ajankohta, Poliittisen historian vuosikirja 2010. Turku, Poliittinen historia, Helsingin ja Turun yliopistot, pp. 11–37.

8   The place of World War II in the grand narrative received a boost after the Cold War with the Soviet Union's collapse, an elaboration of which can be seen in Lauri Haataja (1994) (ed.), *Me voitimme sittenkin. Sodan muisto ja perintö*. Helsinki, Kirjayhtymä. In the selection of themes and historical interpretations of key events and experiences, the narrative cannot be said to have followed a uniform pattern. A common feature nonetheless was to stress the continuing significance of the war for the Finnish people as a whole, in all its complexity.

9   Since the 1990s, the 1955 film version of Väinö Linna's war-novel *Unknown Soldier* (Helsinki, WSOY 1954) has been shown on national television every independence day, portraying the experience of the war of 1941–44 realistically – yet somewhat heroically – through the eyes of ordinary frontline infantrymen.

10 Jouni Tilli has also pointed out the strong polarizing tendency in Finnish Second World War debates. Jouni Tilli (2009), 'Tiloja, linjauksia, retoriikkaa – historiapolitiikan ulottuvuuksia', in *Historiallinen Aikakauskirja* 3/2009, special theme issue 'Historian käyttö' ['The Use of History'], edited by Juhana Aunesluoma & Pilvi Torsti, 280–7.

11 Examples of well-known historians from public debates have been Mauno Jokipii, Heikki Ylikangas and Osmo Jussila, to name some. Their 'impact', to use a contemporary term, could be compared with that of A. J. P. Taylor or Hugh Trevor-Roper in the United Kingdom.

12 A notable proponent of the 'separate war' thesis was the ex-diplomat and writer Max Jakobson, a Finnish Jew, who served at the front. See his memoirs Max Jakobson (1999), *Väkivallan vuodet. 20. vuosisadan tilinpäätös I*. Keuruu, Otava. Also, President Tarja Halonen (2000–12), a left wing social democrat and no friend with the nationalistic right in Finland, supported this view of the war in a speech given in 2005, to the dismay of the Russian ministry for foreign affairs, which protested officially.

13 Eino Jutikkala (1976), *Suomen poliittinen historia 1809–1975 II*, Helsinki, WSOY. Mauno Jokipii (1987), *Jatkosodan synty. Tutkimuksia Suomen ja Saksan sotilaallisesta yhteistyöstä 1940–1941*. Helsinki, Otava.

14 Hannu Rautkallio (1987), *Finland and the Holocaust: the rescue of Finland's jews*. New York, Holocaust Library. This work provided the standard account until the early 2000s, when new findings led to a reassessment of the figures of Jews shipped to Germany. Elina Sana (2003), *Luovutetut. Suomen ihmisluovutukset Gestapolle*. Helsinki, WSOY. A scathing, if not very informed, critique of Finland's complicity in Nazi atrocities and genocide has been provided recently by a Swedish journalist Henrik Arnstad (2006) in *Spelaren Christian Günther. Sverige under andra*

världskriget. Stockholm, Wahlström & Widstrand. A rehearsed, if not much more learned, version of the thesis is the chapter on Finland in Henrik Arnstad (2009), *Skyldig till skuld: en europeisk resa i Nazitysklands skugga*. Stockholm, Norstedts.

15 Lars Westerlund (ed.) (2008), *Prisoners of War Deaths and People Handed Over to Germany and the Soviet Union in 1939-1955*. Helsinki, Finnish National Archives.

16 Antti Laine (1982), *Suur-Suomen kahdet kasvot. Itä-Karjalan siviiliväestön asema suomalaisessa miehityshallinnossa 1941-1944*. Helsinki, Otava 1982.

17 The 'defensive victory' thesis gained ground in the 1990s. See, for example, the memoirs of one of the commanders in the field Adolf Ehrnrooth, *Kenraalin testamentti*. Helsinki, WSOY.

18 Heikki Ylikangas (2007), *Suomen historian solmukohdat*. Helsinki, WSOY, 269.

19 The standard account of the trial is Jukka Tarkka (1977), *13. artikla. Suomen sotasyyllisyyskysymys ja liittoutuneiden sotarikospolitiikka vuosina 1944-1946*. Helsinki, WSOY.

20 This feature of the trial is highlighted by Henrik Meinander (2011), 'A separate story? Interpretations of Finland in the Second World War', in Henrik Stenius, Mirja Österberg & Johan Östling (eds.) *Nordic Narratives of the Second World War: National Historiographies Revisited*. Lund, Nordic Academic Press, pp. 55-77. I am grateful for the author for an opportunity to consult this before publication and two other unpublished manuscripts.

21 Henrik Meinander (undated),'Krigsansvarighetens dimensioner', unpublished manuscript.

22 Wipert von Blücher (1950), *Suomen kohtalonaikoja. Muistelmia vuosilta 1934-44*. Helsinki, WSOY.

23 John H. Wuorinen was professor in history in Columbia University. Ilkka Herlin (1998), 'Suomi-neidon menetetty kunnia – ajopuuteorian historia'. in Päiviö Tommila (ed.), *Historiantutkijan muotokuva*. Helsinki, Suomen Historiallinen Seura, 199-238.

24 C. G. E. Mannerheim (1954), *Marskalkens minnen I-I*. Helsingfors, Schildt.

25 On Kekkonen's vacillating views and public statements while President of the republic, see further Henrik Meinander (2011), 'A separate story?'

26 Stig H. Hästö (1987), *Vuodet kertyvät, pilvet haihtuvat. Omaelämäkerrallista tarinaa ja mietteitä seitsemältä vuosikymmeneltä*. Helsinki, WSOY, 82.

27 Henrik Meinander (2011), 'A separate story'. In a rare speech in 1974, Kekkonen criticized the driftwood theory, but after critical press comment refrained from similar utterances in other occasions.

28 On the cultural representations of the war, see Henrik Meinander (undated), 'Kriget i finländsk historiekultur', unpublished manuscript.

29 Linna's novel *Unknown Soldier* runs now on its 60th edition. It has sold more than 700,000 copies in Finland.

30 Charles Leonard Lundin (1957), *Finland in the Second World War.* Bloomington, Indiana University Press; Anthony Upton (1964*), Finland in Crisis 1940–1941. A Study of Small-Power Politics.* London, Faber & Faber; Hans Peter Krosby (1967), *Suomen valinta 1941.* Helsinki, Kirjayhtymä.
31 Arvi Korhonen (1961), *Barbarossa-suunnitelma ja Suomi. Jatkosodan synty.* Helsinki, WSOY.
32 Koivisto has elaborated his views in his memoirs, also available in Swedish translation. Mauno Koivisto (1998), *Koulussa ja sodassa.* Helsinki, Kirjayhtymä.

12

Conclusion

Allan Little

For Europeans, the Second World War is ever present. For those of us born and raised in the decades after its end, the passage of time seems to darken, rather than diminish, the shadow it casts. In popular histories, in television dramas and documentaries, at the cinema, we cannot get enough.

I am the only contributor to this book who is not a scholar. I am a reporter with some experience of war, and of war in Europe at that. I am old enough now to have witnessed events in the kingdom of news that have since slipped into the realm of history. I have seen how perception and memory shift with the passage of time. I have grown interested in the confluence of history and contemporary events: both in the way that history comes to view events in retrospect and in the ways in which history, or a version of it, can be used to drive contemporary events; how collective memory can be mobilized in pursuit of a contemporary aim.

The war with which I am most intimately familiar – that in former Yugoslavia from 1991 to 1995 – seemed in one sense to be the resumption of a conflict that had not really ended in 1945 but had merely been put on hold. Collective memory – *inherited* memory – played a powerful role in fuelling the cycle of vengeance and counter-vengeance that characterized much of the fighting. Bosnian Serbs consciously evoked the events of the 1940s to justify their actions and in doing so gave to the lexicon of conflict a shaming new metaphor – ethnic cleansing. Even the terminology of the 1940s found its way back into common usage: Serbs and Croats referred to each other pejoratively as *'Ustache'* and *'Chetnik'*, and to their beleaguered former Bosnian Muslim neighbours, menacingly, as 'Turks'.

It is surprising to me that the privations suffered by the Scandinavians, the dilemmas they faced, the compromises they made and the sometimes-heroic stands they chose to take are not better understood in the wider continent. We think we know Europe's northern tier: Scandinavians are peace-loving, egalitarian and moderate; they are impressively committed to social welfare, internationalist in outlook; their democracies are deeply entrenched both institutionally and in popular sentiment. If any of that is so, it is – in large part at least – because a particular sensibility was forged, in each of the four countries, by the experience of the war years. The Scandinavia we know today is, in part, a product of that bitter experience. No other event in history comes close in the enduring significance attributed to it; no event is celebrated so publicly, commemorated so solemnly or debated so vigorously. Finns and Norwegians, in particular, in the decades since the war, have invested those years with something close to a national foundation narrative – the period in which the modern national identity was forged and nation-statehood born.

That makes the study of World War II an anguished and an anguishing business, for the war years have taken on the character of a moral test. The contributions to this book are suffused with the sense that Europe's virtue, its courage, its commitment to uphold civilized values and behaviour were all tested and that everywhere – to varying degrees and in varying ways – were found wanting. Knowledge of that sobering, sometimes shaming, reality has driven much of the political history of Europe in the decades since – from the European Coal and Steel Community through the Treaty of Rome to the European Union and the single currency; from Willy Brandt's silent expression of contrition, kneeling at the monument to the Warsaw ghetto in 1970, to François Mitterrand and Helmut Kohl's symbolic embrace at Verdun in 1984.

How did each of Scandinavia's four nations meet the great moral test of the age? On the face of it, they had much in common as the world crisis closed in. Apart from Finland, they had little or no recent experience of conflict. They had impressively well entrenched democratic institutions. They had maintained, for decades, even centuries, good relations and strong links with Germany, even into the Nazi period. And they were each, in distinctive ways, small countries caught between powerful mutually antagonistic neighbours with no intention of observing their claim to neutrality.

Yet despite the similarities in their predicament, they each acted alone. None offered help to the others. Each responded – initially at least – within the narrow confines of its own perceived national interest. Only Norway can really be said to have formally joined the broader world struggle waged by the western Allies: the others, individual acts of resistance notwithstanding, at best waited out the great challenge. Four nations produced four radically different responses to and experiences of the rise of the totalitarian challenge to democracy – and as a consequence have faced four quite different sets of questions in the years since. We can put them on a spectrum: at one end Norway – occupied by force; then Denmark – occupied with minimal resistance; then Sweden – which succeeded in protecting its armed neutrality; lastly Finland, which fought alongside Nazi Germany.

It looks, arranged like this, like a spectrum of culpability. For each of these nations was culpable in its own way. Much of the soul-searching that has guided historical enquiry since the end of the war has been concerned with the nature and extent of this culpability. The contributions to this book are in one sense an audit of that culpability – of the failure, or inability, of Scandinavia's peace-loving nations to rise to the challenge of defending democracy.

But they are also an audit of mitigation, and finally of redemption. For each of the four also found its own ways of salvaging its essential pre-war self, and of emerging from the nightmare years with some honour, and with strong democratic institutions that would enable them to play their part in the rebuilding of a democratic Europe.

Let us take the issue of culpability first and come later to that of mitigation. Norway, once it had been defeated, gave the world a new term for an old trait. 'Quisling' entered the English language with a lower case 'q': a Norwegian name became a universal synonym for one who commits a despicable and cowardly act of treachery against his own people by collaborating with a detested foreign occupier. Membership of Quisling's *Nasjonal Samling* party among Norwegians rose to 43,000 by 1943 – not a mass movement but scarcely a tiny minority either, out of a population of some three million, and far more than the number who had joined Quisling in the years before the German occupation. As Ole Kristian Grimnes remarks in these pages, 'the awkward question is why so many, that is more than a tiny minority, joined the fascist party and supported the Norwegian fascist government and its Nazification campaign'. Twelve thousand Norwegians also volunteered to join the *Waffen-SS* and fight for the Nazis. Five and a half thousand of them saw action on the eastern front, of whom eight hundred were killed.

Half of Norway's police officers joined the *Nasjonal Samling* or the German SS. The rounding up and deportation of Norway's 760 remaining Jews was largely a Norwegian affair, commanded by Norwegian police; Norwegian civil servants drew up registers of Jews; Germans took custody of the deportees, some only once they were on board the ship in Oslo harbour that would take them to their deaths. Only 25 Norwegian Jews survived.

Norway's economy became integrated into the German war economy. Farms and fishermen supplied the occupying power with produce. Hundreds of thousands of Norwegians took part in German war-related infrastructure projects. Some Norwegians profited from the new opportunities for economic collaboration. Unemployment fell.

This collaboration would diminish only when the tide of military fortune turned against Germany. This would become part of a pattern in Scandinavia: each nation emboldened to distance itself, by increments, from Germany as the hinge of war turned.

In Norway, the pre-invasion political leaders of the country – those who could genuinely claim popular legitimacy, who could genuinely claim to be acting on behalf of the broad mass of the people – had very little opportunity for, or inclination toward, collaboration. Attempts at active engagement by the Germans in the weeks following Norway's defeat and the exile of the King and government did not last long. The State Council formed by those Norwegian politicians who chose to remain and work with the Nazis was replaced by Quisling's unelected *Nasjonal Samling* ministers on 25 September 1940. Thus, the opportunity for collaboration by mainstream leaders disappeared very early – leaving the business of active collaboration only to those who had never commanded popular support among the Norwegian people.

This was not so in Denmark, which quickly decided to cooperate with the occupier. The 'culpability' history has attributed here is quite different in character from that in Norway. In Denmark, the coalition government that was assembled after the invasion consisted of parties that between them accounted for 90 per cent of the popular vote. The arrangement that government came to with the occupying power has vexed generations of Danes since – for it can be said to have been an arrangement made on behalf of the mass of the people and with the support of the general population – and that cannot be said in the case of Norway.

The tone of the accommodation the Danes were to make with the German occupiers was set by Foreign Minister Scavenius's speech on the day on which the coalition was inaugurated in July 1940, in which he spoke of 'the great German victories that have struck the world with astonishment *and admiration*';

Denmark's task, he said, would be to 'find her place in a proper and *mutually active co-operation* with Germany' (italics added). Scavenius persuaded his ministerial colleagues that Denmark should not wait to receive German demands but should pre-empt them with initiatives of its own designed to bolster German confidence in the trustworthiness of the Danish authorities.

Thus in the name of upholding the independence of the country and the integrity of the constitution, Denmark's government knowingly subverted both. The Danish government was required by the Germans to expel enemy embassies, crack down on anti-German propaganda, censor the press, actively discourage the people from engaging in anti-German activity, punish acts of sabotage, outlaw the Danish Communist Party (which had members in the national Parliament), intern hundreds of political prisoners (including elected MPs) in camps, force others underground and encourage Danish citizens to become police informers to help to suppress the emerging resistance movement. This list does not read like the actions of a government that had retained real independence, for Denmark had embraced what Niels Wium Olesen describes in this book as 'the politics of the lesser evil. . . [in which] the transactional character of the German-Danish relationship endowed it with a touch of mutuality and voluntariness'.

Sweden was far more fortunate than Denmark. It retained the substance, as well as the impression, of neutrality – and that brings with it, in retrospect, a different measure of culpability – for Stockholm made its own compromises with Nazi Germany not as a result of occupation but rather to forestall it. Sweden refused to allow the British and French free passage across its territory to help Finland, but it granted Germany transit rights to supply its troops in Norway. Sweden continued to supply Germany with iron-ore until August 1944 – long after the military tide had turned against Germany in the west as well as in the east. Eighty per cent of Swedish exports went to Germany. The Swedish government repeatedly reassured Berlin that the steady escalation of its armed forces was designed to repel any Allied attempt to gain a foothold in Scandinavia, and protested about Allied infringements of its neutrality. It seems reasonable to ask why, when the country had 350,000 troops in frontline field units, and 200,000 in local defence units, Sweden did not turn against Germany earlier. Gradually, Sweden, according to Kent Zetterberg, 'placed herself closer to the side she had always considered the right one, following an ever more pro-western line' – but only towards the end of the war when its outcome was a foregone conclusion. Sweden's policy for the war was, in effect, to wait for others to win it. To defend its neutrality, Sweden had been 'incapable of seeing the war for what it really was – a mortal struggle between democracy and dictatorship, liberty and oppression, good and evil'. Only in April 1945, with Soviet troops already in Berlin and Hitler on the verge of committing suicide, did the Commander-in-Chief of the Swedish Defence Forces declare that Sweden's armed forces were ready to attack German troops in Norway if they did not surrender. Only then.

But it is in Finland that the post-war questions are most troubling and still provoke the greatest controversy, for Finland was the only democracy in effect to make common cause with Adolf Hitler. By contrast with their neighbours elsewhere in Scandinavia, many Finns were reassured, rather than alarmed, by the rise of Nazi Germany, because a strong Germany had always been viewed as a counterweight to Soviet power – a counterweight which the collapse of Imperial Germany in 1918 had removed. The Winter War seemed to vindicate this view. Oula Silvennoinen argues here that because Finnish statehood was predicated on a rejection of Soviet Communism, Finland's 'choice to ally itself with Germany was a foregone conclusion'. Finnish-German co-operation deepened as Germany prepared to renege on its pact with Moscow and attack the Soviet Union. And when, in 1941, Germany did attack the Soviet Union, Finns saw it as an opportunity not only to redeem territory that Finland had lost in the disastrous Winter War, but also to go further. In fighting the same enemy as Nazi Germany, Finland, having been invaded and occupied, became itself an occupying power. It exhibited 'a decidedly opportunistic readiness to gamble, when a lucrative combination of low risk and huge gains seemed to present itself'. In Soviet Karelia, ethnic non-Finns were interned to await deportation, as Finland prepared to settle an immigrant Finnic population in their place. Soviet POWs in Finnish captivity died of hunger and disease. Oula Silvennoinen argues that Finland was not, as it has been traditionally held, simply 'co-belligerent' with Nazi Germany but, in effect, an ally. It began to emphasize the 'separate war' narrative, and to seek a realignment of its loyalties, only when it became clear that Germany would lose the war.

And so despite the enormous differences in the way in which the nations of Scandinavia met the challenge of totalitarianism and war, a pattern establishes itself. Each nation, despite its well-entrenched democratic institutions and traditions, had, by 1945, collaborated with Nazi Germany in its own way. Each had also – again in its own way – taken the opportunity to distance itself from Germany and to identify more and more with the values (if not always the military needs) of the Allies as the tide of war turned in 1943–44. And as a result, each emerged, in 1945, with the machinery of democratic government still in place, in a position to re-establish pre-war democratic institutions and quickly claim membership of the community of democratic nations that was already confronting the new geo-strategic reality – the armed polarization (and partition) of Europe that would come to be known as the Cold War.

In 1945, each of Europe's nations needed a tale to tell itself. Each needed a redeeming narrative on which to build its post-war democratic future. At the liberation of Paris in August 1944, General de Gaulle declared that he had represented the continuation of the real France and that the France that governed from Vichy during the occupation had not been France at all but an aberration from French history. What is more, he said, France – the real France – had liberated herself. It required a wilful act of collective self-deception to believe this to be literally true, for many of the hundreds of thousands of Parisians who lined the streets of the capital to welcome him had, themselves, lined the same streets to cheer the Vichy leader, Marshal Pétain, to the echo during his last visit to the capital in April, only four months earlier.

In Scandinavia, the post-war redemption narrative was perhaps easiest to build in Norway. The King and government had gone into exile in London very early where they had carried on the tradition of constitutional government: they had been given parliamentary authority to govern without the National Assembly until the crisis was over. The merchant fleet was rescued and made available to the Allies, and Norway became a contributing member of the Grand Alliance. Units of the Norwegian armed forces became integrated into the Royal Navy, the RAF and the British army. Norwegian exiles and resistance units at home played a vital role in British-led sabotage operations against the Nazis in Norway (although the military value of these operations would later, controversially, be questioned). Collaboration was limited to a small pro-Nazi elite that had never won an election and had no popular legitimacy. After the war, Norway executed or imprisoned more collaborators, proportionate to its population, than any other nation of occupied Europe, including Communist Yugoslavia. Thus, Norway, in the years after 1945, came to see its response to the challenge of the war years as heroic. For Norway, uniquely among the Scandinavian countries, had remained a belligerent western ally throughout.

Sweden's redeeming narrative was not one of anti-Nazi heroism, but of the triumph of pragmatism, armed neutrality and wise diplomacy. Among Swedes, the war experience has not shaped the country's modern national identity in the way that it has in Sweden's three neighbouring countries. The war years exert a much weaker pull on the collective Swedish imagination. This came to be seen as evidence in itself of the success of the policy of neutrality pursued by the Swedish political elite – a national consensus that was never seriously challenged. Again, the notion that 'small-state realism' had saved Sweden served the purposes of a country that, during the Cold War, sought to identify strongly with the values of the western democracies while remaining neutral in its security and defence policies.

The redeeming narrative was a more challenging business in Denmark. Here, the dilemma faced by the Danish authorities would resurface in Europe 40 years later after a military coup in communist Poland in December 1981. The man who would be (one hopes) Europe's last military dictator, General Wojciech Jaruzelski, seized control of the state in order to save Poland from a much worse fate – a Soviet invasion. After the fall of Communism, Jaruzelski went on to develop a constructive and even friendly relationship with some of Poland's new democratic leaders; and there is a lot to be said for the view that had Jaruzelski not acted, the Soviet Union might well have been ready to impose itself on Poland. But his argument never won popular sympathy and he remains, among most Poles, unforgiven.

The same is not true in Denmark. Here, the government could claim 90 per cent popular legitimacy. Everything it did under the occupation it did in the name of the Danish people and with broad popular support. This was certainly not true of the puppet regime in Norway. The Danish people themselves were, therefore, directly implicated in the compromises that their government, for good or ill, had entered into.

And so Danes did not, in the decades after the war, challenge the popular narrative favoured by those who had led them through the Nazi occupation. They seized instead on an account dominated by heroic, and deft, resistance against overwhelming odds. Hundreds of saboteur novels were published in a matter of months. The story of the rescue of Denmark's Jews became the touchstone of a small nation's refusal to abandon civilized values, even under occupation; so too, the story of the Danish government's eventual resignation in 1943 when the demands imposed by the Nazis became too egregious.

Here, the confluence of post-war strategic imperatives and the writing of history is most pronounced. Throughout the years of the Cold War, the Danes, in common with their Scandinavian neighbours, needed a national story that located them safely and unambiguously in the community of democratic nations. Only after the collapse of Communism did Danes seriously challenge the post-war 'consensual myth': only then did historians seriously raise the question of how Danes would have responded had the Nazis demanded the transportation of the Jews in 1941 or 1942, when Germany was still on an upward military trajectory; only then did Danish historians begin to argue that the Danish government had not resigned, in 1943, on a point of principle but, instead, because it had already lost control of the widespread popular unrest that was beginning to sweep the country. Only then: such, once again, has been the power of contemporary need, in post-war Europe, to shape historical thinking about the war years.

But it is in Finland that the post-war questions remain most haunting and most agonizing. Ninety per cent of the Scandinavians who lost their lives in the war were Finns. Hundreds of thousands of others were forcibly displaced. In order, as they saw it, to defend the integrity of their country's democratic institutions, Finns found themselves fighting *alongside* the power that most in western Europe considered the far greater existential menace to democracy. No other Scandinavian country, after the war, had to face this question: how do we, the survivors and subsequent generations, mourn and, as a nation, commemorate those who died, when we know that they died fighting not for but against the Grand Alliance that defeated the Nazis? For in the narrow national interest they might well have died fighting on the right side of the moral argument, but in the broader struggle for the survival of democracy itself, the moral equation is quite different.

And so Finns, after the war, found shelter in the 'same war' thesis: it is not our fault, their wartime leaders had reassured them, that we face the same enemy as Hitler. After the war, there was enough historical circumstance to draw on to defend this argument: Finland, after all, had not gone all the way with Germany; it had not bowed to German demands to take part in the siege of Leningrad, or to pursue other German objectives that were not strictly compatible with Finland's own, narrower, irredentist aspirations. Finns had also, in the end, turned on the defeated Germans; they had, all along, been 'co-belligerents' rather than allies (surely one of the great, obscuring euphemisms of warfare, like 'collateral damage').

Even now the questions – not even the answers, the questions themselves – divide Finns into viscerally opposing camps. Since the 1970s, historians have asked whether there really was 'continuity' between the Winter War of 1939–40 (the just nature of which is not challenged) and that of 1941; of whether there had been a real choice in 1941; of whether Finns should have sued for peace in the first half of 1944 and accepted the terms offered by the Allies or whether

Finns were hemmed in by the accident of their geography. Even in raising these questions historians have sometimes risked popular opprobrium, for the war experience is still recent and still raw.

And in all four countries, geography was, to some extent, destiny. All four, in the 1930s, would find themselves trapped between two or more mutually antagonistic global powers – in Finland and Sweden's case, between Germany and the Soviet Union; in the case of Norway, Denmark and also Sweden, between the rising continental might of Germany and the maritime strength of imperial Britain.

And all the choices they made, or were forced to make, stemmed from a single geo-strategic circumstance: that in May 1938, they had signed a declaration of neutrality, as post-1919 systems of collective security collapsed – the so-called 'flight from Geneva'. Why, when geo-politics, like nature, abhors a vacuum, did they entrust the safety of their countries to so fragile, so violable, a policy? Why did they place their nations in such jeopardy? Did they believe that, in the event of war between Germany and the western democracies, this policy alone would be sufficient to protect their independence? It was already clear that both sides would have clear strategic designs in the north; that Germany would want to keep Britain's Royal Navy out of Scandinavian waters; that Britain would seek to disrupt Swedish iron-ore supplies to Germany; that, in other words, both sides would seek a presence in Scandinavia, if only to keep the enemy out. Did wishful thinking drive the neutrality policy? Or was it a wilful refusal to address the potential consequences of the coming crisis? Or simply that by 1938 there was no alternative but to hope for a peaceful resolution?

Throughout the democratic world, by 1938, many saw the coming conflict as an existential battle for the survival of democracy itself. This was the guiding preoccupation of Winston Churchill's lonely exile in the pre-war political wilderness. When, two years later, he became Prime Minister, his speeches were remarkable for their explicit championing *not* of Britain's narrow national, or even imperial, interest, but for their conscious evocation of the *universal* interests of western civilization itself. 'Without victory, there is no survival', he told the House of Commons three days after becoming Prime Minister. 'Let that be realized; no survival for the British Empire, no survival for all that the British Empire has stood for, no survival for the urge and impulse of the ages, that *mankind* will move forward towards its goals.' (My italics) In the same month, he warned that 'upon this battle [the coming Battle of Britain] depends the survival of Christian civilization'.

Britain, it is true, was a global power, and the nations of Scandinavia had no such aspirations. Britain still thought of itself as the pre-eminent imperial power in the world, the lead nation of the western world, not yet eclipsed by the emerging United States. In France, too, political leaders assumed that they had some responsibility for defending the values of the western democracies, not only at home but also globally. 'There is a pact, two thousand years old, between the greatness of France and the freedom of the world', General de Gaulle would insist after refusing to accept his country's capitulation to Nazi Germany.

Is it fair to ask why, then, the Scandinavian democracies saw it as legitimate to declare themselves neutral in the coming battle between democracy and dictatorship? Did they believe that if the western powers were defeated, their own way of life could continue nonetheless? The May 1938 declarations of neutrality were sincere attempts by democratic leaders to spare their peoples the horrors of war. But were they not also a moral abdication? Was it not also an assertion that the duty to defend democracy in Europe fell to others, principally Britain and France? Does it not amount to a declaration that Scandinavia would – some conspicuous acts of resistance notwithstanding – simply wait for others to win the war and create a world in which their own very Scandinavian values, their own indisputable commitment to a democratic future, would at last be secure?

Of course, the question is not fair. The judgement it contains relies entirely on hindsight. The western democracies were not ready for war, either, in May 1938 and would continue, for another year and more to do everything in their power to spare *their* peoples the same horrors. 'Appeasement' was not yet a pejorative term in 1938; it was seen as honourable and sane – a policy designed to prevent a catastrophic war. As late as 1940, and after the fall of France, many British parliamentarians, including the Foreign Secretary, Lord Halifax, were still arguing strongly that Britain should seek terms with Germany, through the mediation of Mussolini: this, one might say, was Britain's own 'Scandinavian option', a road, in the end, not taken.

Only in Sweden – where the policy appeared to have 'worked' – did faith in neutrality survive the war. The other nations of Scandinavia would lock themselves into post-war international security arrangements: Norway and Denmark with NATO and Finland with the Soviet Union. After the war, democratic Europe drew its northern tier close, like a shawl around its shoulders. Three of the four would also, eventually, join what is now the European Union (though only Finland would commit itself to the single currency).

Seventy years on, Scandinavia, like much of occupied Europe, is still in the process of becoming reconciled to the realities of the war years. In Russia, after 1991, historians, given access to the state archives for the first time, would articulate a gloriously Russian paradox about the unfettered historical work that was now possible: the trouble with the past, they would say, is that it is dangerously unpredictable.

In Scandinavia, as elsewhere in Europe, professional historians and intellectual elites have challenged prevailing myths and uncovered new evidence about what happened during the nightmare years. The professional historians have had, at best, a limited effect on what the broader populations continue to believe, or choose to believe, or want to believe. After all, as the British historian Julian Jackson has said of France, just because the Resistance was mythologized, does not mean that the Resistance was a myth. Even as generations born long after the end of the war grow into adulthood and challenge the accounts of their parents and their grandparents, World War II remains close, painfully so. And even now, when we look into it, we look into a mirror and see, whether we like it or not, something of our nation's character reflected back at us. Understanding the Second World War, and the moral test it has come to represent, and what it says about who we were and who we are now, remains a work in progress.

Index

Subtitles in bold refer to separate chronological sections under a main heading

Abisko Group 110
Administrasjonsrådet 170
agency, Finnish 8, 209, 211–15
Aldridge, David 43n. 11
Allies
   and Iceland 27
   and iron ore 116
   and Norwegian campaign 7, 20, 91, 105
   Norwegian support for 21, 92, 227
   Scandinavia and 4, 23, 111, 123
   Sweden and 120–1
   and Winter War 18
Altmark, *City of Flint* and *Westerwald* incidents 88
antisemitism 164, 185, 187
Anti-Comintern Pact 29
AOK (*Armeeoberkommando*) *Lappland* 114
AOK (*Armeeoberkommando*) *Norwegen* 114
Archangel 20
Atlantic Wall 153
Auschwitz 9, 173, 214
   Trial 186
Axis Tripartite Pact 64

Barbarossa 21, 57, 59, 104, 208
Berlingske Tidende 146, 154
Best, Dr Werner, German Plenipotentiary (*Reichsbevollmächtigter*) in Denmark 29, 64–7
Blackbourn, David 40
Blücher, Wipert von 208
Bodenschatz, Lieutenant General Karl-Heinrich 112
Boheman, Erik 111, 116–17, 122
Bohemia and Moravia Protectorate 47
bokmål 165

Bosnia 221
Bothnia, Gulf of 134
Brandt, Willy 222
Breivik, Anders 5, 164
Briand, Aristide 81
Bryld, Claus 148, 188
Buhl, Vilhelm, Danish Prime Minister 62–3, 68

Cadogan, (Sir) Alexander, Permanent Under-Secretary at the Foreign Office 111
Carlgren, Wilhelm 117, 183–4, 187
Chetnik 221
Christian X, King of Denmark *see* King of Denmark
Christmas Møller, John 56–7, 59
Churchill, Winston 8, 42, 105–6, 111, 122, 230
Churchill Club 61
Clausen, Frits 56, 63
Clausewitz, Carl von 103
Clemmesen, Michael 42
Cobb, Richard 40
cohabitation, Danish 57, 60, 67, 148, 156n. 4
Cold War 8–9, 24, 72, 74, 109, 149–52, 155, 174, 182, 189–91, 202, 208–9, 211, 213–15, 227–8
   concessions 18
   Denmark in 70
   Finland in 12, 22–3
   Sweden in 9, 18, 25, 102, 110, 115, 118, 166, 180, 182, 184, 187
collaboration with Germany 4–5, 54, 226
   Denmark and 7, 29, 32, 54, 62, 166, 189
   Finland and 31
   Norway and 6–7, 9–10, 93, 95, 163, 166–72, 223–4, 227
   Sweden and 26, 31

constitution
  Denmark 6, 13, 28, 46, 49, 56, 58–9, 64, 66, 68, 225
  Norway 28, 82, 86, 92, 227
  Sweden 101
Continuation War, Finnish-Soviet War 1941–44 21–2, 31, 200
Convoy PQ17 23
counter-narrative
  Danish 148, 189
  Swedish 182
Croats 221

Danish Agrarian Party 50
Danish Communist Party 50, 58–9, 225
Danish Conservative Party 50, 55–6, 59, 67, 148
Danish elections
  March 1943 29, 58, 65
  post-war 68
Danish Freedom Council 29, 67
Danish Nazi Party (DNSAP) 50–3, 55–7, 63, 65, 69
Danish Press Bureau 54–5
Danish Resistance Movement 3, 26, 29, 147, 149, 188–9
Danish Schleswig Party 50
Danish Social Democrats 51
Danish Unity Party 55, 60
de Gaulle, General Charles 148, 227, 231
Denmark
  Pre-war
    exports to Britain 50
  Wartime
    Anti-Comintern Pact 29
    August rebellion 29
    constitution (*see* Constitution, Denmark)
    election (*see* Danish elections)
    foreign policy 52
    Freedom Council (*see* Danish Freedom Council)
    German invasion 3–4, 20, 47–8
    German minority 47, 50
    Jews 6, 29, 64, 67, 69
    press and censorship 54–5
    resistance (*see* Danish Resistance Movement)
    sabotage 26, 29, 49, 55, 60–3, 65–6, 68, 150

  sovereignty (*see* Constitution, Denmark)
  standard of living 51
  State Advocacy for Special Affairs Office 49
  Post-war
    counter-narrative (*see* counter-narrative, Danish)
    DNH research project 9, 149–50, 153
    foreign policy 152
    historiography 51, 147–55 *passim*
    railway sabotage 150
Dorpat (Tartu), Peace of 132

Eastern Front 94, 114, 121, 139, 154, 203, 205, 214, 223
EEC *see* European Economic Community (EEC)
Ehrenstandpunkt 112
Ehrensvärd, General Count Carl August, Commander-in-Chief of the Swedish Defence Staff 123
Eichmann trial 186
Einsatzkommando Finnland 139
Eley, Geoff 40
Estonian war of liberation 131
ethnic cleansing 6, 141, 221
European Coal and Steel Community 222
European Economic Community (EEC)
  opposition to membership of 151–2, 161
European Union (EU) 10, 161, 191, 222, 231

Falkenhorst, General Nikolaus von 20
Federal Republic of Germany 139, 185
Finland
  Pre-war
    anti-communism 130, 138–9
    civil war 5, 130, 132, 138, 200
    Communist Party 130, 206
    foreign policy 134
    Finno-Ugric languages 131
    independence 13, 22, 129–31, 200
    irredentism in 130–2
    Lapua movement 14
    nationalism in 130
    Russification of 129

Wartime
  alliance with Germany   140–1
  Allied aid   105, 135
  Blue-White Book   137
  Continuation War   21–2, 31, 200
  foreign policy   140
  Greater Finland   6, 131, 138, 141
  Moscow Peace of 1940   18
  prisoner-of-war administration
     138–9, 226
  security police   139
  Swedish aid to   106
  war casualties   140
  Winter War, (Soviet-Finnish War)
     1939–40   6, 9, 15, 17–19, 23,
     58, 104–6, 108, 134–5, 137–8,
     142, 174, 200, 203, 206, 216n. 7,
     226, 229
Post-war
  artistic representations of
     war   211
  defensive victory thesis   214, 218n.
     17
  driftwood theory   8–9, 144n. 26,
     204, 208, 210–12, 218n. 27
  Friendship, Cooperation and Mutual
     Assistance Treaty   32
  historical culture   200–3, 210,
     215n. 1, 216n. 4
  post-Cold War triumphalism
     in   214
  war-guilt trial in   207, 211
Finnish People's Republic   17, 24
Finnmark   90, 123, 131
Finno-Ugric languages   131
First World War (World War I)   13, 52,
   72, 75–6, 78, 84–5, 87, 101–2,
   106, 134, 160, 162
Fisher, John, First Sea Lord   77
FORTITUDE NORTH   26
France   8, 14, 18, 32, 40, 47, 52, 79–80,
   85, 91, 102, 106–7, 111, 113, 121,
   134–5, 148, 166–7, 186, 227,
   231–2
Free Danes (*De frie Danske*)   60
Free Denmark (*Frit Danmark*)   59
Freedom Council (Denmark)   29, 67
Friendship, Cooperation and Mutual
   Assistance Treaty (FCMA)   210
Frisch, Hartvig   56–7

Germany
  Federal Republic   41, 139, 185
  'New Order'   25, 53–4
  offensive in the west 1940   111
German-Norwegian relations
  armed forces   83–4
  commerce, mining, technology and
     industry   75
  cultural and intellectual life   165–6
  education and science   165
  Hanseatic League   74
  immigration to Norway   75
  labour movement   77
  Lutheranism (Protestantism)   75–6,
     165
  Weimar Republic   78–80
Gestapo   58, 64, 172
Göring, Hermann   20, 112, 206
Great Britain (United Kingdom)   13–14,
   18, 50, 230–1
  1940 campaign   20, 90–1, 111
  alliance with the Soviet Union   140
  and Finland   18, 21, 136, 140–1
  and Norway   74–5, 77–8, 80, 87–8,
     90–3, 111, 113, 160, 174–7
  Scandinavian history in   41
  and Sweden   40, 101–2, 106, 111, 113,
     123
  and Winter War volunteers   135
Great Patriotic War   200
Greater Finland   6, 131, 138, 141
Greifswald   41
Grieg, Edvard   76, 166
Gulf of Finland   17, 142, 205
Günther, Christian, Swedish Foreign
   Minister (1939–45)   30, 113,
   118, 184
Gustavus Adolphus, King of Sweden
   (1594–1632)   40

Haarr, Geirr   42
Haakon VII, King of Norway *see* King of
   Norway
Hæstrup, Jørgen   149
Hägglöf, Gunnar, Swedish trade
   diplomat   111, 118, 183
Hakkila, Väinö, politician   136
Halifax, Edward Frederick Lindley Wood,
   1st Earl of Halifax, British
   Foreign Secretary   111, 231

Hamsun, Knut 166
Hansen, H. C. 57
Hansson, Per Albin, Swedish
    Prime Minister (1932–36 &
    1936–46) 29, 101, 112–13,
    116, 181, 184
Hayes, Paul 40
Hedtoft, Hans 57
Henningsen, Bernd 43n. 10
Herrington, Ian 40
Himmler, Heinrich, SS *Reichsführer* 171
Historikerstreit 186, 190
historiography, Scandinavian 5, 39–42
    Danish 51, 147–9, 154
    Finnish 213
    Norwegian 75, 78, 189
    Swedish 179–80, 183, 185, 187–9
Hitler, Adolf, Chancellor of Germany
    19–20, 23, 25, 28, 34n. 28, 54, 63,
    66–7, 74, 81–2, 90, 103–4, 106,
    110, 112–14, 116, 134, 203–4,
    209, 215, 226
Hjemmefronten see Home Front
Holocaust 9–10, 27, 104, 154, 157n. 20,
    173–4, 178, 184–8, 190, 194n. 19,
    203–4, 214–15, 217n. 14
Humboldt University, Berlin (*Nordeuropa
    Institut*) 41
Hungary 21, 105, 137, 205

Iceland 13, 26–7, 161
Ingermanland 131
Integrity Treaty (1907) 80
iron ore 18–20, 23–4, 26, 40, 102, 105–7,
    110–16, 135, 183
Islam 3, 164

Jaruzelski, General Wojciech, Polish Prime
    Minister (1981–85) 228
Jews 47, 164, 185–6
    Denmark and 6, 29, 64, 67, 69,
        115–16, 155, 228–9
    Finland and 27, 139, 203, 217n. 14
    Norway and 7, 10, 27, 83, 93–4, 170,
        172–4, 189, 223–4
    Sweden and 104, 115–16, 155, 184
Johnson, Herschel, US Minister in
    Stockholm 116
Jokipii, Mauno 202
Jutikkala, Eino 202, 213

Kalevala, folk epic of Finland 131
Kallax airbase 123
Karelia 16–17, 21–3, 105, 133, 138, 140
    Soviet (Eastern) Karelia 16, 21, 131–2,
        138, 140–1, 204, 226
    uprising (1921–22) 132
Kekkonen, Urho 9, 208, 210–11, 213–14,
    218n. 27
Kiel 41
Killing II, The 3
King of Denmark, Christian X 27–8, 46,
    48, 50, 52, 63, 66, 115
King of Norway, Haakon VII 28, 83,
    90–1, 94, 160, 162, 168, 175, 224,
    227
King of Sweden, Gustav V 112, 120
Kirchhoff, Hans 149
Kiruna-Malmberget *see* iron ore
Kohl, Helmut 222
Koht, Halvdan, Norwegian Minister of
    Foreign Affairs (1935–41)
    83, 88
Koivisto, Mauno 214
Kola Peninsula 131
Kolchak, Aleksandr, Admiral 131
Korhonen, Arvi 208, 212
Kuusinen, Otto 13, 16–17, 19

la Cour, Vilhelm 55–6
Landssvikoppgjør 8, 166–9, 173
Lapland 142
    War (1944–45) 123, 142, 215
Larsen, Aksel 59
League of Nations 23, 80, 83, 87, 134
Lend-Lease 21
Leningrad (St. Petersburg, Petrograd)
    16–17, 21–3, 131, 140, 229
Liberal Agrarian Party (Venstre) 50
Linkomies, Edwin, Prime Minister of
    Finland 141
Linna, Väinö 211, 217n. 9, 218n. 29
Løvland Jørgen, Norwegian Foreign
    Minister 77
Lutzhöft, Hans-Jürgen 31

Mackay, C.G. 117
Macmillan, Harold, British politician 135
Mann, Christopher 40
Mannerheim, Marshal Gustav,
    Commander in Chief and later

President of Finland   16, 102, 207–8, 210
Mannerheim Line   17
Mainila   16
Meinander, Henrik   210
Milorg   28–9, 92–3
Milward, Alan   40
Mitterrand, François   222
Møller, A. P.   146
Molotov-Ribbentrop Pact (Nazi-Soviet Pact, German-Soviet Pact, Hitler-Stalin Pact, non-aggression pact, the pact)   6, 8, 15, 18, 59, 99, 103, 105, 107, 134–5, 174, 203, 226
Moscow Conference 1943   121
Moscow, Peace of 1940   212
Mowinckel, Johan L., Norwegian Prime Minister   79, 81, 83
Munch, Edvard   166
Munch, Peter, Danish Foreign Secretary   47–8, 50, 52
Munch-Petersen, Thomas   40, 106
Munich Crisis   101
Murmansk   20–1, 139–40
Mussolini, Benito   65, 135, 231

Narvik   18, 20, 91, 111, 113, 120–1
Nasjonal Samling (NS)   6, 8, 13, 28, 82, 223–4
NATO   7, 115, 151–2, 160, 231
Nazism
  and Denmark   69, 82
  and Finland   6, 142
  and Norway   6, 164, 168
  and Sweden   7, 180, 184, 188
Netherlands Protectorate   47, 51, 167
neutrality, Scandinavian policy of   5, 10, 14, 27, 87, 102, 222, 230–1
  and Denmark   32, 47–8, 55, 151, 223
  and Finland   9, 211, 213
  and Iceland   26
  and Norway   7, 24, 28, 32, 73, 78, 81, 86–90, 160–1
  Scandinavian declaration of (1938)   14
  and Sweden   4, 6–7, 10, 24–5, 30, 101–5, 107–15, 117–18, 120, 122–3, 166, 179–82, 190–1, 225, 227–8

nickel   23
New Order *see* Germany
Nobel Peace Prize   79, 81, 83
Nordic History Group   41
Northern Norway 1944–45 *see* Finnmark
Norway
  Pre-war, German-Norwegian relations
    armed forces   83–4
    commerce, mining, technology and industry   75
    cultural and intellectual life of   165–6
    education and science in   165
    Hanseatic League   74
    immigration to Norway   75
    labour movement in   77
    Lutheranism (Protestantism) in   75–6
    Nobel Peace Prize   79, 81, 83
    territorial waters   76, 80–1, 87
    Weimar Republic and   78–80
  Wartime
    Administrasjonsrådet   170
    Altmark, City of Flint and *Westerwald* incidents   88
    armed forces-in-exile   89, 92, 96, 227
    1940 campaign and   20, 90–1, 111
    collaboration in   170–1
    economic collaboration (*see* economy)
    economy   25, 40, 89, 95, 161–2, 224
    Finnmark   90, 123, 131
    government-in-exile   7, 28, 74, 90, 92–3, 96, 115, 162–3, 168, 176, 224, 227
    heavy water plant   24, 26, 175
    Home Front *Hjemmefronten* (resistance movement: Milorg, Sivorg)   4, 6–9, 20, 26, 28–9, 92–3, 166–8, 172, 174–7
    Jews   7, 10, 27, 83, 93–4, 170, 172–4, 189, 223–4
    labour camps (forced) in   25, 29, 89, 93
    merchant navy   92
    Milorg (*see* Home Front)
    ministry of police   171

Northern Norway 1944–45 (*see* Finnmark)
Operation Balchen   123
Quisling coup   19–20, 28, 73, 85–6, 94
Reichskommissariat   86, 90, 94–5
Resistance (*see* Home Front)
Rjukan   26, 175
Sivorg (*see* Home Front)
Soviet POWs in   25, 89
Stapo   172
territorial waters   20, 87, 111

Post-war
collaborator trials   169
economy   163–4
historiography   75, 78, 189
Landssvikoppgjør   8, 166–9, 173
narrative   9–10, 160, 167–9, 189, 222, 227
resistance-oriented interpretation   168, 170–1

Norwegian Agrarian Party   81
Norwegian Communist Party   174
Norwegian Labour Party   74, 83, 163, 174
Nygaardsvold, Johan (Norwegian Prime minister)   91
nynorsk   165

Operation SALMON CATCH   21
Ossietzky, Carl von   83

Paasikivi, Juho Kusti   210–11
Palmgren, Raoul   132
patriotic narrative   9, 181–2, 186, 189–91
Paxton, Robert   46, 148
Pétain, Maréchal Philippe   54, 148, 227
Petsamo   22, 132, 136
Pettersson, Tommy   119
Politik als Beruf   69
Poulsen, Axel   3
progressive narrative   181, 191

Quisling, Vidkun   13, 19–20, 28, 32, 40, 73, 81–2, 85–6, 90, 94, 166, 168, 173, 223–4

racial biology   185, 187
Raeder, Grand-Admiral Erich   19, 94, 112

railway sabotage, Denmark   150
Rasmussen, Anders Fogh   10, 152
Rechtsstaat   169
Red Army   16–18, 21–4, 105, 123, 205
losses   18
Red Goose Magazine   61
Renthe-Fink, Cecil von, German Ambassador to Denmark   47–8, 64
Rjukan   26, 175
Roberts, Geoffrey   24
Roberts, Michael   40
Rosenberg, Alfred   19, 94
Ruge, Colonel Otto   84
Russia
civil war in   131
empire   129–31, 200
Orthodoxy in   130–1
Russian revolution   81, 129, 200
Ryti, Risto, President of Finland   31–2, 140, 202, 207–8, 214
Ryvang Memorial Park   3

Saboteur novels   228
Safe-Conduct Traffic   108
Sámi   131
samnorsk   165
Sawyer, Peter   40
Scandinavia
and dictatorships   14, 18, 24
and Hitler   19, 23, 25, 28, 34n. 28, 96, 102, 107, 114, 134, 209
neutrality   5, 10, 14, 27, 87, 102, 222, 230–1
Scandinavian Economic History Review   41
Scandinavian Journal of History   41
Scavenius, Erik, Danish Foreign Secretary   52–4, 56–7, 63–5, 225
Speech 8 July, 1940   53, 224–5
Schlüter, Poul   152
Schulte-Mönting, Erich, Chief of Staff of the German Navy   112
Serbs   221
Serlachius, Gösta, Finnish industrialist   135
Sivorg see Home Front
Skagerrak blockade   108, 113, 136

Sköld, Per Edvin   108
small-state realistic narrative   9, 32, 102,
    180–7, 190–1, 228
SOE *see* Special Operations Executive
    (SOE)
Soviet Union   4, 7–9, 14–19, 21–5, 27,
    30–2, 57–8, 61, 80, 89, 103–5,
    107–8, 116–17, 120–1, 123, 130,
    132–42, 174–5, 199–200, 202–11,
    214, 226, 228, 230–1
  POWs (Soviet) in Finland   138–9
  POWs (Soviet) in Norway   25, 89–90,
    169, 171, 203
Soviet-Finnish War (1939–40) *see* Finland,
    Wartime, Winter War
Special Operations Executive (SOE)   26,
    29, 60, 117, 149, 175
Speer, Albert   153
SS (*Schutzstaffeln der NSDAP*)   28–9, 64,
    94, 139, 153–4, 168, 171–2, 189,
    223
Ståhlberg, K. J. (Kaarlo Juho), President of
    Finland   132
Stalin, Josef, General Secretary of the
    Soviet Communist Party (1922–
    53). From 1941–46 Chairman
    of the Council of People's
    Commissars   14, 16, 19, 23–4,
    103–4, 107–8, 110, 209
Stapo   172
Stauning, Thorvald, Danish Prime
    Minister   48, 50, 53, 57, 62
Stockholm International Forum on the
    Holocaust (2000)   186
Stresemann, Gustav   81
SUAV research project (*Sverige under andra
    världskriget*)   9, 183–4, 187–8
Suursaari (Hogland)   142
Sveistrup, Søren   3
Svenningsen, Nils, Permanent
    Undersecretary, Danish Ministry
    of Foreign Affairs   57–8
Sweden
  empire   130
  neutrality (*see* neutrality Sweden)
  Pre-war
    iron ore (*see* iron ore)
  Wartime
    aid to Finland (*see* Finland,
      Wartime, Swedish aid)

  air force   107, 109, 112, 120
  army   103, 107, 109–10, 112, 120–2
  concessions policy (*see* concessions,
    Sweden)
  Enskilda Bank   30
  navy and coastal defence   110, 112
  occupation threat   30
  protecting power   104
  Realpolitik   7, 102
  rearmament   108–9
  Safe-Conduct Traffic   108
  transit   30, 104, 110, 112–13, 116,
    225
  violations of Swedish territory by
    foreign aircraft   119
  Post-war
    historiography   179–91 passim;
      (*see also* historiography, Swedish)
    small-state realistic narrative   8,
      180–3, 185–6; (*see also* small-
      state realistic narrative)
    Stockholm International Forum on
      the Holocaust (2000)   192, 200
    SUAV research project (*Sverige
      under andra världskriget*) (*see*
      SUAV)
    Swedish Research Council   188
    SweNaz 'Sweden's Relations with
      Nazism, Nazi Germany and the
      Holocaust' (*Sveriges förhållande
      till nazismen, Nazityskland och
      Förintelsen*)   188

Tanner, Väinö   208
Telegram Crisis   1942 63–4
Terboven, Josef (Reichskommissar
    Norway)   28, 94
Terijoki   17
terror corps   153
Thulstrup, Åke   183, 187–8
Treaty of Rome   222
Trommer, Aage   150

U-boat warfare   78
*Udgiverselskabet for Danmarks Nyeste
    Historie* (DNH)   149
United States   21, 27, 74, 92, 102, 113,
    120–3, 135, 137, 140–1, 231
University College London   41
University of East Anglia   41

University of Newcastle upon Tyne   41
Upton, Anthony   40
Ustache   221
Uthmann, Bruno von, German Military Attaché, Stockholm   110

Västerbotten   131
Vergangenheitsbewältigung (the process of coming to terms with the past)   185, 203, 215
Versailles, Peace of   47, 80–1, 84, 134
Vichy   46, 148, 186, 190, 227

Waffen-SS see SS
Wallenberg, Raoul   105

Wallenberg brothers   190
Warring, Anette   148, 153, 188
Weber, Max   69
Wegener, Vice Admiral Wolfgang   87
welfare state   5, 163, 182, 190–1, 222
Weserübung   19, 73, 85–6
White Sea   138
Winter War *see* Finland, Wartime, Winter War
Wittmann, Dr. Klaus   115
Wuorinen, John W. 208, 218n. 23

Ylikangas, Heikki   206
Yugoslavia   221, 227